KNOWING CATS

knowing Cats

**An Anthology for
Unsentimental
Cat-Lovers**

**edited by
ALAN HARVEY**

Taplinger Publishing Company | **New York**

PN
6071
C3
K6

First Edition

Published in the United States in 1977 by
TAPLINGER PUBLISHING CO., INC.
New York, New York   1977

Copyright © 1977 by Alan Harvey
All rights reserved. Printed in the U.S.A.

Published simultaneously in Canada by Burns & MacEachern, Limited, Ontario

Library of Congress Cataloging in Publication Data

Main entry under title:

Knowing Cats.

1. Cats—Literary collections. I. Harvey, Alan.

PN6071.C3K6   1977   808.8'036   76-54407

ISBN 0-8008-4487-4

Designed by Manuel Weinstein

Acknowledgments

*Grateful acknowledgment is made for permission to include
the following material:*

PANGUR BÁN, from *Poems and Translations* by Robin Flower. Reprinted by permission of Constable & Co., Ltd.

GEORGE ELIOT: A MEDICAL STUDY by Jean Stafford. Copyright © 1957 by Jean Stafford. Reprinted by permission of Russell & Volkening, Inc., as agents for the author.

THE PRINCESS by Doris Lessing, from *Particularly Cats*. Copyright © 1967 by Doris Lessing Productions, Ltd. Reprinted by permission of Simon & Schuster, Inc., and John Cushman Associates, Inc.

IMPO by Tay Hohoff, from *Cats and Other People*. Copyright © 1973 by Tay Hohoff Torrey. Reprinted by permission of Doubleday & Company, Inc., and the Estate of the Author.

ABRIDGED DICTIONARY OF BASIC CAT by Louis J. Camuti and Lloyd Alexander, from *Park Avenue Vet*. Copyright © 1962 by Lloyd Alexander and Louis J. Camuti. Reprinted by permission of Brandt & Brandt and A. M. Heath & Company, Ltd.

RHUBARB by H. Allen Smith, from *Rhubarb*. Copyright 1946, © 1973 by H. Allen Smith. Reprinted by permission of Harold Matson Company, Inc.

DAVID by Lloyd Alexander, from *My Five Tigers*. Copyright © 1956 by Lloyd Alexander. Reprinted by permission of E. P. Dutton & Co., Inc., and Brandt & Brandt.

"THE SHE-SHAH" by Colette, from *Creatures Great and Small*. Copyright 1952 by Farrar, Straus & Cudahy. Translated from the French, *Dialogues des Bêtes*, by Enid McLeod. Reprinted by permission of Farrar, Straus & Giroux, Inc., and Martin Secker & Warburg, Ltd.

AGRIPPINA by Agnes Repplier. Reprinted by permission of Houghton Mifflin Company.

HELP! KIDNAPED! by Doreen Tovey, from *Cats in the Belfry*. Copyright © 1957 by Doreen Tovey. Reprinted by permission of Doubleday & Company, Inc., and Paul Elek, Ltd.

FRIMBO ON CATS by Rogers E. M. Whitaker and Anthony Hiss, from *All Aboard with E. M. Frimbo*. Copyright © 1973 by The New Yorker Magazine, Inc. Reprinted by permission of The Helen Brann Agency.

UNCLE WHISKERS by Philip Brown, from *Uncle Whiskers*. Copyright © 1974 by Philip Brown. Reprinted by permission of Little, Brown and Company and Andre Deutsch Limited.

SOLOMON THE GREAT by Doreen Tovey, from *Cats in the Belfry*. Copyright © 1957 by Doreen Tovey. Reprinted by permission of Doubleday & Company, Inc., and Paul Elek, Ltd.

CALVIN by Charles Dudley Warner, from *My Summer in a Garden*, published by Houghton Mifflin Company.

ABNER OF THE PORCH by Geoffrey Household, from *Sabres in the Sand*. Copyright © 1959 by Geoffrey Household. This story first appeared, under a different title, in the *Saturday Evening Post*. Reprinted by permission of Little, Brown and Company and A. M. Heath & Company, Ltd.

THE SHE-CAT by Doris Lessing, from *Particularly Cats*. Copyright © 1967 by Doris Lessing Productions, Ltd. Reprinted by permission of Simon & Schuster, Inc., and John Cushman Associates, Inc.

AMBER by Gladys Taber, from *Amber, A Very Personal Cat*. Copyright © 1970 by Gladys Taber. Reprinted by permission of J. B. Lippincott Company and Brandt & Brandt.

MR. CAT'S IMMOLATION by George Freedley, from *Mr. Cat*. Copyright © 1960 by George Freedley. Reprinted by permission of Howard Frisch.

ACKNOWLEDGMENTS

LILLIAN by Damon Runyon, from *Guys and Dolls*. Copyright © 1930, 1957 by Damon Runyon, Jr. and Mary Runyon McCann. Published by J. B. Lippincott Company.

THE CAT'S BEHAVIOR IN TWO WORLDS by Frances and Richard Lockridge, from *Cats and People*. Copyright 1950 by Frances and Richard Lockridge. Reprinted by permission of J. B. Lippincott Company.

THE CAT by Mary E. Wilkins Freeman, from *Understudies*, published by Harper & Brothers.

CAT WITH A TELEPHONE NUMBER by Fred Sparks. Reprinted with permission from the July 1963 *Reader's Digest*. Copyright 1963 by The Reader's Digest Assn., Inc.

PIAZZA VITTORIO by Eleanor Clark, from *Rome and a Villa*. Copyright 1952 by Eleanor Clark. Reprinted by permission of Pantheon Books, a division of Random House, Inc., and William Morris Agency, Inc.

DICK BAKER'S CAT by Mark Twain, from *Roughing It*, published by Harper & Brothers.

THE LEOPARD CAT by Ludwig Koch-Isenburg, from *The Realm of the Green Buddha*. Copyright © 1963 by The Viking Press, Inc. Reprinted by permission of the Viking Press.

APOTHEOSIS by Carl Van Vechten, from *The Tiger in the House*. Copyright 1920, 1936 by Carl Van Vechten. Reprinted by permission of Alfred A. Knopf, Inc.

ERRATA

LILLIAN by Damon Runyon, from *Guys and Dolls*. Copyright 1930, © 1957 by Damon Runyon, Jr., and Mary Runyon McCann. Published by J. B. Lippincott Company. Reprinted by permission of the American Play Company, 52 Vanderbilt Avenue, New York, with special permission from Raoul Lionel Felder, Esq., New York City; and by permission of Constable & Co., Ltd. (published in *Runyon on Broadway*).

Contents

CONTENTS

Introduction

What *is* knowing cats?

It's what most cat lovers think they do. But I believe that when we say we know our cats we mean that we are knowledgeable about their ways and wiles, needs and desires . . . but knowing? It's a moot point who does the most knowing, master or mistress, or cat, but it doesn't matter. The nearest we can truly come to knowing these elegant creatures is a matter of shared trust, love, and the most intelligent care we can give them. As for our cats, what they know about us is, and I expect, will remain, their inscrutable secret.

What *are* knowing cats?

They are cool cats, independent, and self-possessed. They are usually affectionate and understanding, sensitive to our moods and feelings. They are fearless hunters and defenders of their homes. They are playful and loving and funny—and, alas, vain and selfish. But they are never sentimental. They know exactly where their best interest lies and who can help them in their determined and persistent pursuit of it.

These essential attributes of the knowing cat—determination and persistence—recall my favorite story about a cat who possessed them to an uncanny degree. Francie's story is too brief for the body of this book, but it's too good to omit, so here it is, as told by Margaret Cooper Gay in her classic book on every practical aspect of cat care, *How to Live with a Cat:*

"I can't tell you how to be found by a cat because that's a secret cats keep to themselves. I do know that the cats which choose their own people are the smartest cats of all. When a cat finds you, you may be sure it is a feline of discrimination, judgment, and taste.

"Out of all the millions of people who pass on the streets of New York, Francie chose the two most likely to appreciate him and followed them home. The fact that they disliked cats and ignored him would have discouraged a weaker character than Francie. It was a challenge to him. He warped in and out between their feet, and shouted after them when the door closed in his face. The next evening he ambushed them, swooped out with clamorous greeting, and raced ahead to wait at their front door. Again they shut him out. The third evening they found Francie waiting outside the door to their apartment. The fourth evening they looked for Francie; he wasn't on the street, or on the stoop, or in the hall. He was asleep on their living room sofa. How he got in remains a mystery to this day. The point is that he stayed and convinced his folks that cats were swell."

It is a happy circumstance for the anthologist that the deep bond between cats and many men and women of literature has resulted in so many excellent stories and books about the authors' personal experiences with their favorites.

The finest form a seamless whole in which cat adventures, anecdotes, nuggets of the writer's personal history, and bits of cat lore or practical advice on the care and loving of cats are so inextricably interwoven that it is a challenge to try to carve out a piece without doing injustice to the whole.

It was a special joy to discover a few of these that had not been excerpted before. To my knowledge, nothing from Tay Hohoff's *Cats and Other People*, Gladys Taber's *Amber, a Very Personal Cat*, *Mr. Cat* by George Freedley, *Uncle Whiskers* by Philip Brown, and *Particularly Cats* by Doris Lessing has appeared in any anthology.

If I have done any injustice to these fine books I apologize, and I hope that my attempt to convey something of the personality of both cat and biographer, and of their life together, will encourage readers to seek out these books and read them in their entirety, as they well deserve.

The shorter selections of fact and fiction I have chosen because I like them and they fit the theme of the knowing cat. Some will be new to the reader; others are old favorites that deserve not to be forgotten. Included too, are examples of honest, straightforward reporting about remarkable cats like Bockitay and Uncle Whiskers.

As for poetry, although I agree with that delightfully irascible writer Beverley Nichols that "most of the poets who have written verse about cats would have been better employed composing advertisements for detergents," there is some pleasant verse that I would like to have included. But for reasons of space I have confined myself to an opening poem, a translation from eighth-century Irish, and a closing one, excerpted from the wordy Mr. Swinburne, and both favorites of mine.

The drawings that enhance this book are by the Parisian painter and illustrator, Theophile Alexander Steinlen (1859–1923), who Carl Van Vechten called "Of the moderns . . . probably the greatest of the cat artists." Certainly he is one of the most knowing, revealing with a few telling strokes the very essence of Cat.

ALAN HARVEY

KNOWING CATS

Pangur Bán

I and Pangur Bán, my cat,
'Tis a like task we are at:
Hunting mice is his delight,
Hunting words I sit all night.

Better far than praise of men
'Tis to sit with book and pen;
Pangur bears me no ill-will,
He too plies his simple skill.

'Tis a merry thing to see
At our tasks how glad are we,
When at home we sit and find
Entertainment to our mind.

Oftentimes a mouse will stray
In the hero Pangur's way;
Oftentimes my keen thought set
Takes a meaning in its net.

'Gainst the wall he sets his eye
Full and fierce and sharp and sly;
'Gainst the wall of knowledge I
All my little wisdom try.

When a mouse darts from its den,
O how glad is Pangur then!
O what gladness do I prove
When I solve the doubts I love!

So in peace our tasks we ply,
Pangur Bán, my cat, and I;
In our arts we find our bliss,
I have mine and he has his.

Practice every day has made
Pangur perfect in his trade;
I get wisdom day and night
Turning darkness into light.

Anon: *translated from the
Gaelic by* ROBIN FLOWER

George Eliot: A Medical Study

JEAN STAFFORD

It is only fair to give George Eliot first place in this book, for not only would she undoubtedly be miffed if anyone let on that her story was fourth or fifth (or even second) but because in a way she is responsible for the whole book.

An artful blending of affection and irony, Jean Stafford's wonderful piece displays a precise understanding of cat psychology—at least the psychology of that enchanting minx George Eliot who by her mistress's admission (though she modestly attributes it to friends) is "probably the most beautiful cat in the Western Hemisphere."

A friend read this article years ago in a little-known magazine and, thinking it would make a fine piece for an anthology, made a copy. But the book did not materialize and the copy disappeared. The search for the errant article led me into a few blind alleys until one evening, searching for something else, I consulted my own file, intelligently labeled "Cats"—and there was George Eliot! And here she is, rescued from obscurity for all our pleasure.

The subject of this monologue was not born Mary Ann Evans nor was she united, without legal form, to George Henry Lewes; she did not, furthermore, die Mrs. John Walter Cross. She was born, I regret to say, "Stripey," and she had a long and fertile (*highly* fertile) relationship with a country fellow named Robert until she was obliged (indeed, commanded) to have a hysterectomy. She is still alive, thanks to the miracles of modern medicine, and is, as a matter of fact, staring at me right now with the big grape-green eyes she inherited from her Persian mother. It has been proposed by a good many perceptive people that she is probably the most beautiful cat in the Western Hemisphere; she has a silvery coat and ebony necklaces and ebony bracelets and ebony rings around her tail and her purr, to those attuned, is the music of the spheres.

George Eliot was given to me as a Christmas present by a Nor-

15

wegian friend of mine who, cribbing a line from an I. J. Fox ad, observed that "a small fur piece is a joy forever." When I first saw her, on a sparkling, cold Connecticut day, she was lying with her sleeping siblings, one black and one white (Blackie and Whitey) in a baby's playpen along with a sleeping blond baby (Nils; the Norwegians were better at naming specimens of *homo sapiens* than they were at naming those of *felis domestica*). A great big Norwegian explorer, a guest in the house en route from the Galapagos to Lapland, was playing sweet folk tunes on a fiddle and silver tabby kitten, Stripey, was looking up at him with an expression of wonder, showing, even at this early age, a sensitivity to the finer things of life. We established an immediate rapport and while we have had our ups and downs, we have, on the whole, been much contented with each other for seven years.

I have never had so expensive a Christmas present and by expensive, I don't mean what it cost the Norwegians, I mean what it has cost me. When I go away, I store the silver in the bank for fifty cents a month and I store her in posh cat-houses for a dollar a day. It pleases her to remove parts of her silken coat to, preferably, black surfaces, ideally, black velvet; my cleaning bills and those of my friends (the few I have left) are staggering. She would rather starve than eat anything so non-U as Puss 'n Boots; she despises horsemeat; she is fond of boiled chicken lightly salted, and of cantaloupe; for daily fare she puts up with baby food at 26 cents a jar. Her hospital and medical bills have run into four figures and mine, after getting the bills, have not been inconsiderable—when I am not insomniac, I am in a dead faint.

We lived, she and I, at first in New York, but she was so bored and woebegone, so homesick for the trees of her infancy, that after a few months we moved to Connecticut so that this prominent cat would not perish of inanition. She was immediately transformed by the country air and one would never have guessed that she had ever suffered depression. She patrolled the grounds, routing great oafish English setters whose only goal in life was to overturn my garbage pail and strew my lawn with things I did not want to know existed; she brought me presents of vivisected shrews and deer mice; she climbed the trees and smelled the flowers and chased the butterflies and she purred the livelong day. Robert, an outside cat came with the house and at first George Eliot disdained him. And no wonder, for no cat in the world ever cared less for his personal appearance than Robert, unless it was Pegleg, George Eliot's father, a randy old boy who had fathered thousands. Robert was scarred from fights without number, there were burrs as old as himself attached to his dusty, uncombed coat; he had the shoulders of a bull and the manners of a hired man. I'd invite him to come into the kitchen but he would never accept— he said, in effect, "No thanks, ma'm. I'd like my handout right here on the welcome mat." George Eliot, looking at him through the screen door, said, in effect, "Bumpkin!"

And then, when the peonies were blooming and the weigela was out and the roses were beginning, when the air was heady with all the perfumes and the mysterious noises of spring, George Eliot, nubile and ready to fall in love, fell in love with dirty old Robert. She, so dignified and so fastidious, behaved like the most shameless of tarts and the pair of them made the kind of racket in the picking garden that causes me to blush when I recall it. The results of their rendezvous were Daniel Deronda, Silas Marner, Milly and Flossie (subsequently renamed by the illiterate children to whom they went to live "Blackie," "Whitey," "Stripey," and "Baby"). The delivery, in a coat closet, was difficult, but recovery was uneventful and was far too rapid for my taste; she was only just getting her figure back when she encountered Robert again, and so sprang to life Middlemarch, Adam Bede, Romola—the Spanish Gypsy died soon after birth. George Eliot's pathological philoprogeneity knew no season and no sooner than Stripey, Pinky and Blackie, as they came to be

called, had been indentured to the homes of ailurophiliac children, than she hotfooted it out to the barn to wake up Robert. I had run out of easy targets—the children were duck soup but their parents had begun to snub me—and I had also run out of names. The third group were called Mr. Gilfil, Felix Holt and Scenes of Clerical Life. (They exist today as Stripey, Blackie and Roger.) I refused to let her see Robert again after this confinement because I would not, I could not be confronted with more kittens, one of whom would have to be called Essence of Christianity. I kept her under lock and key until a well-known surgeon of the community could schedule her for an operation. This doctor, whom I will call Dr. Catwalder, had an excellent reputation for his bedside manner with ailing animals, especially cats; cats, I was told, hated to leave his hospital. George Eliot loathed him on sight.

On the day of the operation, he telephoned me to say that she had worms and that he could not perform the hysterectomy until he had cured her of them. Five days later he called again to say that she refused to eat or drink, that she was dying, that it would be a kindness to let her die at home. Sobbing a lot, I went to get her, but before I left the house, I prepared a dainty invalid's meal just in case: some breast of chicken, some heavy cream, some chopped bacon. When I opened the top of her carrier in the kitchen, she leaped out of it with a trilling mew of pleasure, ate everything in sight and asked for more. She washed, checked the house to make sure everything was still there and then pretended that she had never been away at all. Her act had been nothing more nor less than a suicide threat and Dr. Catwalder, when I called to make another appointment, refused to take her on. "There was no transference," he said.

Next we went to a Dr. Catlett whom she loved, or rather, she loved the Mexican burro belonging to Dr. Catlett's children which she could see through the window in his consulting room. He operated successfully and recovery was uneventful. Thereafter she treated Robert like scum.

Dr. Catlett saw her through a kidney ailment (at first he diagnosed it as tubercular in origin but to our relief he found that it was streptococcic—there is, so far as I know, no cat equivalent of Saranac), for tonsilitis and virus pneumonia, for hepatitis, for the common cold. The only disease she didn't have was Asiatic flu and she didn't have that simply because it hadn't yet been introduced to this country by *Life* magazine.

After a few years, George Eliot and I moved from the outskirts into the village itself to a house on a heavily traveled street and for some time I did not allow her to go outdoors since she had had no experience with traffic. But she sneaked out one evening in the early spring and made the acquaintance of a neighboring castrate named Balzac, and she had such a good romp with him, she was so happy to be in charge of the wine-glass elm trees and being in the grass that I began to let her out for a few hours each day. She was sensible about the cars and never went into the road and she took enormous pleasure in climbing a tree outside my second-story study and peering in at me, winking sometimes. Only once that summer was she ill. She was treated for worms by a Dr. Cattell who happened to be nearer than Dr. Catlett and she liked him and she adored his kennel-boy who was probably a substitute figure for Dr. Catlett's burro.

And then an altogether awful thing happened. One evening at dusk, I went out to call my pretty cat and I found a gathering of people gazing down at something in the road. It was my poor George Eliot and I was told by the outraged witnesses that she had been hit by a car that had not slowed down but had sped straight on. The kind people told me to go and call for help and they promised to watch her and reroute cars. I called the ASPCA for an ambulance and they sent it immediately with an interne who carried a net. Sensing this, with the last bit of strength she had left, she leaped into the bushes in front of the house across the road from mine and when he followed her, she streaked away under the porch. The ASPCA man asked leave of the owner of the house to tear down some of the steps and she, a benevolent old Irishwoman who had one time been a belly dancer, said, "Tear down the whole house, but rescue that dear kitty!" The ASPCA man sought her in the darkness with his flash-light and then he turned to me with a sigh and said, "Won't do any good now. She's dying." Hours later my dead cat came home. I heard the faintest of mews at the front door and opened it to find George Eliot limping and reeling, blood-stained and begrimed; she managed to get up the stairs and onto my bed and there she lay motionless, waiting to die on a familiar counterpane. Drs. Catlett and Cattell were both away fishing in Canada and I had no choice but to call her enemy, Dr. Catwalder, rousing him out of a sound sleep. She spent the night in his hospital and in the morning he telephoned to say that he thought her skull was fractured and that she apparently had internal injuries and that she could not possibly live. So again I brought her home for her final rites. For the next forty-eight hours she lay under my bed, refusing to eat, refusing to drink, but trying, stalwart cat, to purr. At last I could bear the spectacle no longer and I called a psychiatrist friend of mine who was a cat lover and told him that I was going to have a nervous breakdown. He did not doubt me for a moment and he suggested that I call a Dr. Catto, a cat specialist with offices on Park Avenue.

Dr. Catto, who drove a Mercedes, paid only house calls. Once he had had a hospital, but he had so many casualties from homesickness that he had abandoned it. He treated patients in New Jersey, in up-state New York, Pennsylvania and Connecticut and he was consulted over long distance by cat fanciers with unwell cats in Hollywood. For eight nights, he called on George Eliot; he injected her with caffein and with penicillin; he swabbed her perforated jaw; he massaged her, prescribed infant glycerine suppositories and he put her on a diet of Junior beef. He left me a handful of oral antibiotics which I took later on myself when I had flu. He saved my cat all right and when his bill came I lay right down on the floor and screamed.

Now she has asthma. Dr. Cattell (the one with the nice kennel-boy) has examined her. Originally he said that possibly she had an an allergy to house dust or to the fumes from aluminum cooking vessels. But after keeping her for some time in his surgery he said to me, "There is nothing *physical* to explain it," and giving me a hard look, he added, "She doesn't have asthma when she's here with us." And the truth is that no one has ever seen her have an attack except when I have been around; last summer I was away for four months and her hostess reported that she did not cough or gasp once. What have I deprived her of? That old bum, Robert, I suppose, who reminded her of her father. Right this minute she is wheezing; she has stopped staring at me and is sitting on the typewriter paper with her back to me, wheezing, and every now and again she glances over her shoulder at me to make sure she's giving me a rough time. Well, she's going to be rid of me for a while. I am going to London and while I'm gone, she is going to be in residence at 10 Downing Street. The fact that it isn't the real 10 Downing Street but is in New York City doesn't matter because she isn't the real George Eliot either and quite possibly she won't know the difference.

The Princess

DORIS LESSING

Doris Lessing's trenchant novels about women in the modern world are greatly admired, and she writes of cats with equal perception in her book "Particularly Cats." Wholly unsentimental, she does not blink at the harsh facts of many cats' lives and some of her stories are not for the squeamish.

Here is a chapter about a selfish, fastidious half-Siamese beauty, who was nameless but often referred to as "the princess." It is especially revealing about the ways of cats when the first whimper of sex becomes a full-throated cry of passion.

I came to live in a house in cat country. The houses are old and they have narrow gardens with walls. Through our back windows show a dozen walls one way, a dozen walls the other, of all sizes and levels. Trees, grass, bushes. There is a little theatre that has roofs at various heights. Cats thrive here. There are always cats on the walls, roofs, and in the gardens, living a complicated secret life, like the neighbourhood lives of childhood that go on according to unimagined private rules the grownups never guess at.

I knew there would be a cat in the house. Just as one knows, if a house is too large people will come and live in it, so certain houses must have cats. But for a while I repelled the various cats that came sniffing around to see what sort of a place it was.

During the whole of that dreadful winter of 1962, the garden and the roof over the back verandah were visited by an old black-and-white tom. He sat in the slushy snow on the roof; he prowled over the frozen ground; when the back door was briefly opened, he sat just outside, looking into the warmth. He was most unbeautiful, with a white patch over one eye, a torn ear, and a jaw always a little open and drooling. But he was not a stray. He had a good home in the street, and why he didn't stay there, no one seemed able to say.

* * * *

In the middle of that winter, friends were offered a kitten. Friends of theirs had a Siamese cat, and she had a litter by a street cat. The hybrid kittens were being given away. Their flat is minute, and they both worked all day; but when they saw the kitten, they could not resist. During its first weekend it was fed on tinned lobster soup and chicken mousse, and it disrupted their much-married nights because it had to sleep under the chin, or at least, somewhere against the flesh, of H., the man. S., his wife, announced on the telephone that she was losing the affections of her husband to a cat, just like the wife in Colette's tale. On Monday they went off to work leaving the kitten by itself, and when they came home it was crying and sad, having been alone all day. They said they were bringing it to us. They did.

The kitten was six weeks old. It was enchanting, a delicate fairy-tale cat, whose Siamese genes showed in the shape of the face, ears, tail, and the subtle lines of its body. Her back was tabby: from above or the back, she was a pretty tabby kitten. in grey and cream. But her front and stomach were a smoky-gold, Siamese cream, with half-bars of black at the neck. Her face was pencilled with black—fine dark rings around the eyes, fine dark streaks on her cheeks, a tiny cream-coloured nose with a pink tip, outlined in black. From the front, sitting with her slender paws straight, she was an exotically beautiful beast. She sat, a tiny thing, in the middle of a yellow carpet, surrounded by five worshippers, not at all afraid of us. Then she stalked around that floor of the house, inspecting every inch of it, climbed up on to my bed, crept under the fold of a sheet, and was at home.

S. went off with H. saying: Not a moment too soon, otherwise I wouldn't have a husband at all.

And he went off groaning, saying that nothing could be as exquisite as being woken by the delicate touch of a pink tongue on his face.

The kitten went, or rather hopped, down the stairs, each of which was twice her height: first front paws, then flop, with the back; front paws, then flop with the back. She inspected the ground floor, refused the tinned food offered to her, and demanded a dirt box by mewing for it. She rejected wood shavings, but torn newspaper was acceptable, so her fastidious pose said, if there was nothing else. There wasn't: the earth outside was frozen solid.

She would not eat tinned cat food. She would not. And I was not going to feed her lobster soup and chicken. We compromised on some minced beef.

She has always been as fussy over her food as a bachelor gourmet. She gets worse as she gets older. Even as a kitten she could express annoyance, or pleasure, or a determination to sulk, by what she ate, half-ate, or chose to refuse. Her food habits are an eloquent language.

But I think it is just possible she was taken away from her mother too young. If I might respectfully suggest it to the cat experts, it is possible they are wrong when they say a kitten may leave its mother the day it turns six weeks old. This cat was six weeks, not a day more, when it was taken from its mother. The basis of her dandyism over food is the neurotic hostility and suspicion towards it of a child with food problems. She had to eat, she supposed; she did eat; but she has never eaten with enjoyment, for the sake of eating. And she shares another characteristic with people who have not had enough mother-warmth. Even now she will instinctively creep under the fold of a newspaper, or into a box or a basket—anything that shelters, anything that covers. More; she is overready to see insult; overready to sulk. And she is a frightful coward.

Kittens who are left with their mother seven or eight weeks eat easily, and they have confidence. But of course, they are not as interesting.

As a kitten, this cat never slept on the outside of the bed. She waited until I was in it, then she walked all over me, considering possibilities. She would get right down into the bed, by my feet, or on to my shoulder, or crept under the pillow. If I moved too much, she huffily changed quarters, making her annoyance felt.

When I was making the bed, she was happy to be made into it; and stayed, visible as a tiny lump, quite happily, sometimes for hours, between the blankets. If you stroked the lump, it purred and mewed. But she would not come out until she had to.

The lump would move across the bed, hesitate at the edge. There might be a frantic mew as she slid to the floor. Dignity disturbed, she licked herself hastily, glaring yellow eyes at the viewers, who made a mistake if they laughed. Then, every hair conscious of itself, she walked to some centre stage.

Time for the fastidious pernickety eating. Time for the earth box, as exquisite a performance. Time for setting the creamy fur in order. And time for play, which never took place for its own sake, but only when she was being observed.

She was as arrogantly aware of herself as a pretty girl who has no attributes but her prettiness: body and face always posed according to some inner monitor—a pose which is as good as a mask: no, no, this is what I am, the aggressive breasts, the sullen hostile eyes always on the watch for admiration.

Cat, at the age when, if she were human, she would be wearing clothes and hair like weapons, but confident that any time she chose she might relapse into indulged childhood again, because the role had become too much of a burden—cat posed and princessed and preened about the house and then, tired, a little peevish, tucked herself into the fold of a newspaper or behind a cushion, and watched the world safely from there.

Her prettiest trick, used mostly for company, was to lie on her back under a sofa and pull herself along by her paws, in fast sharp rushes, stopping to turn her elegant little head sideways, yellow eyes narrowed, waiting for applause. "Oh beautiful kitten! Delicious beast! Pretty cat!" Then on she went for another display.

Or, on the right surface, the yellow carpet, a blue cushion, she lay on her back and slowly rolled, paws tucked up, head back, so that her creamy chest and stomach were exposed, marked faintly, as if she were a delicate subspecies of leopard, with black blotches, like the roses of leopards. "Oh beautiful kitten, oh you are so beautiful." And she was prepared to go on until the compliments stopped.

Or she sat in the back verandah, not on the table, which was unadorned, but on a little stand that had narcissus and hyacinth in earthenware pots. She sat posed between spikes of blue and white flowers, until she was noticed and admired. Not only by us, of course; also by the old rheumatic tom who prowled, grim reminder of a much harder life, around the garden where the earth was still frostbound. He saw a pretty half-grown cat, behind glass. She saw him. She lifted her head, this way, that way; bit off a fragment of hyacinth, dropped it; licked her fur, negligently; then with an insolent backwards glance, leaped down and came indoors and out of his sight. Or, on the way upstairs, on an arm or a shoulder, she would glance out of the window and see the poor old beast, so still that sometimes we thought he must have died and been frozen there. When the sun warmed a little at midday and he sat licking himself, we were relieved. Sometimes she sat watching him from the window, but her life was still to be tucked into the arms, beds, cushions, and corners of human beings.

Then the spring came, the back door was opened, the dirt box, thank goodness, made unnecessary, and the back garden became her territory. She was six months old, fully grown, from the point of view of nature.

She was so pretty then, so perfect; more beautiful even than that cat who, all those years ago, I swore could never have an equal. Well of course there hasn't been; for that cat's nature was all tact, delicacy, warmth and grace—so, as the fairy tales and the old wives say, she had to die young.

Our cat, the princess, was, still is, beautiful, but, there is no glossing it, she's a selfish beast.

The cats lined up on the garden walls. First, the sombre old winter cat, king of the back gardens. Then, a handsome black-and-white from next door, his son, from the look of it. A battle-scarred tabby. A grey-and-white cat who was so certain of defeat that he never came down from the wall. And a dashing tigerish young tom that she clearly admired. No use, the old king had not been defeated. When she strolled out, tail erect, apparently ignoring them all, but watching the handsome young tiger, he leaped down towards her, but the winter cat had only to stir where he lay on the wall, and the young cat jumped back to safety. This went on for weeks.

Meanwhile, H. and S. came to visit their lost pet. S. said how frightful and unfair it was that the princess could not have her choice; and H. said that was entirely as it should be: a princess must have a king, even if he was old and ugly. He has such dignity, said H; he has such presence; and he had earned the pretty young cat because of his noble endurance of the long winter.

By then the ugly cat was called Mephistopheles. (In his own home, we heard, he was called Billy.) Our cat had been called various names, but none of them stuck. Melissa and Franny; Marilyn and Sappho; Circe and Ayesha and Suzette. But in conversation, in love-talk, she miaowed and purred and throated in response to the long-drawn-out syllables of adjectives—beeeoootiful, delicious puss.

On a very hot weekend, the only one, I seem to remember, in a nasty summer, she came in heat.

H. and S. came to lunch on the Sunday, and we sat on the back verandah and watched the choices of nature. Not ours. And not our cat's, either.

For two nights the fighting had gone on, awful fights, cats wailing and howling and screaming in the garden. Meanwhile grey puss had sat on the bottom of my bed, watching into the dark, ears lifting and moving, tail commenting, just slightly, at the tip.

On that Sunday, there was only Mephistopheles in sight. Grey cat was rolling in ecstasy all over the garden. She came to us and rolled around our feet and bit them. She rushed up and down the tree at the bottom of the garden. She rolled and cried, and called, and invited.

"The most disgraceful exhibition of lust I've ever seen," said S. watching H., who was in love with our cat.

"Oh poor cat," said H.; "If I were Mephistopheles I'd never treat you so badly."

"Oh H.," said S., "you are disgusting, if I told people they'd never believe it. But I've always said, you're disgusting."

"So that's what you've always said," said H., caressing the ecstatic cat.

It was a very hot day, we had a lot of wine for lunch, and the love play went on all afternoon.

Finally, Mephistopheles leaped down off the wall to where grey cat was wriggling and rolling—but alas, he bungled it.

"Oh my God," said H., genuinely suffering, "It is really not forgiveable, that sort of thing."

S., anguished, watched the torments of our cat, and doubted, frequently, dramatically and loudly, whether sex was worth it. "Look at it," said she, "that's us. That's what we're like."

"That's not at all what we're like," said H. "It's Mephistopheles. He should be shot."

Shoot him at once, we all said; or at least lock him up so that the young tiger from next door could have his chance.

But the handsome young cat was not visible.

We went on drinking wine; the sun went on shining; our princess danced, rolled, rushed up and down the tree, and, when at last things went well, was clipped again and again by the old king.

"All that's wrong," said H., "is that he's too old for her."

"Oh my God," said S., "I'm going to take you home. Because if I don't, I swear you'll make love to that cat yourself."

"Oh I wish I could," said H. "What an exquisite beast, what a lovely creature, what a princess, she's wasted on a cat, I can't stand it."

Next day winter returned; the garden was cold and wet; and grey cat had returned to her fastidious disdainful ways. And the old king lay on the garden wall in the slow English rain, still victor of them all, waiting.

Impo

TAY HOHOFF

Under the impersonal title "Cats and Other People," Tay Hohoff has written a moving and revealing book, an autobiography in miniature of a woman who has recalled her memories and tells the story of her long and full life as it related to the cherished cats who shared it.

I have chosen her story of Impo, which begins when Tazie was a little girl of eight, growing up in New York with her beautiful mother and dashing father, and her wise and understanding Quaker grandparents. The story ends many years later when Tay is a grown woman with children of her own. It is full of compassion and sadness, too, for when you give a part of your life to creatures you are almost sure to outlive, there are bound to be losses, but they are worth bearing, as Miss Hohoff's courageous book testifies.

I don't know how long we had lived there [Richmond Hill] when Bagheera came. Black from nose tip to tail tip, without a white hair, big and friendly and intelligent, what else could he be called? Steeped in *The Jungle Books* as I was, recognition was instant, and even my mother admitted it, with a laugh. He came to us out of nowhere, stood at the kitchen door asking with polite insistence to be allowed in, ate, washed thoroughly, said "thank you" to my grandmother and Gerda (the daily substitute for Rose and Mary), and then, "rather tentatively," my grandmother reported, stretched out in front of the stove. When she told him it was all right, go to sleep, he lifted his head and she saw that his eyes were emerald-green.

There are cats who avoid children, often from bitter experience, but Bagheera adopted me on sight because I was the smallest human being around. He was the companion I had been hungry for. He never pushed or crowded or made demands at the wrong moment. He slept on my bed and opened his amazing eyes when I said something like, "Oh, Bagheera, what does *inconsequential* mean?" and looked on while I made a check in the margin to remind me to ask the nearest authority when I woke up.

In addition to all his other virtues, Bagheera was a warm, loving cat who demonstrated his affection by rubbing, kissing, snuggling, purring, patting my face. He loved to be rubbed under his chin and even more, to be scratched vigorously behind his ears. He was a great one for kissing and his rough red tongue would tickle my face, hands, arms, until I laughed. I was very happy with him.

Him.

One day when the early spring sun felt deceptively like summer, my grandfather picked me up at school, although I was now allowed to travel without escort, and as the train rattled past the roofs and windows of tenements, stores and warehouses, he said, "I think there may be a surprise waiting for thee at home."

"What?" I demanded.

He shook his head. "It's a surprise."

In a box behind the kitchen stove, out of the draft, were six tiny kittens, each one black from nose tip to tail tip. Bagheera, purring like a steam engine, looked at me proudly. Newborn kittens should not be touched, but I could look my fill. Six miracles . . . seven, counting Bagheera. Superb in her maternal pride, supremely content, she lay at full stretch, accepting congratulations and admiration as her due, while the kittens wobbled and fell and staggered to reach her milk.

But quite soon, I made some excuse and ran upstairs to fling myself on my bed and weep tears of relief. For what seemed to me a long time, I had been worried about Bagheera's increasing girth, his odd shape, his alternating sleepiness and restlessness. I had thought, "If no one, not even Granddad, sees anything wrong it must be my imagination," and had tried to shut my eyes and my mind against a possibility I couldn't face. It had all been needless, and the world was right side up again.

Perhaps adults should think twice before treating themselves to the pleasure of "surprising" a child.

The kittens went from phase to phase of growth at a pace I found unbelievable. I arrived home in the afternoons—not loitering in the playground these days—breathless with anticipation. I was never disappointed. The other children could come and look, which they did with a regularity that drove Gerda nearly out of her mind, but why should I go and play when six kittens were putting on a new circus act every few minutes?

Gerda said, "Miss Tazie, I take whip, beat you out of my kitchen. I promise. Yah. I tell my lady so, too."

"What did she say?" I asked, removing one kitten from the back of a squealing brother—or sister, it was too early to tell.

"She laugh," Gerda said ruefully, and laughed too.

Strictly speaking, the active performers were five. My grandfather said that in most large litters there would be a runt, the one who got kicked around, pushed away from the mother's teats, buried under a pile of fat, well-fed, aggressive siblings, the one who was always out of line and out of step. He picked up Bagheera's runt and looked it over carefully.

"Nothing really wrong," he said. "Well-shaped. I think it's a male —look at that head, wide between the ears, broad in the jaw, or would be if he had enough to eat." He put the kitten next to Bagheera who gave it a casual lick.

I said, "Bagheera doesn't seem to like the—the little one as much as the others . . ."

"I've seen that before. We had a sow on the Farm who killed all her runts—rolled on them. But I've seen the other kind of mother, too. You never can tell. And I've known runts who turned out to be the best of the lot, given a decent chance."

The fame of Bagheera's kittens spread beyond the nearby families. "*All* black, there's not a white hair on any of them."

As the weather warmed and they grew, they were moved out of Gerda's way into a small room used as a catch-all, and this became a Mecca for children of all ages, many of whom I had never heard of. An occasional parent would trail along, but I suspect less to see the famous kittens than out of curiosity about my parents whose parties and comings-and-goings were watched by our neighbors with intense interest. Neither was snobbish, they genuinely liked people, rich and poor, high and low, black, yellow, and white. They chose their friends according to their own tastes, not by the rule book. In a close-knit, conventional community, they were conspicuous and misunderstood.

My grandmother's experience with similar, and uglier, situations, as well as pride in her children, made her sensitive. In the presentation of the five kittens (one would stay with us), she saw an opportunity to soothe ruffled feathers and mute, if not silence, criticism, without, as she put it, "committing us in the future."

"It's unlikely," she said, "that there'll be the excuse of five black kittens again."

"We could mate Bagheera with one of her sons," my grandfather suggested and touched off an argument that ranged from throwbacks to insanity; Egyptian pharaohs and other royal houses; animal inbreeding for specific purposes; the inbred communities in the New Jersey hills, the Ozarks, and eastern Europe. When a foray into botany threatened, my grandmother reversed the talk full circle by mentioning an article she had recently read dealing with future similarities between urban and rural societies.

I was too young to appreciate how cleverly she switched the runaway discussion back on the track, but on later occasions I was to hear and marvel, and watch my grandfather's eyes glow with awareness while, under the mustache that tried to hide the sensitive mouth, flickered a smile that I could not read but made my heart turn over.

Weather permitting, the party would be held on the lawn. She and Gerda would take charge of refreshments and extra help, folding chairs, tables, and so on. My mother would collate and organize the lists of guests each of us would prepare, and send the invitations because "she's the only one of us who writes a hand anyone can read." The date? Oh, yes, July 3, a Saturday.

"That's Tazie's birthday," she went on, "but we won't confuse matters by mentioning that if she doesn't mind."

"I've been telling you for years and years I hate birthday parties—this will be fun."

"So thee has," my grandmother said. "At least, ever since the fat boy ate more cake than even he could hold. This year . . ." she continued serenely, "Ernest will give the kittens to the proper people—the children, of course—and thee must be sure not to get them mixed up. And say something graceful each time, but not long and try not to be too clever."

My father grinned, and said he would try.

"Don't I have anything to do?" my grandfather asked.

"We'll talk about that later. I have some ideas."

His eyes danced. "I was afraid of that."

The party was a dizzy success. My mother set out to charm the women—she didn't have to worry about the men—while my father operated in reverse order. By the time it was over, the entire family could have danced the cancan in front of the Methodist church during Sunday services without a blot on its escutcheon.

We were tidying up the living room, for of course the party had spilled over into the house, when my mother suddenly broke the weary silence by turning on me with a demand to know why she hadn't been consulted about which kitten we were to keep. "After all, I have to live with it too." Generosity was all very well, she rushed on, but in this case it was unnecessary, and selfish too, because

I hadn't taken her into consideration, she hadn't even been *told* until it was too late . . .

I saw my father's right eyebrow go up as he looked at his "two girls." His wife could do no wrong—but neither could his daughter.

I tried to speak, but her voice rose. "Giving the cream of the litter away to strangers," she cried, "and keeping the *runt!* It's just plain stupid."

For a moment no one moved. Then I felt my spine stiffen and my eyes go hot.

"He's mine," I said. "Not thine." I marched stiff-legged to the doorway. Then I turned on my heel and faced her. "I'm going to take him upstairs with me," I told her. "He'll be lonely without the others."

I remember I left a dead silence behind me as I walked down the hall.

* * * *

Carrying the kitten downstairs next morning, I thought about Bagheera. After the kittens were weaned, her behavior became, I thought, odd. She was away for days and nights at a time, was pleasant and affectionate, but as if her mind was on other things.

Gerda had Sundays off and I found my grandmother in the kitchen preparing breakfast. After giving the kitten some milk, which he attacked with enthusiasm, I said, "Where's Bagheera, Nana?"

She turned the sausages and said vaguely, "Goodness knows. I expect she'll be back, when she gets good and ready."

"Doesn't she love us anymore?"

"She doesn't *need* us anymore."

"Has—has anything happened to her?"

"I don't believe so. Not in the way thee means. She has a restless nature, Bagheera." She laughed a little. "Runs in the family, thee knows." She pushed the pan to the back of the stove and sat down. "Come sit on my lap. Thee's getting enormous but not too enormous for that." She was silent for a long moment, watching the kitten and holding me rather tight.

I suddenly realized how small she was. I said, "I am getting too big for thee, darling. I'm getting too big for anything but a man's lap, I guess."

"Well, not quite yet," she said seriously. "That will come, though, and then thee may understand a little more about Bagheera. She's as female as anyone I've ever known. And clever. Beautiful and lovable and clever. It's quite a combination. I don't worry about Bagheera.

If she needs us again, she'll come back." While I was trying to digest this novel view of Bagheera, she went on thoughtfully, "It will be interesting to see how this one turns out. He hasn't had anything his own way. Now he will. What will it do to him? Or for him?"

I buried my face in her soft mass of sweet-smelling hair. My world was steady again. I whispered, "Thanks, darling," and slid off her lap. "What shall we call him? Nana, thee name him, please."

"Impo," she replied promptly.

I shrieked with laughter. "Impo! Why?"

"Because the Imp o' Darkness cannot be Imp o' Light."

I dashed off to meet my parents coming down the stairs. "Nana's named him," I cried. "Just listen . . ."

By early autumn, the runt was bigger, stronger, far more handsome and amusing than his brothers and sisters. His superiority irritated two mothers whose children had made their own selections out of the litter. We had, they claimed, kept the best for ourselves. When this allegation reached our ears, my mother was the first to laugh.

She nicknamed him Puddah. It was exactly the sound he made when he ran up and down stairs. We all slipped into it, and he answered to either. Even in early youth, his character was complex. When he was affectionate, playful, or mischievous, he was Puddah; when he chose to be regal, austere, scornful, annoyed, or bored, he was Impo.

While he was still small and scrawny, I dressed him up and put him in a doll carriage. This performance bored him extremely, but he put up with it, usually. It bored me, too. Unfortunately, someone had given me the idea that the kitten would be a perfect substitute for the dolls I detested—and if a litle girl didn't want to play at being "mama," something was very wrong. This aberration didn't last long, and I don't know whether Impo or I was the more relieved.

Bagheera never returned.

*   *   *   *

During the summer, long weekly letters from my grandmother had kept me up to date on what she called the "Progress of the Imp o' Darkness" and—from what I could decipher, often with Sally's help —Impo seemed to have been well named. Letters from my grandfather were shorter but more legible. I was warned that I would find a cat no longer in the kitten class. Nothing was said that led me to believe he would remember me, and I girded myself to accept the probability that he would not.

It was a waste of energy. It was I who hardly recognized him.

There are few things in life more heart-warming than to be welcomed by a cat. I didn't expect it then, and I have never quite learned to take it for granted. Demonstrations of affection come easily to the canine, but the feline nature is different, more reserved, more sensitive to its own dignity, more egotistical. Stress is laid on the hardship he has suffered by your absence. (Of course, you have turned yourself and half your dearest friends into nervous wrecks in the effort to keep his life as normal as possible. He then insults the Angel of Mercy by turning his back after eating and settling down for a long winter's nap. "He" is used loosely; any of them will do it.) I had had no experience with that parenthetical comment when I came home that autumn, but I expected the worst.

Impo went all out to show me that his world was now complete because I had returned to it. There were no hard feelings. He followed me from room to room, he purred, he sat in my lap—it was like holding a young panther—he came to bed with me in the usual place, at my feet. The first night I rather missed my lumpy country bed and the whispered talks Sally and I had when we were supposed to be asleep, but Impo suddenly got up, walked the length of the bed, kissed me, purred in my ear, and went back to his own place. The timing was perfect, even if accidental.

What my grandmother hadn't attempted to convey in her letters was his physical development. He had been handsome enough since he left off being a runt; now the only word for him was "magnificent." His coal-black coat shone like highly polished leather. He carried his long, luxuriant tail like a banner or swished it like a dueler's sword, twitched the very tip in moments of concentration, and waved it like a flag in a high wind when he was excited. When you learned the language, his tail was a fairly accurate index to the momentary contents of his active mind.

He was as clever as a monkey at opening doors, pails, boxes. If interrupted, he would walk away, only to return when interference had subsided. He had very little discrimination about "mine" and "thine." My father had brought back from Cuba a pair of fine, soft, handmade gloves which he liked very much. So did Impo. He absconded with one, but when my father surrendered and tossed him the other, he merely sniffed at it contemptuously.

Someone sent my mother a delightful little pillow from Belgium with a fine lace slip over a pink-covered cushion rather strongly scented with expensive perfume. Impo apparently decided the smell was deadly poison. He would sit for long minutes silently regarding the pretty object with baleful green eyes. Everybody, except my grandfather, thought this was amusing and my mother teased him by rubbing the pillow under his nose and then snatching it away. He made no attempt to grab it with his claws. He simply pulled his head back and continued to look.

"I wouldn't do that," my grandfather said, "if thee wants to keep the thing."

One morning she came into the living room to find lace, pink cover, and cushion in ribbons and shreds on the floor. Impo was crouched beside the wreckage. Enraged, she chased him around the room, shrieking imprecations and half crying, until Mr. Thomas, standing in the doorway, said quietly, "Better save thy breath to cool thy porridge, daughter."

Cats, in general, are dramatic animals, but I have never known another who dramatized the ordinary acts of everyday living with such gusto. If he wanted to go out, he would stand at a door—preferably one as far from any of us as possible—and scream. "Hurry! Hurry! If there's an accident, it won't be my fault!" Sometimes he chose to be suspicious of his food, looking over his shoulder and hunching himself, nibbling thoughtfully: "Poison? Stuff been around too long?" Another nibble. "Doesn't taste quite right. Tricking me into something new, are they?" Then getting down to it: "Oh, well, a fellow can't live forever."

He worshipped my grandmother and whenever she sewed, he would sit in front of her, watching every motion of her hands, and purring. While I was in the country, Impo had taken to sitting on my grandfather's lap, and when I came back with every intention of reverting to this lifelong habit, Impo was annoyed. He flounced, he glowered—or, if that was the way I wanted it, why couldn't we *both* be there? We compromised: when I was away, he sat there, when I was home, I did.

All young cats, and many older ones, play special games of their own. Impo ran the gamut of emotions while chasing, losing, finding, tossing, a small rubber ball or a piece of crumpled paper. When someone brought him a catnip mouse, his excited activity was so excessive my grandmother wearily suggested that we all move out and leave the place to Impo until the catnip smell faded.

The instinctive urge to dramatize, to play up to a situation, was not lacking in any of us except my grandfather (and even he had broken Ahab to harness and shown him off in public). Impo was in his natural environment. The one whose need for drama surfaced most frequently was my mother, who had first rejected him.

Any intelligent cat will show shades of difference in its treatment of the individuals it lives with, and Impo made the distinctions particularly plain. He understood that he and I belonged together. He wasn't unhappy without me, but with me he was content and complete. When I came home from school he was waiting. When I was hounded by commands to "go outdoors and get some exercise," he went with me. When I read he sat on my lap; my father speculated on what he was absorbing from the books that rested on his back. I've never known a cat who didn't love to sit on papers, and I did my homework under difficulties. The games we played sometimes turned rough, and as he had the more efficient weapons I often went to school with scratches on my hands and arms and even my face.

*   *   *   *

As everyone knows who has done it, moving from a big place into a small one is physically, mentally, and emotionally wearing. . . .

Impo was the only one who enjoyed it. After Macgregor went home with Karl, he looked around, sniffing, and occasionally made small noises in his throat. But the excitement of cartons and barrels served as compensation. There were new hiding places and dark corners from which to spring at passing skirts, and my mother wailed, "Macgregor may have been a nuisance while you were packing up at the Island—but at least you'd see him!"

Would Impo adjust to indoor life? He couldn't be allowed out of the apartment, if he got on the street he'd be run over, someone might steal him . . .

"Oh, for heaven's sake, stop worrying! Thee's always worrying about something, and none of it ever happens."

"I come by it honestly, anyway," I retorted. "Straight from thee and Nana." We were all on edge. Except Impo.

He took to apartment living like a duck to water. We were on the top floor of a building on a hill. There was a glimpse of the East River, plenty of sky, pigeons flapped past the windows and were, I believe, the first birds Impo ever paid attention to. He didn't even try to go out in the public hall, much less down the stairs.

The subway was almost brand new. The stations were clean, the cars clean and well-lighted. The trains weren't crowded and ran in an efficient, orderly manner, only stopping where they were supposed to. I loved it. But the trip was long, and three of us started out together very early in the morning and came home late. For much of the time, my grandmother was alone. "With Impo," she always said, when the subject came up. . . .

Except for marketing—which she whisked through with efficient celerity—trustee meetings and interviews at the school, she had little to occupy her time except reading. And thinking. The other occupant of the top floor was an old maid recluse who kept her door barred and demanded detailed identification before she opened it even a crack. What could Impo do if anything went wrong? My mother and I took to coordinating our social lives so that one of us would get home early, but it was difficult.

We didn't think much in those days about crime, and if there were drug addiction (as there probably was), it wasn't generally discussed. But there were maverick criminals then as there are now. There was a chain on the front door which my grandmother was supposed to slip into its notch when she was alone. She consistently forgot it. When the bell rang late one dark cold day, she trotted down the hall and flung the door wide open.

She stood about five feet two inches. A tall man looked down at her, his eyes shadowed by a slouch hat. She said pleasantly that she thought he must have come to the wrong apartment. He put both hands on the door frame and leaned over her. At the other end of the long, dim hallway, lamps in the living room glowed cheerfully.

The man put his foot over the threshold. "Don' wanta hurt any li'le old lady," he muttered.

She stood without moving as he gripped her shoulder. He started to swing her out of his way, and then everything seemed to happen very fast. With his free hand, he snapped down the hall light switch and in the dark she reached out to steady herself against the little table by the door and felt it shake under a sudden weight, although she had heard nothing and, momentarily blinded by the darkness, could see nothing. Then, by a trick of light from the living room lamps, she saw his eyes shift and stare and his hand dropped from her shoulder.

Out of blackness that was blacker than the dark hall blazed two vicious green eyes. The spell was not broken by a sound or a motion, there was only silence and the eyes.

With an incoherent exclamation, the man turned and ran down the stairs. She waited until she heard the street door slam shut. Then she closed our door—and put up the chain. With the hall lights on again, everything seemed normal. Walking regally towards the living room was just a black cat, a big cat, a very black cat, but . . .

Once in the living room, she sat down. "I don't know why," she said later, "but I felt a little tired. The whole thing hadn't taken seconds, after all." We had finished dinner before she embarked on a recital of "something that might have been rather unpleasant," and we listened in appalled silence, while Impo sat in his usual place on the sideboard, watching us through slitted eyes and occasionally nibbling at a bothersome claw.

"But really," my grandmother was saying, "I do wish you could have seen Impo, I could hardly see him until I turned on the hall lights and he almost scared me— three times his size and his tail . . ." She spread her hands exaggeratedly, "And it was lashing back and forth, like a whip. I could almost hear it crack. He was magnificent. I wish you could have seen him. But," she added, "if you'd been here, it wouldn't have happened, would it?"

My mother and I looked at each other. *She had enjoyed it!* They didn't talk very much about those strange, dangerous years in the hostile southern mountains—could she possibly regret that they were over? We had an uneasy feeling that we had deprived her of the kind of life she wanted.

She said, speculatively, "I wonder what Impo would have done if the man had actually pushed his way in? What does thee think, Tom?"

My grandfather had listened without comment, almost as if his mind were on something else, but now he turned in his chair to look

at the black cat. Impo had relaxed into a cozy, by-the-fireside position
with his paws tucked under and only the tip of his tail twitching to
prove he was still awake. As my grandfather moved, the emerald
eyes opened wide to stare straight into the other male animal's face.
For some reason, I shivered.

"Oh, well," said my grandfather coolly, "he might have flown at
the man. At his eyes, probably. Good thing the fellow was a coward.
Sarah, if there's any coffee left, may I have another cup?"

We moved to Brooklyn. It was better for everybody, my grandmother in particular. There were no stairs, the school and the Meeting
—of which she was an Elder—were within walking distance. The
neighborhood had changed, but it was here she had grown to woman-
hood, and we became used to finding her entertaining some old
gentleman who had sought the favors of "the Brooklyn Beauty," and
had not forgotten. My grandfather regarded these visitors with a
twinkle and, we thought, compassion. After all, he had been the
victor.

The apartment was sunny and pleasant, and in those days in a
residential area it was actually desirable to be only a few feet above
street level. Impo was the first cat I knew who became enamored of
traffic. The window sills were wide and he would sit for hours with his
nose glued to the pane. People began to look for him, children hung
on the areaway railing and called to him. He swished his tail, washed
elaborately, rose to his full height standing on his back legs. This
called forth o-o-ohs and ah-a-a-hs. He was not above showing off. . . .

Europe was consuming itself in the trenches on the Western Front,
in open warfare and revolution in the east. There was no longer any
doubt that soon the Yanks would be coming to set everything right.
This was my generation's war, and it may have been just as well we
didn't know there would be precious little peace in all the years of our
life.

My grandmother took it very hard. The fires of her overactive
imagination were fed daily by the firsthand reports and the photo-
graphs that filled the newspapers. People who couldn't stop talking
about the war kept her nerves on edge, but were easier to endure than
those who, as she said, behaved as if everything that was happening in
Europe was an obscene smell it would be impolite to notice.
Domestic help was hard to get and she took refuge in housework. Her
standards were high and she wouldn't lower them by a single notch.
My mother cried out in protest, "Stop pretending thee's Rose and
Mary rolled into one! Thee'll kill thyself."

It amounted to that. A stroke paralyzed her vocal cords and left her nearly helpless. My mother had a good job with the city; her salary was important. I wanted to stay home, my job wasn't all that lucrative. We couldn't understand everything she said, but at the mere idea, her agitation was extreme and at first it had seemed best to give in to her.

During this interim period, whoever managed to get home first would find Impo close to her chair, and she made us understand that he had been "right there" all the time we were away. She pointed to her watch, running a finger around the dial—"every minute." Touching his head with one hand and her own face with the other—"watching"—she would smile at me and nod and then shake her head emphatically, which we took to mean that he was all right, he wasn't sickening as he had when he watched me hiding from the fact of my father's death. *She* was not hiding from anything—perhaps that made the difference.

Impo took it better than we did. One evening—the repetition of this scene became unendurable—I burst out to my mother that the lack of the little money I was earning couldn't matter by comparison with ending this horror, someone must be with her and I was electing myself no matter what anyone thought or said.

My mother said, "It's got past the point where I can argue. Thee's too young—but yes."

Impo was glad to have me. He still stayed near her and when I had to go out on an errand, returned to his post at her feet.

One evening she seemed so alert, my mother and I became gay and made jokes, and she laughed. During that night she died, alone with her husband. We never knew at what hour it happened, or how. They were together, as they would have wanted it.

*   *   *   *

On the rebound from a love affair with a boy about my age, who looked like a Greek God and whom my mother detested with a fervency she might have put to better use, I became engaged to an acceptably older man she liked very much and thoroughly approved of. I thought I knew him quite well and liked him enough to imagine that we had—or could have—much in common. A minor physical disability had kept him out of the services (which it would not have done in the wars to come), and I saw a good deal of him. Emotionally battered, I had obtained what I believed I most desired: my mother's unqualified approbation.

After we were engaged, Lewis bought a house in the Chelsea

district on a street that was favored by artists, writers, decorators, architects, and such. Renovated and painted, the houses were a delight to the eye. The apartment on Amity Street was dismantled, my grandfather would "visit around" until the house was ready for him, my mother leased a cozy little flat, and we moved in. With Impo.

There was a back yard which he regarded with some interest. There were cats on the back fence. They peered down at the huge, coal-black stranger with green eyes and a long thick expressive tail. I watched the proceedings nervously. Impo had not been face to face with another cat since Richmond Hill. He didn't *look* elderly, but he was. I conjured up horrors. After the first inspection, the neighborhood cats—a scrawny bunch but formidable in number—went quietly away. To talk over strategy, I thought darkly.

Lewis and Impo were polite to each other, but no rapport developed. Nevertheless, the next day, a Saturday, when I came back from a necessary shopping excursion uptown, Lewis met me, doubled up with laughter. It seemed Impo had asked to go into the back yard and had immediately reverted to his country habits. Lewis considered that admirable and left him to it.

A while later, he heard a noise such as Hell must ring with and on looking out the living room window he saw a battle royal. The local cats' strategic plan had clearly been to mount a mass attack on this black, oversized interloper. I listened to his dramatic replay with growing alarm and had turned to dash for my beloved's mangled body, when Impo appeared in the doorway. He was rather rumpled and there were some bits of fur missing, but he was puffed up with self-satisfaction. Nothing on earth can look as smugly pleased with itself as a cat.

"My God," said my husband, the male animal speaking, "what a sight! You should have seen it. The old boy walloped the hell out of them. I thought I'd have to help one of them get up the fence . . ."

Impo ignored him and rubbed against my ankles, asking to be picked up and made much of. I hoped the ice between husband and cat had been broken for good and all, but it froze up again later although Lewis boasted happily about "our cat" to anyone who would listen. Basically incompatible personalities seldom get beyond a live and let live compromise.

My husband was an honest, upright man. He was interested in the aesthetics of architecture, painting, and other visual arts. He had humor and told an off-color story superbly. He had many devoted friends among his own sex. He was kind but lacked the sensitivity that lifts kindness above a pedestrian virtue. I was genuinely fond of him, but lonely. He cared nothing about music and knew less, he liked to "keep up" with the new books, he loved the theater and vaudeville (this was a real bond between us), and he deserved better than to have me for his wife.

We spent several months in Europe, had a marvelous time, and I came home happier than I had expected to be, and pregnant.

The area of Chelsea where we lived was part of the old Moore estate. Bishop Clement C. Moore had perpetrated " 'Twas the night before Christmas, when all through the house/Not a creature was stirring—not even a mouse . . ." I think, though I'm not sure, that mice and rats won't live under the same roof. If so, there wasn't a mouse stirring in our house; it was infested with rats. The place was within gunshot of the waterfront, most of the houses were nearing the century mark, there was no cellar. The winter was exceptionally bitter, and I think that was one of the years when the dock workers struck and an unusually large number of freighters were tied up along the River. Did other houses in the block suffer a similar curse? It seems likely, and I suppose a primitive sense of social shame kept our neighbors silent—as it did us.

The beasts were annoying enough when they stayed inside the walls, but when overcrowded conditions (I suppose) drove some of them from their living quarters into ours, our attitude hardened. On the first morning after we moved in, I had come face to face with a large, stinking, grayish monster who was busy knocking over milk bottles in the basement vestibule. I stamped my foot and, if I remember correctly, said "Scat!" It snarled at me and, probably out of sheer surprise, vanished down a hole. Lewis had plugged one hole with thick, broken glass and now we tried to find other places to apply the same remedy.

Then we got in an exterminator. The rats laughed and the house was almost uninhabitable for a week. Impo was a complicating factor; there was no way of knowing whether he was as immune as the rats proved to be. Short of moving out, we seemed doomed to live with the dirty brutes.

Very soon a new and much more serious complication was the presence of an infant daughter. I don't remember exactly when the rats' search for Lebensraum became a major force, but she was still small enough to sleep in our room where there was a Franklin stove that could be kept warm all night with cannel coal. But the warmth (more or less fictitious) of our room was mere camouflage for the real reason. John Elliott having commandeered me for volunteer work at the Hudson Guild the first moment I set foot in Chelsea, I had seen what rat bites could do to a baby. Lewis had not; his imagination was not prodded by visual memories.

The first time I heard Impo howling in the kitchen region, I ran downstairs barefoot, for he sounded *in extremis*. The rat he held between his paws was beyond *extremis*; it was thoroughly dead. Impo's tail was lashing with pleasure and pride. Shivering and giving a passing thought of wonder at the stupidity of a rat who would leave the cozy walls for this, I wrapped the ugly thing in a piece of newspaper and dropped it in the garbage pail, lavishing on the noble rat killer every loving compliment I could get past my blue lips.

It would be a wild exaggeration to say that the same scene was enacted every night—it just seemed so to me. He would howl like twenty demons until he heard me on the stairs. I kept newspapers handy and became adept at wrapping corpses without touching them. I told my grandfather (we were again under one roof) that I would be a splendid helper if the city were struck by an eighteenth-century yellow-fever epidemic. He growled that it wasn't much to joke about in this house; rats had carried the fever from the ships and could again. When I came back from these expeditions I would find that he had left his room across the hall and was leaning over the crib (Lewis slept more or less peacefully through most of these episodes), just "making sure," he would whisper apologetically; he knew it was silly but he felt better if he knew she was safe.

I didn't think it was silly. This was his first great-grandchild and he "fair worshipped" her, as my next door neighbor said, but he would have done the same if she had been a waif from one of the old-style tenements near the Guild. He said he thought Impo prowled through the house, but the cat was so silent when on the hunt, and so black, that he couldn't be certain. He rather wished Impo had continued to sleep in the crib—she had been really safe then.

On the coldest night of that winter I pulled the covers tight over my head and pretended I didn't hear the weird jungle cry from the kitchen. The air in the room, with the Franklin stove working overtime, felt frozen when you breathed it. The baby, I knew, was all right, under layers of blankets, and the crib tented over with a quilt. She wouldn't smother, her nose wouldn't be frost-bitten. She was my real responsibility and I would not—repeat NOT—go downstairs. I went back to sleep.

Perhaps the unwonted silence wakened me, for I was conscious when something heavy, smelly, and slimy hit me accurately in the middle of my back. I almost screamed. I couldn't turn over on top of the—the thing, so I knocked it on the floor and then looked down into a pair of blazing green eyes. Impo was furious. He spit. He spit at *me!*

I heard my grandfather stirring in his room. I got out of bed. It's difficult to be haughty when you're shivering from head to foot, but I tried. Making sure I hadn't pushed the ghastly object onto my slippers, I got into my dressing gown, picked up a piece of paper by the stove and, ignoring Impo, I rolled the rat in the paper and left the room. My grandfather, standing under the dim hall light, looked surprised.

I gestured at Impo, with the hand holding the body.

"He *threw* it at me," I told him through teeth chattering with cold and indignation. "He *spit* . . ."

My grandfather leaned back against the door frame, and laughed.

I was enraged. I stamped down the stairs—as well as one can stamp in woolly slippers—after Impo, who was halfway to the kitchen. I dropped the dead rat in the garbage pail, slammed down the lid, punched it tight. I don't believe in the resurrection of the body, but I wasn't taking any chances with this one.

When I got upstairs I found my husband, awakened by the ruckus, and my grandfather trying to smother their laughter.

I said, "Look at Ann. If her nose is blue it may be frost bitten. I think you put salt on it," and crawled under the covers as far down as I could get.

*   *   *   *   *

A threat of eye trouble that might become serious if he didn't get away from the drafting table set Lewis thinking about another jaunt to Europe. The first time we had skimped on London and Paris, to concentrate on Italy. Two months, including the leisurely boat trips, should allow time to have a real taste of the two cities. Coggie, competent both as nurse and housekeeper, was devoted and sensible; our top floor had been turned into a flat for my mother, my free-lance work was unimportant, so why was I dragging my feet? What was there to stop us?

There was nothing, except an aged cat who was sleeping too much and eating too little. My mother pointed out that he might be expected to live until I came home; two months was not long. Coggie was a little miffed. If I were willing to trust the children to her, why not a cat? My husband did not say very much, but he was bewildered and hurt: I was putting loyalty to a cat above loyalty to him. He walked away, buried himself in a newspaper or made a telephone call, when I began to explain that Impo had been an integral part of my life for many years more than he, it was not a question of loyalty but of love . . . I would reach this point in the unvoiced argument and pull myself up short. Pleas for a mere delay in the sailing date fell on deaf ears; a friend would be traveling with us and must be considered. And, they said, what made me think I could time all this so neatly? Unless, of course, I were to take the sensible course, the merciful way out? Theoretically, I agreed—but not for Impo. I am not given to foreknowledge; the "second sight" my grandmother apparently possessed, had passed me by. I did not forecast a day or an hour, but I knew, and Impo knew that we had very little time left. I have never regretted for an instant that I was a neglectful mother, wife, and daughter during those final days and nights, before he opened his emerald eyes for the last time, and went into the dark.

We sailed on the appointed date.

Abridged Dictionary of Basic Cat

DR. LOUIS J. CAMUTI AND LLOYD ALEXANDER

*Among all these knowing cats, there is room for an excep-
tionally knowing man, a veterinarian who specializes in cats
and has contributed much to veterinary knowledge. Believing that cats recover more quickly in their own homes,
Dr. Louis J. Camuti prefers to make house calls on his
patients and his fees are commensurately high. In fact, he is
quite probably the vet who treated Jean Stafford's George
Eliot after her near-fatal accident.*

*I have chosen the chapter from his entertaining book
"Park Avenue Vet" in which Dr. Camuti reflects on the
cat's independent nature and its relationship to people and
gives his Abridged Dictionary of Basic Cat.*

How do cats get along with us? Since no cat has ever been psy-
choanalyzed or written his memoirs, we can only observe from the
outside and try to guess what happens on the inside.

My own guess is that independence is the most important single
attribute of a cat's personality, the one aspect always present and
always coloring his attitude toward humans. . . .

Nothing succeeds like success, and for thousands of years, cats have
been eminently successful loners. They have developed the physical
characteristics they needed in an enterprise of this kind and have refined
them to the highest degree. They are literally built to be independent.

But independence doesn't preclude active relationships with
humans. Humans are often very interesting, and cats observe them by
the hour. Most of the time, cats seem to know what we're up to and
what they can expect of us. Cats have the uncanny knack of knowing
which side their bread is buttered on, which human is a soft touch,
and which one isn't. . . .

Cats have developed a number of ways of communicating with
people; they have more techniques than a Method actor and can ring
in countless elaborations or variations. I offer the following:

ABRIDGED

DICTIONARY OF BASIC CAT

(Any cat owner can add to these)

Affection

I've already touched on the various ways a cat can say "I love you." Purring, rolling, kneading are good standard cat language, all in current usage. But, like individual humans, individual cats have struck on personal ways of showing affection. One small example concerns a brown tabby kitten who, after exhausting the purring-rolling repertoire, in a final surge of joy would run off and find an old sock and carry it back to his owner. Cats bring offerings of mice and other small game to their favorite humans; possibly the sock was the nearest equivalent which the kitten could find on the spur of the moment. In any case, bestowal of the Order of the Sock was the highest compliment and honor. The human responded by cries of wonder, admiration, and appreciation for this magnificent tribute, while the cat, wearing an expression of "Oh, it's really nothing, nothing at all," helped the human examine the sock in great detail, as if demonstrating its remarkable virtues.

Anger

Cats, unless in pain or badly frightened, seldom show complete out-and-out anger toward humans. But they don't hesitate to express annoyance and irritation. This usually results from human intrusion on the cat's train of thought: petting the cat when he doesn't want to be petted; picking him up when he doesn't want to be picked up; or, in fine, doing anything contrary to what the cat has in mind at any given moment. To a cat, interference is not to be tolerated, and he lets you know about it with unmistakable warnings: ears flat and pointing backward, tail lashing. If you want to get down to fine points, there might even be a correlation between the speed and number of tail twitches and the degree of the cat's annoyance with you.

If more serious matters are involved, such as unwanted attention to new kittens, the cat adds growling and hissing to the tail-and-ears business; a swat with a paw may be used for emphasis. Cats don't often bite (except me) unless the human has committed a capital offense: hurting a cat is one, or making him feel seriously threatened. I see more of this than most owners because, under treatment, cats don't accept the it's-all-for-your-own-good philosophy.

Announcements, Important

Cats constantly make important announcements, issuing statements and directives of all types. Usually, they concern the subjects covered in the rest of this glossary, but sometimes it's impossible to guess exactly what a cat has on his mind. One owner reports that her cat, at regular intervals, appears in the room, walks up to her and mews once or twice, or simply sits down in front of her and gives a quick glance of inspection. Nothing is required from the human, and I suppose this behavior would correspond to a friend's telephoning just to say hello and find out how things are going.

Emergency announcements are something else again; as with anger, the signs are unmistakable. Watch-cats, such as my friend Hercules, growl and race back and forth when strangers approach. When a cat weaves between your legs when you walk, there's a good chance that something is up and you'd better look into it.

Window-sitting cats make important announcements about events outdoors, and they use a specialized language depending on what they want to call attention to. Most cats chatter: an amazing combination of clickings and smackings, chattering of teeth, jiggling of the jaw plus slight coughing noises. All this to signal an animal in sight. Usually, the animal is a small one, a squirrel or bird. A dog strolling across a cat's field of vision is more likely to bring forth still a different sound, a long, sustained growl. Seeing another cat may result in a loud hiss-growl combination; some cats grow so indignant that they almost bark—a choppy, strangled sort of hack.

A cat's invitation to a romp is, to my ear, one of the most delightful of cat sounds: a melodious, high-pitched plunk combined with a short trill. One of my clients owned a cat who usually chose the middle of the night to issue this invitation. But the owner found it so irresistible that, in spite of the hour, he would stagger out of bed and, half blind with sleep, toss his pet's felt mouse back and forth until the cat tired of the game. Afterwards, the owner would stumble back to bed. (The owner rose early in the morning; the cat, naturally, slept late.)

Disgust

"Turning up the nose" is a drab, limited phrase to use in describing a cat's reaction to something he doesn't care for. Cats can assume the most eloquent expressions of pure disgust with a single motion of the head and a slight flaring of the nostrils. When presented with food that for one reason or another isn't exactly to his taste, a cat may try to cover it up as if he were burying excrement. The worst part of this gesture is that the cat knows perfectly well he is only making a gesture. He makes no serious attempt to scratch up the floor; a few symbolic passes are enough to convey his opinion. One owner reports that she put a plate of food on the kitchen floor, then left the cat alone with it. Returning after a few minutes, she found that her cat had dragged a small throw rug into the kitchen and carefully draped it over the plate.

Flattery

Some writers praise the cat as an animal which never flatters and never plays the hypocrite. I disagree. A cat can be the world's most shameless flatterer and cajoler when he has an ulterior motive in mind (see Out and Hunger). The best way a human can evaluate this is to check through a list of things the cat might possibly want. If none seems applicable, the human may accept the cat's attentions as sincere and representing the cat's high esteem for the human—as of that particular moment.

Greetings

A cat's greetings can be a simple mew of recognition, wild rolling, ecstatic kneading, or nothing at all. I know of one couple still puzzled over their cat's reaction to their absence. Whenever they went out for an evening, the cat welcomed them back with happy bleatings and leg-rubbings as if they had been away for a year. After two weeks' vacation (the cat stayed at home with a sitter), they looked forward to a warm reception. The cat ignored them completely, hardly stirring from his place on the armchair. The most he offered was a blasé glance; these people had seen him behave in a more friendly manner with total strangers. Next day, after they had been out for an hour's shopping, the cat climbed all over them.

Hunger

Cats learn early that many blessings flow from the refrigerator. Some of them sit in front of it when they're hungry; others choose subtler methods. I know of one cat who yawns repeatedly when he's hungry. Another nibbles his owner's fingers. Still others trot back and forth impatiently between the kitchen and wherever the owner hapens to be, yowling all the while. A cat in search of his dinner will use every trick of flattery—the passionate glance, the resonant purr. Never ask a hungry cat whether he loves you for yourself alone.

Jealousy

Jealousy is not an exclusively human emotion. Cats, for all their independence and self-sufficiency, are as prone to jealousy as people.

I'm thinking of one family, where the cat singled out the man of the house as his favorite person. Each time the man took his two children on his lap, the cat observed this domestic scene with annoyance, crouching on the floor, looking up with flashing eyes (naturally green, but also filled with obvious vexation). After a few moments, the cat joined the party, sliding in between the children at the risk of being slightly squashed. He hooked his claws into his owner's shirt and hung there. The children eventually got down; the cat stayed, purring triumphantly.

Another cat was jealous of his owner's canary. Most of the time, the cat paid no attention to the bird, never tried to climb into the cage, and in general treated the canary with indifference. But this cat's attitude changed whenever the owner dared to have any dealings with the other pet—filling the seed cup, changing sand and, above all, speaking lovingly to the bird. Then the cat would jump on a side table and furiously give the bird-sighting signal. Beyond this, fortunately, the cat did not go. The canary died peacefully of old age. The owner reports that the cat seemed noticeably relieved.

Out

This is where I, personally, do not believe a city cat should go. Cats allowed to roam freely outdoors are likely to pick up fleas, worms, or other parasites, get in fights, or be run over. Still, if the owner has any amount of ground, it's impossible not to yield to a cat's entreaties. A cat's demands to be let out are as imperious as his demands for food. The most obvious sign of Out is reaching for a doorknob or scratching at the door, but I know of one cat who chose a more indirect approach. After begging at the door and being flatly refused, the cat bided his time for a little while then jumped to a shelf covered with knickknacks. If the owners happened to be in the living room, they naturally removed the cat from the shelf. But, as soon as their backs were turned, the cat jumped up again; he hooked a paw around one of the objects and pushed it to the floor. In exasperation, the owners turned the cat out of doors, which was exactly where he wanted to be. The owners; after a certain amount of smashed china, caught on that the cat was doing it deliberately. They let him out whenever he asked. However, when they weren't quick to comply, the cat would leap to the shelf and rattle a fancy candy dish or porcelain figure. This cat had all the instincts of a blackmailer.

Another type of appeal to go Out is the quietest—and sometimes the hardest to resist. Here, the cat just sits and stares at the door. He waits. And waits. And waits. Motionless, his tail curled around his haunches, he keeps on waiting until the human, driven frantic by this peaceful, passive, and maddening patience, leaps up and lets the cat Out. Can we imagine a subtle smile of victory on the cat's face, a certain smug cast to the whiskers, the look of a cat who has finally succeeded in doing exactly what he intended to do?

The opposite of Out is In, and that is where cats want to be during the times they are not Out. This sounds plausible enough, but it is a complicated business with cats. Most cats, when they are Out want to be In, and vice versa, and often simultaneously. One writer has observed that cats are always on the wrong side of the door. I believe it. And there is no mistaking a cat's In signal. It is usually vocal and loud, sometimes accompanied by thumps on the door or window.

This thumping process is a mystery to many cat owners, for it sounds as if the cat were indignantly rapping on the door with small fists. Most people don't see how it's done because, obviously, the cat is outside when he's doing it. But a friend of mine, walking past his own front door happened to catch his cat in the act, and reports that the cat simply stood on his hind legs and beat a tattoo with his front paws. What the cat really wants, I suppose, is to go and come as he pleases, with doors left open winter or summer. Since most households aren't organized to put up with this, some of my clients have installed cat-ports, round holes cut into the base of a door and covered with a stiff material that bends in or out depending on which way the cat is pushing. Cats quickly learn to use these door-holes, and I supose it is convenient for all concerned. In my opinion, the owner should have more control over the cat's exits and be able to keep track of him at all times. Aside from that, there's a kind of exhilaration in matching wits with a cat who wants to go Out (although the human often loses), and it's a shame to spoil it.

Sex

Despite their reputation, I don't believe cats are especially preoccupied with sex. Like other animals, a cat's sexual urge is periodic. For a good part of the time, they are content to eat, sleep, and enjoy life's other attractions. Humans, in a romantic fervor, have offered to climb mountains, swim oceans, or cross deserts, and would very likely be at a loss if they had to prove their words by actions. Cats make no such claims, nor do they swear eternal fidelity. But once the urge is on them, they will take more risks and overcome more obstacles than the most ardent human. They are more purposeful than postmen: rain and sleet will not keep them in, nor will minor architectural details such as doors and windows. I have known tomcats who have slashed their way out of screened porches to keep a rendezvous. Some of the worst injuries tomcats suffer result from mating-season brawls. An unaltered male, whatever his size, is firmly convinced he can lick any cat in the neighborhood.

But I think cats have acquired a Don Juan reputation partly because they're so noisy about their affairs. They yodel, wail, and scream; their voices tremble up and down the octave. The females are the worst offenders in this, at least when they are confined to quarters. To my mind, no animal is more persistent, beseeching, and demanding than a female cat in season. They are, by turns, raucous and dulcet; they yowl like sirens one moment, then lower their voices to heart-rending sobs. They roll voluptuously or sink forward on their front paws, their hindquarters raised in the air. Female cats are occasionally sex-conscious about humans, too.

One of my women clients has a female tabby who despises men—most of the time. But when the cat is in season, no woman may come near her. Even the cat's owner is growled at and threatened with unsheathed claws. The cat won't eat as long as her owner is in the same room.

With men, at those times, the tabby is all flirtatiousness and seductiveness, cooing, rolling, and blinking up at them with hot, soulful eyes.

I remember ordering a daily dose of pills for this cat. Everything went well until the cat came in season. The owner didn't dare touch her and finally had to call the elevator man to come and help.

Of all a cat's desires, a female's plea to be allowed out for a wild fling should be the easiest to understand. This is not necessarily so. I still smile when I think of a classic situation involving one of my clients, owner of an expensive pedigreed longhair. This woman telephoned, full of alarm at her cat's behavior. To make the story perfect, she was unmarried, very proper, and this was her first cat.

She described the symptoms perfectly, then asked me to come over as soon as possible. "I think the cat's having some kind of fit," she added.

Knowing the cat's age, I had expected her to come in season just about this time. I was confident that the cat's problem came from a purely biological urge and nothing else, and I explained this to the owner.

There was a moment of silence. I could almost feel the hot blast of indignation over the phone.

"Dr. Camuti! You know Kitty would never do a thing like that!"

In fairness, I must add that this owner became reconciled to the knowledge that the most elegant longhair and the humblest alley cat are sisters under the fur. I suppose a vet's office is as good a place as any to learn the facts of life.

I could continue my glossary indefinitely. There are so many things that cats have to tell us, obvious and simple, or subtle and complex. But I think these few examples prove my point, that cats are definitely with us, that they communicate clearly to those of us willing to watch and listen.

For all a cat's independence, there is still a part of his personality that reaches out toward us, quietly asking for our love and wanting it very much. Cats have learned to talk to humans; I only hope that more humans will learn how to answer them.

Rhubarb

H. ALLEN SMITH

This anthology would be a poor thing indeed if it didn't include something on Rhubarb, master of claw and fang, and imperious millionaire owner of the most raffish baseball team in history.

April in New York. Weather. Scenery. The first cat-owned big-league baseball team in recorded history was ready to open its season.

Clarissa Wood insisted that she supervise preparation of the owner's field box, situated immediately behind the home team's dugout at Banner Field. She wanted a cat-sized throne done in platinum and black velvet set up in the middle of the box. She wanted to order a cedar tree from Mount Lebanon in Syria and have a scratching post made from it and placed in a conspicuous position. She contended that Rhubarb's jewel-encrusted sanitary tray should be placed in a small enclosure at the back of the box, out of sight of the populace.

One by one her ideas were knocked down.

Len Sickles had a good deal to say about the arrangements. He told Eric that whenever the new owner of the Loons was present at Banner Field for a baseball game, he, the owner, would have to be within easy reach of the Loon players. That, said Len, was a primary consideration.

"These goons of mine," the manager explained, "are playing ball like they were the nine Apostles. They are inspired. They believe that this cat brings them luck. And they insist that Rhubarb's gotta be somewhere close to the dugout, so they can run up and touch him."

Whereupon Eric invented a gadget. Rhubarb's pedestal was built into the structure of the box and against the back wall of the dugout. A small hole was cut into the wall, communicating between dugout and owner's box, a hole just big enough to accommodate a man's hand. Of necessity the hole was down near the floor of the owner's box, and Rhubarb, if placed beside it, where the players could reach through and touch him, would have been out of sight all the time. The gadget solved the problem. It was a cat elevator. Normally Rhubarb's pedestal extended above the roof of the dugout, giving the cat a clear view of the playing field and giving the fans a clear view of the cat. If an emergency arose, a tight spot, a clutch, a situation in which a player felt the need of touching Rhubarb, he turned a crank and the pedestal would sink, with Rhubarb on it. The player who wanted to touch Rhubarb for luck poked his hand through the aperture to do the touching, then withdrew it and cranked the pedestal back into its normal position. This arrangement obviated use of the silver cage, a situation that gave Eric some worry. He decided that some physical restraint would have to be put on the cat, so a strong fishline was hooked to a heavy staple in the wall of the box, with a snap fastener at the other end for Rhubarb's collar.

As for the sanitary tray. Eric vetoed Miss Wood's scheme for hiding it away out of sight.

"Rhubarb owns this ball club," he told her. "That means he owns this ball park—every inch of it. If he wants to he can walk right out to home plate, or the pitcher's mound, and go. The fans will love it."

Miss Wood was incensed over the very thought of such a thing. "In the first place," she said, "someone would have to go with him and have him on his leash. I assure you, Mr. Yaeger, from the bottom of my heart, that a cat will not do such a thing while on a leash. Furthermore, who is going to take him out there in front of all those rowdy people?"

"I wouldn't mind doing it myself," Eric assured her. "I have my hammy moments."

"You are being most unreasonable," she said. "The very idea of that sweet kitty-cat having to do his business in front of the public horrifies me."

*   *   *   *

St. Louis was to oppose the Loons on opening day, and Eric led Rhubarb's entourage to Banner Field two hours before game time.

The party went first to the executive quarters, and Rhubarb was introduced for the first time to his own private office. He seemed bored by it. Then Eric led the way to the Second Guess Club, a large room where the sports writers gathered before and after games. For this momentous occasion the sports writers were reinforced by a horde of feature writers, all of whom were clamoring for the right to sit in the owner's box. Some of these feature writers tried to pull an old dodge on Eric.

"My city editor," one young woman said to him, "assigned me to sit in the box with Rhubarb. I've simply got to do it. If I don't I lose my job. My city editor said so. And I've simply got to keep my job, Mr. Yaeger. I'm the sole support of my old mother who's dying of heartburn, and——"

"Nuts, sister!" Eric brushed her off. "I used to work on newspapers myself."

* * * *

It was time to get down to the field. The stands were already packed as Eric came up through the Loons' dugout with Rhubarb in his arms. A roar of welcome greeted them. Eric walked across the grass toward the St. Louis dugout, stopping near home plate to hold the cat above his head, so all could see. The roar redoubled in volume.

At the visitors' dugout Eric came up against an unpleasant situation which he should have anticipated. St. Louis was the traditional enemy of the Loons, and Eric quickly recognized a strong undercurrent of animosity toward the cat. Several of the players, presumably the more superstitious members of the St. Louis team, ducked into their dugout and disappeared. Eric heard one man growl, "Git that goddamn Joner outa here!"

Dick Madison, the St. Louis manager, furnished the tip-off on what to expect. The St. Louis gang was going to use ridicule as its chief weapon against Rhubarb. Madison minced up to Eric, took off his cap, and executed a low sweeping bow. Then he stepped back into the dugout and returned with a mousetrap. It was probably the biggest mousetrap ever manufactured—being about four feet long and two feet wide. It was already set and baited with a wedge of yellow cheese that probably cost around a dollar eighty-five. Madison clowned his way out toward home plate and daintily set the trap down on the grass. Then he stood up and gestured with his right arm, indicating that Rhubarb was to help himself to the cheese, a present from his host of St. Louis admirers. The crowd roared with laughter.

Meanwhile the St. Louis players had quietly gathered at the dugout entrance. Now they formed a conga line and started to dance. Each man was carrying a long cattail, and the fans were highly amused as the line of capering players curved and circled around the field. Eric wasn't greatly amused.

"Cute," he said acidly to Dick Madison. "Very, very cute!"

"Ah, shuddup!" said Madison. "Go scratch yourself a hole in the ground, you cat nurse, and crawl in it and cover yourself up!"

Eric felt like popping him one, but he had his arms full of cat. He chose the course of discretion and hurried back across the grass to the Loons' dugout. Here he encountered an explosive situation. Len Sickles was having difficulty keeping the Loons in hand. They wanted to open proceedings by swarming onto the field and beating the brains out of their opponents for making fun of their owner.

They gathered excitedly around Eric, and some of them talked reassuring baby talk to Rhubarb.

"Yes, Rhubarb!" crooned Benny Seymour, the coach. "You sweet liddle Rhubarb you! You sweet thing! Pay no attention to them filthy bastards, honey! We'll fix 'em for you! Yes sir, we will!"

Others expressed similar sentiments. Eric was somehow pleased with it all. The boys were one hundred per cent back of Rhubarb. Old Thad had never commanded such loyalty.

The others were already in the owner's box, and Eric took Rhubarb to his pedestal. The cat was behaving like a gentleman. He sat on the pedestal for a while, looking around at all the color and activity and noise, and then he hopped over into Eric's lap and went to sleep.

Eric had to wake him up when the time came for the game to start. The line-ups were being announced over the loud-speaker system. The announcer called attention to the presence of the new owner of the Loons. Eric put the cat back on the pedestal, and Rhubarb stretched himself and yawned for the edification of the crowd. . . .

Rhubarb now appeared to take an interest in the proceedings. He sat up and watched the Loons take the field. Goff was pitching, and the St. Louis center fielder, Peterson, was the first man to face him. Peterson connected with the first ball thrown to him.

A split second after the bat cracked against the ball something cracked in the owner's box. Rhubarb shot forward, the fishline snapped, and the yellow cat streaked into right field.

It was the fastest Eric had ever seen Rhubarb move. The ball went to the right of the first baseman, and Rhubarb was on it before the right fielder could reach it. The fielder ran up, then stopped in bewilderment. Rhubarb was trying to seize the baseball in his teeth, and the fielder's perplexity was so great that he could do nothing but stand there helplessly. Meanwhile Peterson was quickly circling the bases.

Then a new element of confusion entered the picture. Someone in the St. Louis dugout played the visitor's trump card. They turned loose a bulldog. At the same moment someone in the right field bleachers tossed a terrier over the fence.

Both dogs went for Rhubarb full tilt.

The stands, the dugouts, the players on the field, the game officials —everyone was in an uproar.

Rhubarb looked up from the ball and saw the bulldog coming at him. He feinted, pretending that he was about to flee in the direction of his box.

The bulldog was lost. He swerved, and as he swerved Rhubarb hit him, clawing and biting. The dog let forth a scream of anguish just as the terrier arrived on the scene. That shriek did something to the terrier. He put on the brakes, skidded to an amazed halt, took another quick look just to make sure, then wheeled around and started for what he hoped would be some secluded spot fifty miles away. But Rhubarb was after him like a bullet, leaving the bulldog lying on the field, yelping and bleeding. Now came the terrier's turn. The cat ripped and whipsawed him up one side and down the other.

People were beginning to pour onto the field, and the din was deafening, yet above it all sounded a howl of pain that came from no dog. The High Commissioner had jumped over the wall of his box; he had taken about five quick steps with his eyes fixed on the distant ruckus. He had stepped squarely into the big mousetrap, and the thing had almost torn his leg off.

Willy Bodfish was the first occupant of the owner's box to reach the scene of combat, and he succeeded in prying Rhubarb loose from the terrier. The fallen dogs were removed from the arena, and back in the box Eric got Rhubarb into his cage while police were herding the more excited fans off the field. There was an immediate and acrimonious conference in front of the Loons' dugout involving the umpires, the High Commissioner (free of the trap but sorely wounded), officials of the league, managers of both teams, and most of the players.

Dick Madison was hot with fury—so enraged that he simply jumped up and down on the ground.

"That's my kid's dog," he screamed in anger. "That cat's killed him! Leave me at him!"

They finally had to seize and restrain Madison. Len Sickles, too, had his dander up and was howling that he was going to punch Dick Madison's head off.

"I saw it!" yelled Sickles. "Everybody saw it! You turned that dog loose outa your own dugout!"

There was a prolonged and angry consideration of ground rules. The High Commissioner stood by, glaring at Dick Madison, for he had seen where that damned trap came from. The umpires, after a whispered conference with the High Commissioner, announced that Peterson was not entitled to a home run. He was not entitled to anything. Madison went into a new tantrum bordering on epilepsy over this fresh manifestation of man's inhumanity to man. His players milled around with fists clenched, eager to start a fight. Madison wanted to take his team and leave, go back to St. Louis, and never again have any relations with the Loons.

The argument over Peterson's status—whether or not he was entitled to at least a hit—went on for fifteen minutes.

"It was an act of God," said the High Commissioner.

"Then, by God, we get a home run out of it!" bellowed Madison.

"You'll get a bust in the nose out of it," yelled the High Commissioner. "What the hell do you mean by leaving that trap out there for me to fall into? Look what it did! Ripped my pants leg clear off! I oughta kill you and then bar you from baseball for the rest of your lousy life! Peterson gets no hit. I rule that Peterson must return to the plate and we start all over again. And"—he gave Eric an ominous glance—"if that cat gets onto the field again, I'll outlaw you and the cat and your whole damn team so you won't even be able to get into the Piedmont League!"

"That cat won't get onto the field again," said a stranger, stepping forward. "I seize this cat in the name of the law."

The stranger looked around for a cat to seize in the name of the law, but Rhubarb was some thirty feet away in his cage.

"Now what?" said Eric.

"Hand over that cat," said the stranger. He pulled back his coat and exhibited a shield. "I happen to be the sheriff of this county. Judge Loudermilk of Surrogate's Court commands the appearance of one Rhubarb Banner forthwith, for examination before trial, in the case of Tatlock versus Banner."

"You're crazy!" cried Eric. "You can't examine a cat before trial! What'll you examine him for, fleas?"

"All I know is I got my orders," said the sheriff. "The cat goes, and he goes right now."

"Furthermore," Eric argued, "this doesn't look legally proper to me. Maybe you've got a subpoena. But you can't come out here and seize Rhubarb like this."

"I've got a subpoena," said the sheriff, "and if that cat was a human I'd serve it on him and be done with my duty. But this cat ain't a human. It's a case where I got to make up my own rules as I go along. Judge Loudermilk wants Rhubarb Banner, and Rhubarb Banner he gets. Let's get going."

And so Rhubarb and Eric and Polly and Doom and Clarissa and Willy trooped out of the stands and got into automobiles and drove to downtown Manhattan. Back at Banner Field the opening game of the season was started anew, and the Loons, deprived of a cat to touch, lost it by a score of 12-0.

David

LLOYD ALEXANDER

*Lloyd Alexander was fortunate to have in his life the cats
who frolic through the pages of his charming book "My
Five Tigers." Each had its own interesting and well-defined
personality. But my favorite is David, the demonic little
half-Siamese whose meeting with Rabbit and Heathcliff, the
already established cats, was pure bedlam despite Alexander's intention to "go by the book" and introduce the new
kitten gradually.*

*The skirmishes among them, and particularly between
the burly Heathcliff and his tiny tormentor, are vividly described, as is the dramatic turnabout in behavior that resulted in an enduring love affair.*

*Since this is David's story, I have omitted the account of
Heathcliff's sudden tragic death, but in the last section the
sensitive reader will recognize the change the loss of his
friend wrought in David and will sympathize with his wistful nightly vigil at the open cellar window.*

We located David through an advertisement in the "Pets" column of
the local paper, and he is the only one of my cats able to account for
at least half of his ancestry. His owner, a charming, elderly lady,
usually raised only pedigreed Siamese. But she admitted she wasn't
spry enough to keep track of a Siamese queen in season. David's
mother, a cat of distinguished lineage, had slipped out of the house,
yielded to the blandishments of an anonymous trifler, and produced a
litter of kittens who would never know their father. None bore any
resemblance to the queen. They came out tabbies, tortoise-shells and
unclassifiables. All but David. Although his blue eyes had a slight in-
fringement of green, he showed the typical triangular head, elongated
body and whip tail, and would have cut a fine figure as a Siamese except for his color. He was entirely black.

We agreed to adopt him. During the ride home, I learned he had
another Siamese characteristic: a loud mouth. He yelled and bleated
all the way. I carried him, still grumbling, into the living room where

he fought his way out of my arms, ran off in several directions at once, and finally hid under the couch.

Books on the subject advise introducing a new kitten gradually. I had every intention of doing so. Before going after David, we made sure that Rabbit and Heathcliff were both outside. I had planned to lock David in the workroom, allowing the older cats to get acquainted with him in easy stages. But I forgot about the windows.

As soon as David came out of hiding, he spotted Heathcliff peering in from the outside sill. As luck would have it, Rabbit was there, too. Chattering like a monkey, David sprang to the window and stuck his head through the slats of the venetian blind. The startled Rabbit bristled and began a long, menacing growl. Heathcliff spat, hissed and made terrible faces while his sideburns trembled wrathfully. I immediately carried David into the workroom, but too late. My plans for a leisurely introduction were shattered when the two big cats came thumping up the cellar steps and laid siege at the door.

Heathcliff clawed violently at the woodwork and Rabbit made noises like a lynching party. In despair, I abandoned the advice of my cat manual, deciding this was a case of every man for himself. I opened the door. Confronted with the chattering black kitten face to face, Rabbit and Heathcliff turned tail and raced away.

Rabbit took to his barberry office and refused to come out even for dinner. Heathcliff perched on top of the piano and glared at the newcomer. None of this bothered David. He strutted through the rooms, sniffing and chuckling, and ate a hearty meal alone in the kitchen.

*   *   *   *

For a kitten, his legs were especially long and coltish. He was so black that when he closed his eyes he seemed to make himself invisible. In repose, he kept a vague smile on his face—but it turned into a diabolical grin when he started on a rampage. For ears he had enormous black triangles on either side of his head, like batwings, and I half expected him to be airborne at any moment.

His voice fascinated me most. He spoke a mixture of Siamese and alley cat, suiting the expression to the occasion. A hoarse mew was simply a demand for attention; but in the kitchen, at meal times, he sat back on his lean haunches, opened his mouth as wide as he could, and made a noise like "Frank! Frank!" If we kept him waiting, he turned on his special cry of "Caaake!"—pronounced with much stuttering on the C's and K's, and a very long middle vowel. In addition he would utter a sneezing sound, "Chuff!", which I learned to imitate pretty well.

I reached a point where I could almost converse with him; and if he were in the mood, we could keep it going for several minutes.

I could never master the chattering aspect of his speech. He had a way of curling back his lip and agitating his lower jaw—with a result impossible to write down.

The rest of the time, he bleated intermittently—a surprising, sheep-like cry. At this period, casting about for his name, I settled temporarily on "Frank Blacklamb." But "Frank" never stuck; it wasn't his type. And "Blacklamb" made awkward calling. His official name didn't come until Heathcliff was up and about.

I don't know whether cats have psychosomatic illnesses. Some authorities say they do. If I weren't convinced Heathcliff had a very physical bout with flu, I could easily be persuaded it was all in his mind.

As soon as he could stand, Rabbit demanded to go out; while Heathcliff lingered in the workroom, eating and drinking heartily, purring loudly whenever he saw me, but hissing like a viper at the sight of the black kitten. He seemed so reluctant to leave that I feared he would become an imaginary invalid and spend the rest of his life there. I transported him to the living room. Cackling like a mad cat, David ran to greet the old fraud.

Heathcliff rose, shaking his paws ferociously. David charged like a bull and the older cat found himself ignominiously tipped over: a blue Goliath. David was named.

From that point, David discovered he was able to vanquish the two Philistines by rushing at them as fast as he could. Small enough to slip under their guards, he pummeled their bellies or swung from their necks by his paws. Even Rabbit sometimes came out second best. (He solved this problem by staying outside, as far from the kitten as possible.) But Heathcliff seemed torn between a desire to remain indoors and avoid David at the same time. An impossible wish. The kitten sought him out in every corner.

Whenever possible, Heathcliff defended himself by smacking David about the head. The black kitten would withdraw, sit down for a moment and then, like a man suddenly realizing he's been insulted, turn back with a cry and bore into the blue cat again.

I had no doubt that Heathcliff despised the newcomer. If I held David on my lap, Heathcliff would be uncivil to me for an hour after. And if I dared to pet the kitten, Heathcliff shot me glances of rage, jealousy and general bad temper that were almost human.

If he found the situation untenable, it was no easier for me. First, I was afraid the older cat might decide to inflict major damage. For all his technique, David was a lightweight. Heathcliff could have shaken him like a mouse had he wanted to. Worse, I felt I had done my old friend a disservice, whatever my intentions. Heathcliff made it plain he was not amused.

At the same time, I hated to send David away. His quiet moments were rare, but all the more welcome. He would perch on my shoulder, half dozing, while I sat reading, occasionally raising his head to whisper "Frank!" When I answered him, he would reach down and pat my cheek with his paw. Or else, he would curl beside me and stay motionless, respectful as an Etonian, a proper lower-form boy in a black suit. And he never stopped smiling—only at those times the grin appeared especially wistful.

But a new kitten demands a certain amount of time and attention, plus a great deal of pampering. So does an older cat, for that matter; and as long as Rabbit and Heathcliff remained antagonistic, I felt I was robbing them of something they were entitled to as original settlers. Heathcliff still refused to join David on the bed; he had abandoned the fishing game ever since the kitten jumped into the box with him; and Rabbit ignored everybody.

For two weeks the house remained an armed camp, without even the rumor of a truce. Blue and black shapes streaked past me like angry comets: Heathcliff spitting and growling desperately, David after him, yelling gleefully. I decided, half-heartedly, to find another home for the kitten. Janine made a few telephone calls but we couldn't locate anyone who needed a small cat in a hurry. So David remained in the house on a day-to-day lease.

The cats settled the problem in their own way, during a warm afternoon toward the end of the month. I had taken David into the garden with me. He was still a little nervous outdoors, and he played cautiously among the plants, hooking up twigs with his flexible paws, looking questioningly at me as if he wanted to be assured of doing the right thing.

Heathcliff, spending an idle moment near his castle, spotted us and followed along at a good distance. He never approached me when David was present, and he sat a few yards away, watching gloomily. I don't know what entered his mind at that instant. Perhaps he realized his knowledge of the grounds gave him an advantage over the kitten —at least he couldn't be maneuvered into tight corners. He got up suddenly and galloped toward David.

At the sight of this blue locomotive, David gave a cry and sprang away. They chased each other in wide circles around the lawn: Heathcliff, his ears tight against his head and mighty tail streaming behind;

the kitten pedaling his spindly legs as fast as possible. David tried a piece of fancy footwork—jumping in the air, intending to hit the ground at a run and sprint off in another direction. For once, he miscalculated.

The older cat swarmed over him, cuffing and swearing. For a second or two I lost sight of the kitten in a whirl of blue fur. David finally managed to crawl out and raced for a sanctuary. The nearest one was Barkis' old dog house. Only David didn't go inside. The house had been set on four bricks, one at each corner, and the space between earth and floor was large enough to accommodate only one very narrow cat. So David crawled underneath.

Heathcliff strode up triumphantly. He tried to fish David from under the dog house, but the kitten moved to the far end. Getting out was a tight squeeze. Heathcliff had plenty of time to reach whichever side David chose, and the blue cat patrolled the walls. Whenever the kitten poked out his head, Heathcliff gave him a solid smack. David ducked in again. Once, David succeeded in getting his shoulders free. Heathcliff pounced on his neck with both feet.

I was ready to step in as referee and declare the match over. But Heathcliff moved away of his own accord, and the chastised kitten slowly pulled himself free. He went over to the big cat, sniffed at him and gave a little chirp. Instead of recoiling in horror, my old friend sniffed back. Both sat down and stared at each other for a while. I went into the house and they followed me. From that day on, they were never apart.

* * * *

David's pampering continued even to the most sacrosanct and vital functions of a cat's life: eating. Siamese are reputed intense eaters. Although David was only half a Siamese, he inherited most of their greediness and reinforced it with the perseverance of an alley cat. Since Rabbit ate at the drainboard and Heathcliff on the floor, we made a separate place for David on the kitchen window sill. In this way, the big cats had at least a fighting chance of finishing their meals in peace.

But David gobbled his meal in a few seconds, then jumped to the floor and began embezzling Heathcliff's food. (He once tried it with Rabbit and was cuffed severely for his insolence.) He sidled up to Heathcliff's plate with the smoothness of a cardsharper, edged closer and closer, purring deceitfully until, as if by accident, he found his nose in Heathcliff's plate. He had such an oily, river-gambling and stock-watering way about him that he was soon nicknamed "Honest John."

Heathcliff, usually possessive when it came to his rations, never raised his voice to the kitten. If Janine hadn't interfered at the crucial moments, the old cat might have gone half hungry. She held off the eager kitten until Heathcliff had almost finished; as soon as she let him go, he sneaked over to the plate. Heathcliff, to my surprise, always made room for him, and the old humbug and young swindler shared the few remaining morsels.

Sometimes I feared that all these indulgences could only have a bad effect on David's moral character. By winter time, he had become what breeders call a senior kitten. In human terms, a juvenile delinquent. The lower-form boy was now replaced by an adolescent, long-legged sport in a charcoal gray sack suit. He still impressed me as a British type—but a young gentleman who is rusticated from Cambridge, smokes too many cigarettes and drives a red MG. David, very much a Small Black Kitten, began to take to himself the prerogatives of a Large Black Cat.

*   *   *   *

David became a cat suddenly. At least, it seemed that way to me. Perhaps I had been used to seeing him flat on his back in the arms of Heathcliff or Rabbit, or clucking for a late saucer of milk. But I noticed his graduation shortly after he began spending his days on the lawn. There were no longer any mad pursuits after the squirrels. David operated as carefully as Rabbit now, silent and wary, economical in movement. Even his appearance underwent an abrupt change. He stood as tall as the older cat, his body even longer. The black fur glistened over his muscles. More green had mixed with the blue in his eyes, giving them a color of sea water. And he walked as sedately as a young curate.

He seldom ventured beyond the garden, but found enough to occupy him on our own grounds. The mouse academy came back in business with a new and enlarged enrollment. And David did not overlook the garter snakes. They had grown, too, and he must have caught the biggest ones to bring inside.

For his own private retreat, David chose a trellis at the far end of the grounds. I could watch him climbing the whitewashed slats until he reached the top. There he sat like a pillar saint, watching butterflies, and extending a paw as they skimmed past.

That spring, David also received his baptism of fire—administered, naturally, by Felix Cat. The hoodlum had kept to himself for most of the winter; bunkered down in Felix' barn, most likely. For a time, I had even forgotten about him. But the warm days brought him out again. I could hear him yowling and raging through the bushes in the evenings; in the daytime, he watched over the lawn from a hideout in Felix' vegetable patch.

One afternoon, I saw David sunning himself at the roots of a mulberry tree. He enjoyed lying in the dry dust and he sometimes rolled in it until his back turned earth color. With his eyes closed and his chin resting on one paw, he was oblivious to the approach of the gray tom. From the window, I could see Felix Cat sneaking closer. David never moved. I opened the window and shouted at him, whistled, and waved my arms. Felix Cat was out of range; otherwise, I would have tossed crockery. The gray cat a few feet away, David finally sat up and yawned. By the time I got out of the house and turned the corner of the tool shed, Felix Cat had sprung.

Intentionally, or by luck, David stood and Felix Cat missed his target. As soon as he turned to charge again, David caught him full in the whiskers with a set of unsheathed claws. Yelling like a demon, David rushed against the intruder. For the first time, I saw Felix Cat pinned to the ground. The battle lasted only a second. Felix Cat dis-

engaged himself and streaked away. David straightened his coat and went back to sleep. Heathcliff had taught him well.

In spite of such interruptions, David seemed more at peace outdoors than in the house. With us, he was strangely aloof and rarely wanted to stay longer than a few minutes. If we tried to hold him on our lap, or pat him as he walked about the rooms, he would shy away and run to the cellar door. He had long since learned the trick of getting out of the broken window. Like Rabbit, he now came and went as he pleased.

The world upstairs had little attraction for him. He took his meals without enthusiasm and seldom visited the toy box. Human activities only annoyed him. If the sound of my violin irritated Heathcliff, my typewriting had the same effect on David. When he did happen to be in the house, he left as soon as he heard the tapping of the machine. Visitors distracted him. Hard enough to keep inside when only Janine and I were present, it was almost impossible when we had company.

For no apparent reason, he disliked certain people more than others. One of my neighbors dropped in just as David was finishing his dinner. As we sat in the living room, David emerged from the kitchen, took one look at my guest and reared back. He spat, growled and crept away. At first, I thought something else had startled him at the same time. But, a few days later, when he saw the man on our lawn, his reaction was the same. His attitude deeply distressed my neighbor, certainly the mildest of individuals who never would have dreamed of contradicting a cat.

David gave up sleeping on our bed regularly. When he wanted quarters for the night, he made his way to the top of an old wooden cupboard in the cellar. There was just space enough between the top of the cupboard and the rafters for him to squeeze in. And he stayed there, his paws neatly folded, only his head visible. Before going to sleep, I always went down to his apartment to make sure he was all right. Each time, I tried to entice him upstairs. He only blinked at me and bleated softly.

Cats are supposed to enjoy comfort, and I could never understand why David preferred his cupboard to our innerspring mattress. I soon learned the reason. He had company.

Not only company, but visitors in fairly large numbers. David had become host to the neighborhood's cats.

I discovered his secret about three o'clock one morning, when Janine and I were awakened by a loud crash in the cellar. I went to the head of the stairs and turned on the light. A mackerel cat observed me from the broken window. The noise had been caused by the collapse of a pile of fruit baskets; and from behind the pile another kitten appeared. In the midst of it all, David sat on the cellar floor, grinning like a night-club manager.

The visitors scrambled out the window and David returned to his cupboard.

I didn't object to his entertaining a few friends, but these parties continued almost every night. How and where he found his friends I do not know. My older cats had always avoided their own kind, but David welcomed them. In a short time, I came to recognize the habitual visitors: a ginger cat of David's age, a small tortoise-shell and a mud-colored cat beyond description. A fierce-looking bobtail also showed up frequently.

David was not always a genial host. Wakened out of a sound slumber by angry yells, I would go downstairs and find David wrestling with one of his guests. Once, I discovered him in the bitter embraces of another black cat exactly his size. Half asleep, I couldn't tell which was which, but the affair looked like a serious fight. For ten minutes, I chased black cats around packing boxes and barrels. I maneuvered one to the window and started to shoo him out—until I caught a glimpse of greenish blue eyes and heard the reproachful "Cake!"

These cats were generally members of the younger set and David had no real trouble with them. But the parties were spoiled when the old toms, grizzled veterans of garbage can raids, began to muscle in. The cellar became a branch of the club house. Led by Felix Cat, this faction turned David's drawing-room parties into sordid brawls, during which the elder cats chased away the young ones and bickered among themselves afterwards.

I could invariably tell when Felix Cat or one of his henchmen entered the cellar. Those times, David's growl rose loud and prolonged—more like a dog than a cat. At the head of the stairs, he bristled and made threatening gestures while some burly thug stared up from the top of an orange crate.

Even though David's social club had become a hangout for racketeers, he persisted in spending most of his nights in the cellar: hoping, possibly, that Heathcliff would sooner or later pop in through the open window.

"The She-Shah"

COLETTE

*The unique and marvelous writer Colette was blessed with
an extraordinary, instinctive rapport with all animals. In her
perceptive study of Colette's writings, Elaine Marx says, "In
the rich animal literature of France . . . Colette occupies
a very special place. Her originality is that she attempts to
portray, not only a particular species, but within the species
an individual animal which she knows."*

*But of all animals, Colette loved best the cat, who in-
habits many of her finest stories. Her masterly novel of
passion and jealousy, "The Cat," is probably best known to
cat-loving readers, but they should find that shameless flatterer the She-Shah from "Creatures Great and Small" no
less captivating.*

"This cat, d'you mean? Why of course it's a male! This isn't the first
time I've sold a cat, you know. Don't you see his round head? And
how wide apart his ears are set? Look, he's already got a little lion-
face! And haven't you seen what big strong paws he has?"

Yes, we saw. We saw everything, except the one thing we should
have seen. With the result that, a fortnight later, the little Persian
cat, the Lord Cat, in short the "Shah," turned into a female, of a
delicate blue the colour of cigarette smoke and the silvery flower of
the sea-holly.

"It's a female! Whatever shall we do with her?"

"Why, what had you thought of doing with a male?"

"Oh, I don't know. Nothing special. We wanted to put a green
collar on him, and spoil him a lot. And besides, he was to be called
'the Shah'!"

"Well, there's nothing to worry about. You'll call her 'the She-
Shah' and you'll put a green collar on her, and feed her on milk with
sugar in it until she swells up as tight as a balloon, and all she can do
is to fall asleep on a yellow silk cushion."

One gets used to anything. "The Shah" has become "the She-
Shah." We address her tenderly as "My She-Shah, my little She-

Shah"; we're always proclaiming that "She's so beautiful, this She-Shah"; and sensible people—by which I mean those who possess neither dogs, nor French bull-dogs, nor collies, nor a Persian Shah—regard us with contemptuous pity.

She is indeed a Persian She-Shah, and it's easy to see she doesn't come from this part of the world. She grows at a great pace, but more in girth than height. Low on the ground, she's soft and agile, with a plume of a tail as long as herself, ears set low and a short velvety nose.

In play she is rather fierce, quickly losing her temper, and when she is angry she looks as though she were enjoying a physical pleasure, closing her eyes, clenching her teeth, and gripping her prey hard. She is always ready to look us in the face, and her sweet menacing eyes, grey-green as young willow-leaves, gaze steadily, deep into ours.

It amuses her to knead the thick coat of the big collie bitch with her paws, as one kneads dough; she gets on well with Great Danes, bulldogs, and even with noisy children. But certain musical sounds, and certain stealthy, hardly perceptible noises, terrify her so that her very fur takes fright and ripples with nervous shivers. If one opens and shuts a pair of scissors in front of her, she yawns and yawns. She is a mass of oriental superstitions: two fingers splayed out like horns are enough to put her to flight; but I've hung a little branch of pink coral on her collar to reassure her.

She is, in short, a very affected She-Shah, a princess of the harem with no wish to escape. A very female She-Shah too, coquettish and demure, absorbed in her own beauty which increases daily. Was there ever a more superb She-Shah? Slate blue in the morning, deepening to periwinkle at noon, in the sunlight she is iridescent as a pigeon—mauve, pearl-grey, steel and silver. In the evening she transforms herself into shadow, smoke, or cloud; she floats lighter than air and as impalpable, flinging herself over the back of an armchair as though she were a filmy scarf. And she glides along the wall like the reflection of a nacreous fish.

That is the hour when we like to believe her a fairy or some Eastern spirit, a genie or an afreet. We address childish prayers to her in the most high-flown language; we even go so far as to call her Sheherezade! But the hour is not yet come when our marvellous She-Shah will throw off her electric silky coat, her osprey whiskers, her blue squirrel-tail and her claws of polished jade.

"Now remember, on no account open her basket in the train!"

"Nonsense, you must open her basket the minute the train starts. If you don't, the She-Shah will have an epileptic fit!"

"Be sure to give her milk in the carriage!"

"Oh dear no, don't give her any milk on the journey or she'll be sick!"

"And when you get there, don't let her out for two days. Otherwise she'll make for the open country and you'll never see her again."

"What an absurd idea! Don't you believe it. You let her out as soon as you get to the country. A cat—and particularly a She-Shah— already recognises her home."

Weighed down with responsibilities, and distracted with all this conflicting advice, we set off with our familiar and tyrannical spirit, that fragile jewel, our precious She-Shah, towards the grey-green sea and the Brittany springtime, so eager to flower that sometimes it outstrips the springtime of the South.

Although it is still early in March, the honeysuckle, clinging to the rocks above the waves breaking in foam below, has already opened its green and brown leaves, like so many round, listening ears. There are pale primroses like greenish gold, and thorny brooms with red berries; there are violets, and paper pink Spanish thrift smelling like the flower of the apricot; and there are . . .

But there are also, on the roof of our house, a team of men repairing slates, and in the bedroom more workmen half-naked, busy with the parquet floor, while in the bathroom two jovial plasterers are making a jigsaw puzzle with square blue and white tiles. What's more, in the courtyard there are some wicked young boys, stirring a thick milk of dazzling chalk, a toffee-like cream of cement, and fanning the flame of a forge.

"Heavens above! Whatever will the She-Shah do with all these people about! She'll never eat or drink or sleep again! She'll die of fear, she's so delicate! And come to that, where is she? Where's the She-Shah? Where's the She-Shah?"

The She-Shah's lost, as we might have expected. We're so overcome that we have to spend some time lamenting before we can start looking for her. Then off we go, running and flying and tearing in all directions. We question the well, the deep wood, the shadowy attic, the musty cellar, the stable, the garage, the rocks of the Grand-Nez and the rocks of the Petit-Nez. We promise rewards to the beplastered day-labourers who mix the mortar. We accuse the watchdog and send the French bull-dog bitch, who has no sense of smell, off on an imaginary scent. We listen to the wind which dries our silent tears, and we vent our misery in bitter reproaches.

"I told you so! We oughtn't to have let the She-Shah out so soon."

"What's the good of saying all that now? The She-Shah's lost. As a matter of fact I had a sort of presentiment when we were on our way here. She ought never to have left Paris, a She-Shah of such rarefied breeding as that, who always ate from a bowl of Chinese porcelain and drank from a Venetian glass. Why, almost anything could hurt her—too bright a light, a gust of wind, a raised voice . . ."

"Well, it's no good, let's go in, and leave me to weep in peace for my She-Shah, my beautiful She-Shah!"

Back to the house we go. But at the bend of the path, we fall suddenly silent and stare with all our eyes!

In the middle of a circle of workmen sitting on the ground and eating their lunch, all among the hobnailed boots plastered with mud, the corduroys rigid with plaster, the blue overalls and the faded blouses, between the jugs of cider and rough wine, the greasy papers and the knives with their boxwood handles—there, smiling and very much at home, with her tail upright and her whiskers curling, in the midst of a din of oaths and coarse laughter, is the She-Shah, the divine She-Shah, gorged with cheese-rinds, rancid bacon and sausage skins, purring, spinning round after her tail, and playing to the gallery of masons.

Bockitay

ROBERT E. PINKERTON

Kathrene and Robert Pinkerton were an attractive couple,
both writers, who shared their New York apartment with
two handsome and affable Siamese cats. The Pinkertons had
enjoyed a remarkably adventurous life, beginning soon after
their marriage when Robert Pinkerton built a log cabin in
the Canadian North Woods that was their home for sev-
eral years.

Robert Pinkerton was an incomparable storyteller and
many of his most entertaining anecdotes over cocktails and
dinner were about Bockitay, the cat who contributed so
much to their joy in the wilds. The best of these stories
were published in the magazine article reprinted here.

It has been suggested by cynics that the true basis of a human being's relationship with a pet is vanity—the satisfaction derived from the animal's dependence and resulting loyalty. Perhaps . . . but it wasn't that way with our cat. Hers was a courage, a competence and a self-reliance I have not seen in any other animal. She never asked or accepted anything from humans, and managed to impress the idea that she and the Pinkertons were three individuals sharing life on equal terms.

Even our finding her was extraordinary. Indians alone shared our stretch of Canadian bush, more than 200 miles in length and nearly as wide. A few railroad people lived along a newly built transcontinental line, but they never strayed from their narrow gash in the wilderness. Yet as we paddled up a remote river one cold, rainy day at the summer's end, we heard a kitten call.

We couldn't believe our ears. We must have mistaken a bird's cry. It was impossible for a cat to reach that spot. No white people had been there, and in many years I had not seen a cat in an Ojibway wigwam. Even if it did reach there, it could not have survived. But as we waited, paddles poised, we heard the mew again.

We had the usual ideas about cats: they hated water and were wholly dependent on humans for food, shelter and all the fine comforts they demand. Compassion swept over us, for rain had been falling all day and certainly a kitten lost in that wilderness would be wet, miserable and starving. We knew she was a kitten from her call. As we turned the canoe to the bank, we thought of a name for her— Bockitay Goshigonse. *Bockitay* is Ojibway for hungry and *goshig* is cat, *onse* being the diminutive.

She came out of the brush and looked at us. Her color was gray and white. She was small, no more than ten weeks old, we decided, and she was wet. But we were firm in our ideas then and blindly failed to perceive that Bockitay was not bedraggled and did not show any indication of being miserable. She looked at us curiously and calmly.

We wrapped her in a wool shirt and tucked her beneath the deck in the bow of the Peterborough canoe. Our one idea was to get her warm and dry, as any cat we'd known would want to be, and feed her. We whittled strips of meat from a quarter of venison; she smelled them and turned away. She got out of the shirt, hopped onto the bow and began to wash herself. We wrapped her again, and again she would not stay. Evidently she did not want to waste any of that moisture and she sat in the rain and completed her toilet. It was late and we had many miles to go, so we gave up and let her remain there on the bow.

We reached home just before dark. We had cleared a site for the cabin I was to build and the tent was pitched at the forest edge, with a cooking crane in front. I started a fire and Kathrene hurriedly warmed condensed milk and meat. We knew that when introducing an animal to a home it must be fed at once and made to understand it is welcome and will be well cared for, and we did want Bockitay to like us and be our cat.

When Kathrene set the saucers of food on the ground, Bockitay looked into each dish and turned away. It was dark now and she walked out of the firelight and into the forest.

We felt she had scorned us as a family. Our best had not been good enough. We wondered what more we could have done.

After a few minutes she returned and laid a mouse before the fire. We started to praise the hunting prowess of so tiny a creature, but she didn't wait to hear our comments. Soon she returned with another mouse, and it was not long until four lay in a neat row before the fire.

"Now what in hell does that mean?" I asked in amazement.

"Just what it says," Kathrene said. "She's telling us she can get her own food."

It must have been that. Though Bockitay sat at that campfire many nights, she brought no more mice to it, nor did she eat those four. A pound of cat simply had demonstrated that she was able to take care of herself, and this she did through the years she was with us. Never did she show an interest in our meals, nor would she eat anything we offered except when she participated in the kill, as she loved to do.

Recital of this incident later lifted so many brows that we ceased mentioning it, but I am telling it now because it is so indicative of Bockitay. That evening, however, her independence disturbed us. We'd intended to get a cat after the cabin was built, as mice will overrun a home in the bush. Now we had a proven mouser, but would she stay? Did she approve of us? Certainly she did not behave like any cat we had ever seen.

Days passed and we had no assurance. Bockitay never rubbed against our legs, arched her back, purred or acted in the least way as cats do when they ingratiate themselves. She went about her business and we rarely saw her except at night when she came to the campfire. Then we, not the cat, tried to be ingratiating, and found ourselves helpless. She ignored offers of milk and food, was unimpressed by petting or cuddling, and did not enter the tent. The campfire interested her and she quickly learned to judge its condition. As soon as the blaze began to die, she curled up on the warm ground close to the ashes. In the morning, she was gone before we wakened.

After a week, we went to the railroad for mail, and we still didn't know if we had a cat. Our doubts grew when we met Pete Connelly, an old prospector friend, and learned her history. Pete had seen an Indian woman, who lived in a town far to the west, camping for the night on the river near where we found Bockitay. She had a cat and kittens in her canoe. Pete said the kittens' eyes had been open only a few days. Evidently Bockitay had strayed into the brush when the woman went on that day. Checking dates, we discovered we had been right in thinking she was about ten weeks old when we found her. It is remarkable that she showed no fear of us, for she could have had little or no memory of humans. She was weak and unsure physically, had little or no instruction from her mother. Her only equipment was instinct and the animal urge to live. Abruptly weaned and not yet having tasted meat, she had to stalk and kill her own food. The forest had many animals that would have killed and eaten her on sight or scent, and she had not learned to climb a tree and was too weak for defense. Undoubtedly she went through many days and nights of terror and hunger.

But when we found her, she was competent and assured. We spoke of it on the way home from our mail trip in the dark. Perhaps Bockitay had thought we would not come back and had wandered off. After all, we weren't important to her. The courage of her fight to survive appealed to us strongly and we wanted her to be our cat, yet how could Bockitay be anyone's cat? We had talked ourselves into believing she would be gone when the canoe slid in toward the beach. We trailed the paddles, waiting, and then it came, that kitten call we had heard on the river. The canoe touched and she jumped in with a little chirrup of welcome.

Having accepted us, Bockitay began to share our life, but in accordance with her ideas of the situation. As she supported herself, we could have nothing to say about her conduct, nor did we attempt to, but she never did anything to cause us distress or inconvenience. Though she was glad to see us when she returned from hunting, she never used cat enticements. She liked to be stroked but never suggested it, did not jump to a knee and demand a comfortable place for a nap. If we picked her up, she'd not object, and she'd purr occasionally, but she didn't ask for attention. We never saw her "knead bread," that peculiar alternate flexing of the toes of the forefeet common with all cats and a sign of extreme bliss or great affection.

We never saw Bockitay play. Not even as a kitten did she chase her tail. She never knew kittenhood. At an age when other kittens are still nursing, she roamed a forest hunting her food, and when they are "cute," cuddly and attention-demanding, she was an accomplished huntress. What meaning could a ball of string have for her?

Yet we refused to understand this until the cabin was built and the three of us were together one dirty night. Bockitay prowled restlessly, something we had not seen her do before, and we decided she needed amusement. I rolled a bit of paper and dragged it about the room with a string. She looked as if she thought I had gone a little mad. Though a cold rain was falling, she asked to be let out.

Ten minutes later she returned with a small toad. She poked its rear end with a paw, but after it had made a couple of jumps, she curled up and went to sleep. It was as if she had said, "My God! If I must play a fool game, at least I'll have something alive."

Bockitay was a huntress, and to hunting she devoted her life. She had no other interest except her association with us, and as her ability increased, so did her pride in it, and her shame if she made a mistake. We saw one example of this in the first weeks.

Chipmunks had been plentiful in the clearing, but she quickly cleaned them out except for the clever old grandaddy of the lot. At last she caught him and carried him to an open space, where she looked around to make sure no shelter for her prey was available. Satisfied, she set him down, only to have him scoot between her legs and into a pile of brush behind her. It was the one place where she had not looked.

I am ashamed to say we laughed and thus added to Bockitay's deep chagrin. She didn't get over it until she had caught the chipmunk several days later. Now she went to a wide place in the clearing and turned around twice, looking over every bit of ground, before she set him down and exacted the penalty for her past defeat. That was Bockitay. She didn't make the same mistake twice. She couldn't have done so and survived.

We knew little of Bockitay's hunting, however, and we never saw her at work after she had rid the clearing of chipmunks. We knew only that she never asked for food, never ate anything we offered, never showed signs of hunger. She refused milk and would not drink water from a saucer, but went to the lake or ate snow. Weather didn't stop her and if it caused her to go hungry, we didn't know it. Snow depth varied from one to three feet, we had five months without a thaw, and a government thermometer at the railroad registered 52 to 56 below zero each winter. Yet not once did we know her to forgo her daily and nightly hunts.

Where she went, we never learned. Except for her sober conduct and serious attitude in and around the cabin, she acted much as any house cat, but several times we saw her leave the clearing, and as she entered the forest the transformation was astonishing. She became instantly a savage, preying creature of the wilds, crouching as she walked, her belly almost dragging. She made no sound and paused often to look around. Her expression was of complete ferocity.

Hunting was her passion and her life, and her attitude toward us changed when she learned that we, too, hunted and brought home meat. It pleased her, though she would never touch it, and she began to take a greater interest in our activities.

We made several trips of two to five days the first fall and whether we returned at noon or midnight, she had heard that telltale click of a paddle on the gunwale of a Peterborough and was at the shore to greet us. After the cabin was built, our life was more regular. All three were busy. We paddled in supplies, laid out trap lines, cut wood and hunted meat, but Bockitay performed her tasks with greater competence and far less fuss, and because she did everything for herself and made no demands on us, she considered herself an autonomous member of the trio. She shared the cabin with us and came in every evening at suppertime for a wash before the fire. But she left each night, and whenever a rain fell she went out at once. After our own feet had rustled dry leaves, we understood, but she seemed to have known always that rain softens them and permits silent stalking.

Because we did not know how far Bockitay hunted, Kathrene did not set a trap or a rabbit snare within a mile of the cabin. Evidently that was enough, as she never found a sign that Bockitay had visited the trap line. Kathrene shot and snared snowshoe rabbits for bait and for the table and had ten to twenty of the big hares lying frozen on the roof. Bockitay expressed great satisfaction in examining them and pride in the fact we had stored so much meat, but she would not touch them.

She must have encountered many animals in the forest and we still wonder what happened. Weasels were abundant, and a more blood-thirsty killer doesn't live. Mink, fisher, otter, lynx and foxes were near us, and any one of them would have delighted in killing a cat. Wolves were plentiful and before dawn one winter morning twenty swept through the clearing and onto the lake. It would have been impossible for Bockitay not to have encountered wolves, yet we never saw a tooth or claw mark on her.

She was fearless. A dog team came to the cabin and she walked up to the leader and smelled noses with him. Kathrene was given a beautiful thoroughbred collie, a vain but clever creature who was an utter bitch in every sense of the word. Belle immediately attempted to lord it over Bockitay, and got a lesson she never forgot. Bockitay had only contempt for the dog, and her expression when she saw Belle beg for and eat our food was a delight. Later we acquired a team and once had nineteen sleigh dogs when the Canadian Geological Survey asked us to care for two teams. Dogs were chained all about the clearing, but Bockitay conducted her life as if they were not there. Four bad actors broke loose one night when we were gone and killed four others. We do not know what Bockitay did, but she was unimpressed when she saw the results of the carnage.

Having a dog team did not touch our strengthening relationship with Bockitay. Dogs, as she expressed clearly in her manner, were senseless creatures that scared game by yapping and howling.

This sense of oneness with us increased as time went on and though she rarely showed affection as cats commonly do, we knew in other ways her devotion was great. Her jealousy of us grew and ultimately became savage. After two years, our mothers and sisters arrived for a three weeks' visit and their presence in the cabin infuriated her.

Kathrene always wore riding breeches and Bockitay had never seen anyone in dresses. She disappeared the second day and we did not see her again. A friend called for our guests with his new motorboat and after we had waved farewell and were walking back to the cabin, Bockitay came out of the forest and entered with us. She sat in her usual place before the fire and washed, settling at once into the old routine. Evidently she had been watching from the forest each day, and ever afterward she hated anyone in skirts.

Through it all, Bockitay's passion for hunting increased, though she boasted of her prowess only once each year. In early summer, when young snowshoe rabbits began running about at night and old ones sat on trails and thumped, we knew we were due for the annual ceremony of praise. We couldn't escape it because, as Bockitay might need the shelter of the cabin if pursued by a more powerful hunter, I had built a two-way swinging door in the screen of our bedroom window. Thus she could always get in or out, even if we were away, and through that door each spring she dragged her first young rabbit.

We got up. We had to. She'd leap to the bed and rub it across our faces, and no scolding or covering of heads would stop her. So we'd light a lamp in the living room, Bockitay would lay down her prize and all three would walk around it and admire. After a decent interval, we'd go back to bed, and in the morning we'd find her on her back, her belly distended, with all four feet in the air. She'd lie like that until night. This happened each spring, but we never found a hair, a drop of blood or a bit of bone on the floor. The rabbit was all inside Bockitay, and she wouldn't go hunting that night. Though she must have killed scores of young rabbits each summer, we saw only the first.

As Bockitay's passion for hunting formed a strengthening bond between her and her humans, she developed a special adoration for me. I claim no credit, for I know it was due only to the fact I could bring home the greatest game in the forest, a moose. That, in her world, was the supreme achievement. She knew the heavy rifle had something to do with this and if I carried it she would try to follow me. When late at night I brought home the antlers and the choice cuts of a moose in the canoe, she would meet me, purring furiously, and sleep on the meat until morning. She never touched it, only seeming overjoyed that we had so much.

She liked to follow Kathrene around the clearing on short hunts and if a big snowshoe rabbit was killed, she would fight savagely for it. Evidently she believed she had participated in the kill. She would take only the liver. We never knew whether she caught the big hares— they were larger than her—but she must have done so. As soon as Kathrene shot one, Bockitay would pounce on it, rip open one side, reach in unerringly and pull out the liver. Her knowledge of rabbit anatomy was perfect.

These rabbit hunts were kept close to the clearing, for we did not want Bockitay to get in the habit of following us and reach the traps. We went farther for ruffed grouse and at last she decided to hunt them with us.

Shooting partridge was pretty much of a chore. Kathrené killed about 200 each fall with her .22, and she didn't dare bring home one not shot in the head. One year she got 75 from the windows and doors of the cabin. She was in a hurry the day Bockitay decided to accompany her and she tried to slip away. Bockitay was determined to make a test case of it and at last Kathrene gave in, thinking she would circle back quickly and shut the cat in the cabin. Bockitay started ahead along a trail and after a few yards she sat up on her haunches and stared to one side, motionless. Kathrene heard the familiar cluck of a disturbed bird. She shot it. She shot the six we needed for a meal, each shot made when Bockitay stopped to sit up and look. After that we'd amuse ourselves, and give Bockitay great pleasure, by taking her on short hunts around the clearing.

She didn't retrieve the birds or go near them after they were killed, but when they were dressed she demanded the livers and wouldn't touch any other part. We never knew whether she killed grouse when alone, but we believe she did—she knew so much about them and was so fond of the livers. Once she and Kathrene got six grouse in the clearing and Bockitay watched with great distress while the birds were quickly dressed. At last she regurgitated four mice and waded into the livers. From this and many similar incidents, we reasoned why Bockitay ignored all food except what she killed, or saw killed. She wanted it hot. She wanted the odor and taste of meat with the animal heat undiminished. She would go hungry rather than eat anything else.

This participation in our hunting and her admiration of me as a killer of mammoth rabbits nearly finished our life in the Canadian wilderness. Perhaps Bockitay wished to see me haul down a moose and suck its life blood or rip out its liver, to share in what she considered the greatest triumph in life. In the end, she decided to witness it.

We had seen a bear swim across the mouth of our deep bay and I set a trap near the far point. Each morning when I'd take the rifle and paddle across to look at it, Bockitay would accompany me to the lake. It was nearly two miles around the shore to the trap, and the direction in which I started off by water was opposite to what one would take by land, so I never thought she would try to follow. A few days after the trap was set, we went to the railroad for mail. Bockitay saw us off, but when we returned after midnight she failed for the first time to greet us. We were disturbed and walked around the clearing, calling her name. We wakened late and she had not come in. After breakfast we searched again and finally got in the canoe and paddled along the shore, hunting her. While we were out, we decided to cross the bay and look at the bear trap.

When we landed I heard Bockitay call but was only amazed she could have come so far. That she might be in the trap I never imagined until I saw her. The big jaws had closed on her right hind leg close to the body. If she had sprung the trap with her forequarters, she would have been killed instantly. As it was, three thick, inch-long teeth in the jaws had penetrated her haunch. She was held upright, couldn't move. And she had been like that for twenty-four hours!

When I bent over her, she began to purr as if all were well. I, the mighty hunter who brought home the largest game in the forest, certainly could handle this situation. Her reliance in me didn't help, any more than did the thought that she was in the trap solely because she had sought to share in my hunting, for I knew this was the end of Bockitay. It was impossible those heavy jaws had not crushed the leg bone at the joint. She couldn't be saved. I'd have to shoot her. I said so.

Kathrene, who was weeping, made passionate protest. The leg might not be broken. There was a chance. There had to be!

We had not brought trap clamps or rifle and I paddled home for them. When I returned, I carried a cushion. We laid her on it when the jaws fell apart and hurried to the canoe. A little way from shore, blood began to flow into the leg and Bockitay, frantic with pain, clawed Kathrene's face and neck. The pain was so great when we reached the cabin that I dissolved three-quarters of a grain of morphine and injected it. Soon she slept.

That was a day! We did not dare examine the swollen leg and I was convinced the bone was shattered, that I would yet have to steel myself to pull the trigger. Bockitay did not move until nearly dark, when she wakened, famished for water. She had not drunk for two days and a night. As she had never taken water from a dish, only from the lake, I carried her to the shore and set her down.

Maddened by thirst, she walked into the water—walked in belly-deep. And with that thirst, and pain deadened by morphine, she walked on all *four* legs!

While she drank her fill, and we saw that the miracle had happened and the bone was not broken, we knew we must change our plans. I had to leave next day for three weeks to guide two moose hunters from the States, so we had arranged for Kathrene to visit a friend on the railroad. Now, to care for Bockitay, Kathrene would remain at the cabin, alone, while I was gone. That question settled itself.

We did not dress Bockitay's wounds. We never dressed our own cuts, scratches and bruises. Our sleigh dogs got badly slashed in fights but were never infected. So far as we were able to learn, that was a germ-free world. We knew Bockitay would take care of her hurts.

When I came home in mid-November, she was hobbling about, hunting again. She was, Kathrene reported, the grouchiest patient anyone ever had. Denied the complete independence she had always known, she stormed and fumed and snarled, and tried repeatedly to get outdoors. She refused all food prepared for her and twice each day Kathrene had to shoot a partridge so she could have the hot meat she desired. At last she escaped from the cabin and, hopping on three legs, resumed her independent life.

That winter, when life in the cabin was normal again and Bockitay had fully recovered, we spoke of the fact she had never seen another cat, that perhaps she was not wholly content as she did not live a full life. We'd heard of a trapper who'd left the country, deserting a tomcat, and I spent a day breaking trail in deep snow to his cabin. It was a tough journey, but when I returned after dark I forgot my weariness in anticipation of Bockitay's joy in having a companion.

She was across the living room as I entered, washing her face. When I set the tom on the floor she froze, looking over her raised paw, and for at least sixty seconds she did not move. Then she did, like lightning, and she gave that tom a fearful mauling. We couldn't stop it and opened a door to let him escape. Bockitay came back after a while, furious. She scolded for an hour, letting us know she would not permit an addition to our trio. Next day I tracked down the tom and shot him. Before I pulled the trigger I apologized, explaining it wasn't his fault, that a jealous female refused to share her people.

In the end, Bockitay succumbed to love. We prepared to visit the States before our daughter was born and as we expected to be gone three or four months, we sent Bockitay to Jack Colberg, a trapper friend forty-five miles away. She could have supported herself at the cabin as always, but we knew she would be lonely and could not understand, and we did not wish to risk an accident. She liked Jack, too, had seemed to recognize a kindred hunting spirit. But we didn't know Jack had a tomcat.

We returned in later winter and on the way met a friend, a Chicago surgeon, who had been visiting Jack. Bockitay, he told us, had just died. He had performed a post-mortem and found she had developed rickets during those first weeks of starvation alone in the forest and the pelvic structure had been so distorted that she could not have kittens.

Life, which she had met with such courage and success, had finally betrayed her.

Next day we returned to the cabin with the dog team, and even with the baby to occupy us, it was a tough homecoming. Bockitay had been there before the first log was rolled into place, and never again would we hear her little call of greeting at the lake shore. She wouldn't drag her first rabbit through the bedroom window when spring came or share the warmth of the fireplace each night. That little furred bundle of courage and competence and complete independence had been part and parcel and symbol of the North to us, and she still is.

Robert Pinkerton has told of Bockitay's dislike for skirted women and how, when their mothers arrived for a visit, she took off for the woods.

In her fascinating book about their life in the wilderness, "A Home in the Wilds," Kathrene Pinkerton tells what happened after their guests left.

I was not alone at the cabin a half hour before Bockitay walked down the trail. She approached with caution. Her wary stalking of the cabin would have outraged both mothers. I dashed out to assure her we were free from women, but not until she had verified this by a careful reconnoiter through every window did she walk inside—and announce with a cheerful chirrup that she was home again.

The two weeks of bush life made Bockitay even more devoted and for days she scarcely left the cabin. She became my almost constant companion through grouse hunting season. She pointed like a bird dog and would freeze into a rigid stance when grouse were ahead in the thick brush. And that cat checked on shots. I dreaded her contempt for a miss much more than Robert's. I was a good many up on him in the score we kept. Grouse shot through the head counted one, those hit in the eye scored double, and my bird shot through the body brought a penalty of five.

Agrippina

AGNES REPPLIER

Agnes Repplier's beloved Agrippina is certainly the epitome of the cool, demanding cat. But I think Miss Repplier is unduly severe when she calls her contemptuous and questions her affection.

Of Miss Repplier's affection there is no doubt. Her classic book on the cat through the ages, "The Fireside Sphinx," is history at its best, recounted with intelligence and humor, and ranging over literature and art with graceful erudition. It is dedicated to the memory of Agrippina: "She was dearly loved and early lost and the scanty honors years of toil have brought me I lay at her soft feet for entrance fee."

This version of Agrippina is slightly abridged; I have regretfully omitted some of the author's pleasant wanderings in literary byways.

She is sitting on my desk, as I write, and I glance at her with deference, mutely begging permission to begin. But her back is turned to me, and expresses in every curve such fine and delicate disdain that I falter and lose courage at the very threshold of my task. I have long known that cats are the most contemptuous of creatures, and that Agrippina is the most contemptuous of cats. The spirit of Bouhaki, the proud Theban beast that sat erect, with gold earrings in his ears, at the feet of his master, King Hana; the spirit of Muezza, whose slumbers Mahomet himself was not bold enough to disturb; the spirit of Micetto, Châteaubriand's ecclesiastical pet, dignified as a cardinal, and conscious ever that he was the gift of a sovereign pontiff,—the spirits of all arrogant cats that have played scornful parts in the world's great comedy look out from Agrippina's yellow eyes and hold me in subjection. I should like to explain to her, if I dared, that my desk is small, littered with many papers, and sadly overcrowded with the useful inutilities which affectionate friends delight in giving me at Christmas time. Sainte-Beuve's cat, I am aware, sat on his desk, and roamed at will among those precious manuscripts which no intrusive hand was ever permitted to touch; but Sainte-Beuve probably had sufficient space reserved for his own comfort and convenience. I have not; and Agrippina's beautifully ringed tail flapping across my copy distracts my attention and imperils the neatness of my penmanship. Even when she is disposed to be affable, turns the light of her countenance upon me, watches with attentive curiosity every stroke I make, and softly, with curved paw, pats my pen as it travels over the paper,—even in these halcyon moments, though my self-love is flattered by her condescension, I am aware that I should work better and more rapidly if I denied myself this charming companionship.

But in truth it is impossible for a lover of cats to banish these alert, gentle, and discriminating little friends, who give us just enough of their regard and complaisance to make us hunger for more. M. Fée, the naturalist, who has written so admirably about animals, and who understands, as only a Frenchman can understand, the delicate and subtle organization of a cat, frankly admits that the keynote of its character is independence. It dwells under our roof, sleeps by our fire, endures our blandishments, and apparently enjoys our society, without for one moment forfeiting its sense of absolute freedom, without acknowledging any servile relation to the human creature who shelters it. "The cat," says M. Fée, "will never part with its liberty; it will neither be our servant, like the horse, nor our friend, like the dog. It consents to live as our guest; it accepts the home we offer and the food we give; it even goes so far as to solicit our caresses, but capriciously, and when it suits its humor to receive them."

Rude and masterful souls resent this fine self-sufficiency in a domestic animal, and require that it should have no will but theirs, no pleasure that does not emanate from them. They are forever prating of the love and fidelity of the dog, of the beast that obeys their slightest word, crouches contentedly for hours at their feet, is exuberantly grateful for the smallest attention, and so affectionate that its demonstrations require to be curbed rather than encouraged. All this homage is pleasing to their vanity; yet there are people, less magisterial perhaps, or less exacting, who believe that true friendship, even with an animal, may be built up on mutual esteem and independence; that to demand gratitude is to be unworthy of it; and that obedience is not essential to agreeable and healthy intercourse. A man who owns a dog is, in every sense of the word, its master; the term expresses accurately their mutual relations. But it is ridiculous when applied to the limited possession of a cat. I am certainly not Agrippina's mistress, and the assumption of authority on my part would be a mere empty dignity, like those swelling titles which afford such innocent delight to the Freemasons of our severe republic. If I call

Agrippina, she does not come; if I tell her to go away, she remains where she is; if I try to persuade her to show off her one or two little accomplishments, she refuses, with courteous but unswerving decision. She has frolicsome moods, in which a thimble, a shoe-buttoner, a scrap of paper, or a piece of string will drive her wild with delight; she has moods of inflexible gravity, in which she stares solemnly at her favorite ball rolling over the carpet, without stirring one lazy limb to reach it. "Have I seen this foolish toy before?" she seems to be asking herself with musing austerity; "and can it be possible that there are cats who run after such frivolous trifles? Vanity of vanities, and all is vanity, save only to lie upon the hearth-rug, and be warm, and 'think grave thoughts to feed a serious soul.' " In such moments of rejection and humiliation, I comfort myself by recalling the words of one too wise for arrogance. "When I play with my cat," says Montaigne, "how do I know whether she does not make a jest of me? We entertain each other with mutual antics; and if I have my own time for beginning or refusing, she, too, has hers."

This is the spirit in which we should approach a creature so reserved and so utterly self-sufficing; this is the only key we have to that natural distinction of character which repels careless and unobservant natures. When I am told Agrippina is disobedient, ungrateful, cold-hearted, perverse, stupid, treacherous, and cruel, I no longer strive to check the torrent of abuse. I know that Buffon said all this, and much more, about cats, and that people have gone on repeating it ever since, principally because these spirited little beasts have remained just what it pleased Providence to make them, have preserved their primitive freedom through centuries of effete and demoralizing civilization. Why, I wonder, should a great many good men and women cherish an unreasonable grudge against one animal because it does not chance to possess the precise qualities of another? "My dog fetches my slippers for me every night," said a friend triumphantly, not long ago. "He puts them first to warm by the fire, and then brings them over to my chair, wagging his tail, and as proud as Punch. Would your cat do as much for you, I'd like to know?" Assuredly not! If I waited for Agrippina to fetch me shoes or slippers, I should have no other resource save to join as speedily as possible one of the bare-footed religious orders of Italy. But, after all, fetching slippers is not the whole duty of domestic pets. As La Fontaine gently reminds us,

"*Tout animal n'a pas toutes propriétés.*"

We pick no quarrel with a canary because it does not talk like a parrot, nor with a parrot because it does not sing like a canary. We find no fault with a King Charles spaniel for not flying at the throat

of a burglar, nor with a St. Bernard because we cannot put it in our pocket. Agrippina will never make herself serviceable, yet nevertheless is she of inestimable service. How many times have I rested tired eyes on her graceful little body, curled up in a ball and wrapped round with her tail like a parcel; or stretched out luxuriously on my bed, one paw coyly covering her face, the other curved gently inwards, as though clasping an invisible treasure! Asleep or awake, in rest or in motion, grave or gay, Agrippina is always beautiful; and it is better to be beautiful than to fetch and carry from the rising to the setting of the sun. She is droll, too, with an unconscious humor even in her most serious and sentimental moods. She has quite the longest ears that ever were seen on so small a cat, eyes more solemn than Athene's owl blinking in the sunlight, and an air of supercilious disdain that would have made Diogenes seem young and ardent by her side. Sitting on the library table, under the evening lamp, with her head held high in air, her tall ears as erect as chimneys, and her inscrutable gaze fixed on the darkest corner of the room, Agrippina inspires in the family sentiments of mingled mirthfulness and awe. To laugh at her in such moments, however, is to incur her supreme displeasure. I have known her to jump down from the table and walk haughtily out of the room, because of a single half-suppressed but wholly indecorous giggle.

Schopenhauer has said that the reason domestic pets are so lovable and so helpful to us is because they enjoy, quietly and placidly, the present moment. Life holds no future for them, and consequently no care; if they are content, their contentment is absolute; and our jaded and wearied spirits find a natural relief in the sight of creatures whose little cups of happiness can so easily be filled to the brim. Walt Whitman expresses the same thought more coarsely when he acknowledges that he loves the society of animals because they do not sweat and whine over their condition, nor lie awake in the dark and weep for their sins, nor sicken him with discussions of their duty. In truth, that admirable counsel of Sydney Smith's, "Take short views of life," can be obeyed only by the brutes; for the thought that travels even to the morrow is long enough to destroy our peace of mind, inasmuch as we know not what the morrow may bring forth. But when Agrippina has breakfasted, and washed, and sits in the sunlight blinking at me with affectionate contempt, I feel soothed by her absolute and unqualified enjoyment. I know how full my day will be of things that I don't want particularly to do, and that are not particularly worth doing; but for her, time and the world hold only this brief moment of contentment. Slowly the eyes close, gently the little body is relaxed. Oh, you who strive to relieve your overwrought nerves, and cultivate power through repose, watch the exquisite languor of a drowsy cat, and despair of imitating such perfect and restful grace! There is a gradual yielding of every muscle to the soft persuasiveness of slumber; the flexible frame is curved into tender lines, the head nestles lower, the paws are tucked out of sight; no convulsive throb or start betrays a rebellious alertness; only a faint quiver of unconscious satisfaction, a faint heaving of the tawny sides, a faint gleam of the half-shut yellow eyes, and Agrippina is asleep. I look at her for one wistful moment, and then turn resolutely to my work. It were ignoble to wish myself in her place, and yet how charming to be able to settle down to a nap, *sans peur et sans reproche*, at ten o'clock in the morning!

These, then, are a few of the pleasures to be derived from the society of an amiable cat; and by an amiable cat I mean one that, while maintaining its own dignity and delicate reserve, is nevertheless affable and condescending in the company of human beings. There is nothing I dislike more than newspaper and magazine stories about priggish pussies—like the children in Sunday-school books—that share their food with hungry beasts from the back alleys, and show touching fidelity to old blind masters, and hunt partridges in a spirit of noble self-sacrifice for consumptive mistresses, and scorn to help themselves to delicacies from the kitchen tables, and arouse their households so often in cases of fire that I should suspect them of starting the conflagrations in order to win applause by giving the alarm. Whatever a real cat may or may not be, it is never a prig, and all true lovers of the race have been quick to recognize and appreciate this fact.

"I value in the cat," says Châteaubriand, "that independent and almost ungrateful temper which prevents it from attaching itself to any one; the indifference with which it passes from the salon to the housetop. When you caress it, it stretches itself out and arches its back, indeed; but that is caused by physical pleasure, and not, as in the case of the dog, by a silly satisfaction in loving and being faithful to a master who returns thanks in kicks. The cat lives alone, has no need of society, does not obey except when it likes, pretends to sleep that it may see the more clearly, and scratches everything that it can scratch."

Here is a sketch spirited enough and of good outline, but hardly correct in every detail. A cat seldom manifests affection, yet is often distinctly social, and likes to see itself the petted minion of a family group. Agrippina, in fact, so far from living alone, will not, if she can help it, remain for a moment in a room by herself. She is content to have me as a companion, perhaps in default of better; but if I go upstairs or downstairs in search of a book, or my eyeglasses, or any one of the countless things that are never where they ought to be, Agrippina follows closely at my heels. Sometimes, when she is fast asleep, I steal softly out of the door, thinking to escape her vigilance; but before I have taken a dozen steps she is under my feet, mewing a gentle reproach, and putting on all the injured airs of a deserted Ariadne. I should like to think such behavior prompted by affection rather than curiosity; but in my candid moments I find this "pathetic fallacy" a difficult sentiment to cherish. There are people, I am aware, who trustfully assert that their pets love them; and one such sanguine creature has recently assured the world that "no man who boasts the real intimacy and confidence of a cat would dream of calling his four-footed friend 'puss.'" But is not such a boast rather ill-timed at best? How dare any man venture to assert that he possesses the intimacy and confidence of an animal so exclusive and so reserved? I doubt if Cardinal Wolsey, in the zenith of his pride and power, claimed the intimacy and confidence of the superb cat that sat in a cushioned armchair by his side, and reflected with mimic dignity the full-blown honors of the Lord High Chancellor of England.

Agrippina, I am humbly aware, grants me neither her intimacy nor her confidence, but only her companionship, which I endeavor to receive modestly, and without flaunting my favors to the world. She is displeased and even downcast when I go out, and she greets my return with delight, thrusting her little gray head between the banisters the instant I open the house door, and waving a welcome in mid-air with one ridiculously small paw. Being but mortal, I am naturally pleased with these tokens of esteem, but I do not, on that account, go about with arrogant brow and boast of my intimacy with Agrippina. I should be laughed at, if I did, by everybody who is privileged to possess and appreciate a cat.

As for curiosity, that vice which the Abbé Galiani held to be unknown to animals, but which the more astute Voltaire detected in every little dog that he saw peering out of the window of his master's coach, it is the ruling passion of the feline breast. A closet door left ajar, a box with half-closed lid, an open bureau drawer,—these are the objects that fill a cat with the liveliest interest and delight. Agrippina watches breathlessly the unfastening of a parcel, and tries to hasten matters by clutching actively at the string. When its contents are shown her, she examines them gravely, and then, with a sigh of relief, settles down to repose. The slightest noise disturbs and irritates her until she discovers its cause. If she hears a footstep in the hall, she runs out to see whose it is, and, like certain troublesome little people I have known, she dearly loves to go to the front door every time the bell is rung. From my window she surveys the street with tranquil scrutiny, and, if boys are playing below, she follows their games with a steady scornful stare, very different from the wistful eagerness of a friendly dog, quivering to join in the sport. Sometimes the boys catch sight of her, and shout up rudely at her window; and I can never sufficiently admire Agrippina's conduct upon these trying occasions, the well-bred composure with which she affects neither to see nor to hear them, nor to be aware that there are such objectionable creatures as children in the world. Sometimes, too, the terrier that lives next door comes out to sun himself in the street, and, beholding my cat sitting well out of reach, he dances madly up and down the pavement, barking with all his might, and rearing himself on his short hind legs, in a futile attempt to dislodge her. Then the spirit of evil enters Agrippina's little heart. The window is open, and she creeps to the extreme edge of the stone sill, stretches herself at full length, peers down smilingly at the frenzied dog, dangles one paw enticingly in the air, and exerts herself with quiet malice to drive him to desperation. Her sense of humor is awakened by his frantic efforts, and by her own absolute security; and not until he is spent with exertion, and lies panting and exhausted on the bricks, does she arch her graceful little back, stretch her limbs lazily in the sun, and with one light bound spring from the window to my desk. Wisely has Moncrif observed that a cat is not merely diverted by everything that moves, but is convinced that all nature is occupied exclusively with catering to her diversion.

* * * *

It were an endless though a pleasant task to recount all that has been said, and well said, in praise of the cat by those who have rightly valued her companionship. Théophile Gautier's charming pages are too familiar for coment. Who has not read with delight of the Black and White Dynasties that for so long ruled with gentle sway over his hearth and heart; of Madame Théophile, who thought the parrot was a green chicken; of Don Pierrot de Navarre, who deeply resented his master's staying out late at night; of the graceful and fastidious Seraphita; the gluttonous Enjolras; the acute Bohemian, Gavroche; the courteous and well-mannered Éponine, who received M. Gautier's guests in the drawing-room and dined at his table, taking each course as it was served, and restraining any rude distaste for food not to her fancy. "Her place was laid without a knife and fork, indeed, but with a glass, and she went regularly through dinner, from soup to dessert, awaiting her turn to be helped, and behaving with a quiet propriety which most children might imitate with advantage. At the first stroke of the bell she would appear, and when I came into the dining-room she would be at her post, upright on her chair, her forepaws on the edge of the tablecloth; and she would present her smooth forehead to be kissed, like a well-bred little girl who was affectionately polite to relatives and old people."

I have read this pretty description several times to Agrippina, who is extremely wayward and capricious about her food, rejecting plaintively one day the viands which she had eaten with apparent enjoyment the day before. In fact, the difficulty of catering to her is so well understood by tradesmen that recently, when the housemaid carried her on an errand to the grocery—Agrippina is very fond of these jaunts and of the admiration she excites—the grocer, a fatherly man, with cats of his own, said briskly, "Is this the little lady who eats the biscuits?" and presented her on the spot with several choice varieties from which to choose. She is fastidious, too, about the way in which her meals are served; disliking any other dishes than her own, which are of blue and white china; requiring that her meat should be cut up fine and all the fat removed, and that her morning oatmeal should be well sugared and creamed. Milk she holds in scorn. My friends tell me sometimes that it is not the common custom of cats to receive so much attention at table, and that it is my fault Agrippina is so exacting; but such grumblers fail to take into consideration the marked individuality that is the charm of every kindly treated puss. She differs from her sisters as widely as one woman differs from another, and reveals varying characteristics of good and evil, varying powers of intelligence and adaptation. She scales splendid heights of virtue, and, unlike Sir Thomas Browne, is "singular in offenses." Even those primitive instincts which we believe all animals hold in common are lost in acquired ethics and depravity. No heroism could surpass that of the London cat that crawled back five times under the stage of the burning theatre to rescue her litter of kittens, and, having carried four of them to safety, perished devotedly with the fifth. On the other hand, I know of a cat that drowned her three kittens in a water-butt, for no reason, apparently, save to be rid of them, and that she might lie in peace on the hearth-rug,—a murder well planned, deliberate, and cruel.

> "So Tiberius might have sat,
> Had Tiberius been a cat."

Only in her grace and beauty, her love of comfort, her dignity of bearing, her courteous reserve, and her independence of character does puss remain immutable and unchanged. These are the traits which win for her the warmest corner by the fire, and the unshaken regard of those who value her friendship and aspire to her affection.

Help! Kidnaped!

DOREEN TOVEY

> Traveling with cats is often a problem. John D. MacDonald
> describes a trip with Roger and Geoffrey to the family sum-
> mer home in "The House Guests." "We had learned during
> the few necessary local trips how loudly and bitterly both
> cats objected to riding in a car. This was the longest one yet.
> . . . They made the trip hideous. They complained with
> every breath. By the time we got there Geoff was down to
> a breathy baritone rasp." But MacDonald agrees with me
> that cats will travel well if you start them early.
>
> I accustomed my Tar Baby to riding in a car by taking
> him everywhere with me from the time he was a young
> kitten, and in later years he made several all night auto
> trips in perfect contentment. The only condition he in-
> sisted on was to ride on my lap under the steering wheel.
>
> Tar Baby also enjoyed trains as much as I do. Once the
> train started, I let him out of his carrier, snapped the leash
> on his harness, and looped it over my wrist. He would sit
> quietly for hours, sleep, or stare out the window. I was never
> asked to put him in the baggage car.
>
> Which is by way of prologue to two entertaining accounts
> of traveling with cats. In "Cats in the Belfry" Doreen Tovey
> tells of taking her first Siamese, Sugieh, on a motor trip.
> The second selection, "Frimbo on Cats," from "All Aboard
> with E. M. Frimbo," describes two train trips with cats.

My grandmother loved animals and had, fortunately, not encountered
Sugieh to date, so we had no difficulty in fixing that up. What we
hadn't bargained for was that since that first journey out from town,
when she sat sedately on my lap watching the traffic with wide-eyed
interest and occasionally—hypocrite that she was—smirking affectionately up into my face, Sugieh had developed a Thing about cars.

The moment I got into the car with her the morning of that ill-
fated trip, before Charles had even so much as pressed the starter, she

began to yell. Charles patted her on the head as she sat on my lap and told her not to be a silly girl, she knew she liked carsy-warsies. With Sugieh, of course, that was just asking for trouble. By the time we got to the top of the hill leading to the main road she was standing on her hind legs, clawing frantically at the window and shrieking for help. Charles said it was the noise of the bottom gear upsetting her; once we got on the flat road she'd be all right. I have no doubt at all that Sugieh understood every word we said, because by the time we were halfway to town and the road had been flat as a pancake for miles all the other drivers were gesturing violently at us as they passed, threatening to punch Charles's nose for swerving all over the place and not giving signals, and Charles himself was shouting that if I didn't get that damblasted cat off his neck she'd have us up a telegraph pole. It was even worse on the return trip. . . . We drove home in silence, shaken by the impact of one small Siamese kitten on that tranquil Victorian household, while in the back seat Sugieh continued happily with her game of Kidnaped. This time, while there was nobody else about, she sat there quite quietly, bolt upright with her paws together, her tail tucked primly round them, and the expression on her face of a dowager duchess returning from the theater. The moment she saw lights, however, whether in a house or a passing car, she flew to the window, pressed herself pathetically against it, and screamed wildly for help. She staged a magnificent performance going past a cinema just when the late-night audience was coming out, beating her paws against the window with a frail, pathetic frenzy that would have done credit to Lillian Gish. But where she really excelled herself was when we drew up at the traffic lights at the busy town center. Most Siamese sound uncannily like human babies when they cry, but Sugieh that night outdid any Siamese or human baby I have ever known. She sobbed, she wailed, she howled, until people on the pavement began peering into the car with set faces looking for the little orphan who was apparently being simultaneously beaten, starved, and tortured inside. By that time, needless to say, Sugieh was out of sight, doing her ventriloquist act from under Charles's seat. The only thing that saved us from being mobbed by a crowd of angry passers-by was the last-minute changing of the lights and the fact that Charles, having been something of a racing driver in his gilded youth, was away off the mark like a shot.

Frimbo on Cats

ROGERS E. M. WHITAKER AND ANTHONY HISS

You look at all these city dwellers who proclaim their admiration for cats, and then you walk around town in the summer and see all the abandoned beasts on the streets. People should know that they can take their cats with them when they go away. Cats travel beautifully —unlike wines of the country. At the time I had my thirteen Persians, my mother was living in suburban Philadelphia, up in Germantown, and I used to travel back and forth weekends with the cats. The Pennsylvania Railroad porters were very snooty about cats in the parlor cars. They wanted them kept in the cages. So I transferred to the Reading Railway, which had a ferry across the Hudson and an hourly service with a parlor car to Philadelphia. I'd get off at Wayne Junction and take the local train up to my mother's house. I'd take maybe two or three or four cats down to Germantown with me in the parlor car, and the porters on the Reading were noble old boys. It wasn't long before the cats were allowed to prowl up and down the parlor car. I had a strict understanding with them that they could not jump in the lap of any customer except me. It was all right if they wanted to prance up and down and jump in an empty chair. This was the strict understanding on which they traveled. Or else they stayed home.

So one day I had three Persians—big beasts. My three very best. They were like a team of chariot horses, running up and down the carpeted parlor car at full speed. Finally, in their last sprint, they went nose, head, and tail down the aisle and landed on the top of a chair and began hissing and yowling at each other.

And a woman cried, "Porter, porter! What is all this?"

And he looked at her contemptuously and said, "Why, them's Mr. Frimbo's Persians, of course."

Now I've got one more story. You see, I was brought up in the English countryside, where animals, and particularly cats, are considered the equals of people, as they should be. Cats there accept you as their equals, too. It's a very nice relationship. We used to travel up and down constantly between the countryside and London, sometimes with the cats in tow. My father, who had a season ticket because he was commuting to the City, always traveled grandly in first class, but my mother, who was economical, often traveled third, with me. The English, you know, decided to abolish one of the three classes, so they abolished second class. That gave you the choice of going either first or third, not first or second—the real English attitude.

One afternoon we were coming back, most unusually, first class with my mother, and the ticket examiner, who knew us because we always took the same afternoon train, looked surprised at my mother's traveling first. He thought she had moved up arbitrarily from third. So he said, "Traveling first today, Ma'am?" And she said, patting the cage in which Thomas, our big cat, was sitting, "Yes. Thomas wouldn't hear of going third."

Uncle Whiskers

PHILIP BROWN

It is impossible to know how many cats trapped in the horrifying physical condition of Uncle Whiskers could make such an incredible adjustment. Fortunately this one had a patient protector who aided his recovery and deserves our gratitude for setting down this unadorned, factual account of his cat's amazing achievements in the book, "Uncle Whiskers," from which this excerpt is taken.

If Uncle Whiskers was bewildered and baffled by the turn of events which had changed him, almost overnight, from a whole and active cat into less than half a cat and sorely crippled at that, let me admit that I, too, was bewildered and baffled. It was all very well to ask oneself whether or no one had done the right thing in not insisting that the horribly maimed creature should be destroyed, but the die had been cast. Uncle Whiskers, whatever his plight, was very much alive. True, he had lost one leg completely and the remaining front one was, at the moment, as useless for any kind of locomotion as the missing limb, but the rest of him, as they say, was bonny enough, yet all he could achieve by thrusting with his mobile hind legs was to tumble over himself in a most undignified and frustrating way. What made it so irksome to watch his vain efforts was that Uncle Whiskers simply could not understand why they failed to work.

The pressing problem was to decide how we were going to surmount the difficulties at least sufficiently well to ensure that the unlucky cat could enjoy a reasonably full and happy life—and it had to be a question of "we," for although I was confident that I would be able to help Uncle Whiskers on his road to recovery, very much was bound to depend upon the cat himself. Most cats can be independent when they choose. The accident had rendered Uncle Whiskers, at least for the time being, very much dependent. Any recovery to normal was bound to be slow; I was not too optimistic that Uncle Whiskers could ever live anything like a full life again. But it was a challenge that would require close relationship with the cat and a good deal of trust, if not actual faith, by both parties if there were to be any prospect of a tolerably successful outcome. Probably for the first time in my life I felt some genuine affinity to a cat. The very fact that we were, so to speak, in the job together made something of a compact between us. It was a challenge, anyway, so far as I was concerned and life would be boring without its difficulties and problems.

During the first week following Uncle Whiskers' return from the vet, however, I did little about the challenge beyond a good deal of serious pondering and watching the cat. Uncle Whiskers was, for the present, immobile. So he had to have his food brought to him; he had to be carried to and from his earth-box to relieve the calls of nature (which he did not like at all, for he had always been allowed to go outdoors to perform these essentially private functions) and had to be carried up to our bedroom each night and down again in the morning. He did something to relieve the tedium of his restricted life by washing himself. He was a slim, lissome cat and he became visibly more and more elastic as the days passed. One evening, only a few days after his return, whilst lounging on the rug by the fireside he suddenly surprised us by raising himself on his hind legs, his tail stuck straight out behind him as a sort of third leg, stretching himself upwards and upwards, the paralysed front paw drooping down across his chest and the stump of the amputated leg visibly moving beneath the stitched scar. This movement ended in a somewhat ignominious collapse but it was, in embryo form, the start of one of his greatest and unique performances—the ability to sit upright on his haunches for minutes on end, looking around and taking notice of all that might be going on around him. Yet all that was in the future, unknown to us then; he was still incapable of making any co-ordinated progress in moving in any direction whatsoever.

Before the vet returned at the end of the week Uncle Whiskers successfully resolved one problem, that of washing his face. Cats wash their faces by licking a front paw, then rubbing it over their faces and around their ears, repeating the process until that part of their toilet is completed. Unfortunately Uncle Whiskers had no use whatsoever in his only remaining front paw. He could not even direct it to his mouth, let alone wash over his face with it. So he resolved this difficulty by licking the paw as it lay, crumpled back on itself, on the ground, after which he vigorously rubbed his face on it. It was not the approved feline method but it was equally effective, all the same, and very soon his appearance was as clean and spruce as it had ever been.

When the vet returned to remove the stitches at which Uncle Whiskers had bitten and worried in vain for a week, the cat looked in much better fettle than at any time since the accident a fortnight earlier. He not only did not object to the whipping-out of the stitches but was actually purring with delight before the job was done. The vet expressed great satisfaction with his general condition but was more dubious about the state of the remaining front leg, on which I felt that the mobility of the cat must ultimately depend. The nerves had been severed, there was a radial paralysis and the vet was highly doubtful as to whether it could ever serve him as a third leg. I was a bit depressed but Uncle Whiskers went on singing his heart out and then repeated, his "sitting-up" trick, balancing himself more securely this time, moving his head to look this way and that, purring away with merriment. At least he was no ordinary cat. I knew that the vet had done a remarkable job and he was clearly pleased that the cat had not been put down. I admit that I felt rather less confident about the future. Even if Uncle Whiskers was, more or less, fit and well, he surely could not enjoy the many years of life that, with luck, lay ahead of him if he were virtually incapable of moving away from any spot where we might set him down.

I realised at the outset that only Uncle Whiskers himself could strive to overcome this handicap of immobility. What I had to do was to try to encourage him to make the effort, however painful and possibly futile it might be for both of us. So my wife and I decided that, whilst we would carry him about the house as required throughout much of the day, bringing him his breakfast and light luncheon in the dining-room, we would call him to his dinner in the kitchen. If, within a reasonable time, he did not succed in making much progress towards his objective then we would carry him the rest of the way but, each succeeding day, we resolved that he must do better than on the preceding one.

It was, by any standards, a pitiable performance to watch. Although he seemed to be steadily gaining strength in his already powerful hind limbs, Uncle Whiskers could achieve little or nothing with his paralysed front leg, spending most of his time stumbling over himself, sometimes still turning a complete somersault, ending up by facing in entirely the wrong direction to that in which he was desperately trying to go. But he persisted with a gameness that was admirable and although, at first, he would take ten minutes to cover a yard (at the end of which time we just could not stand it any longer and gave him a lift to his journey's end) at the end of a week or two he succeeded, however slowly and laboriously, in covering the half-dozen yards into the kitchen and the feasting.

It was during this early period of his rehabilitation that Uncle

Whiskers soon became really adept at sitting upright on his hind legs. In point of fact, much of his forward progress, in those early days, consisted of sitting upright on his haunches, stretching himself up to his fullest extent (some two feet) and then diving forward in the direction he wanted to go. He would then shuffle his hind legs up until they were almost under his chin so that he was bent in a sort of tight bow-shape, whereupon he would sit up, stretch again and dive forward. Slow he might be, but Uncle Whiskers soon got over the initial clumsiness of this new sort of locomotion. Within two or three weeks, if he wanted to get somewhere "on the flat," he would make his goal in his own good time.

One evening when we had had our own meal and then called him into the kitchen for his whilst we were doing the washing-up, we left Uncle Whiskers lapping away at a saucerful of milk. As far as I remember we were watching a programme on television. The cat did not come back into the dining-room but we were not worried, feeling that he was content enough, probably washing himself, and would return to the fireside when he chose to do so. But when we switched off the television he was still missing, so I went out to the kitchen. Uncle Whiskers was not there. So a search was organised and we eventually found him, curled up and fast asleep, on the end of our bed. He had managed not only to get along the hall to the foot of the stairs but had then surmounted all seventeen treads, had moved into the bedroom and finally leapt on to the bed unaided. It was a November night to remember! I woke him up, stroking him and making congratulatory noises. Uncle Whiskers was delighted, purring away like a rattling nightjar and rolling about in an ecstasy. So far as he was concerned, he conveyed the impression that there was nothing much wrong with the world!

Two things were rapidly becoming clear. The first was a somewhat depressing one. There could now be little doubt that the cat's sole remaining front leg was going to remain pretty useless. He had no feeling in it and no muscular control over it, either at the elbow or the wrist; the hand (I suppose one ought to call it the front foot) was uselessly and rather grotesquely turned over on itself and he was incapable of extending or retracting any of the claws. Nor was he able to sharpen the claws against the bark of a tree, as most cats do, so that it became necessary to cut the claws back about once a fortnight with a pair of nail-clippers. It was his habit, as soon as the claws grew long, to start biting them vigorously with his very sharp teeth, which was always a reminder to get the clippers out. He never objected to having his claws cut; on the contrary, he lay over on his back and usually began purring the moment one started on this simple task.

The front limb, however, was not *wholly* useless. The muscles of the shoulder and part of the upper 'arm' were still intact and as strong as ever. There was hope to be got from the fact that Uncle Whiskers soon started to attempt to use this limb from the shoulder, first pushing down on it in order to raise his chest clear of the ground and then immediately "throwing" it forward as far as possible. He then half-pulled himself forward, relying on waddling on his back legs to complete the effort. Once he had discovered his ability to move in this manner he began to make rapid progress. He suddenly learnt that, by this means, he could go up a flight of stairs even more rapidly than he could move forward on level ground. So, to hasten his rehabilitation by exercising his muscles and helping him to co-ordinate his movements, I used to get out a ping-pong ball in the evenings. Taking both the ball and the cat to the foot of the stairs, I would then take the ping-pong ball and toss it up the stairs, gently enough to ensure that, nine times out of ten, it did not rebound from the wall at the top and come plop-plopping back down the stairs.

The moment he saw me throw the ball Uncle Whiskers scampered

up the stairs after it as fast as he could go. On reaching the landing
at the top he would scuffle about with the ball until, sooner or later,
it came bouncing down. He followed its descent in spirit, peering
wide-eyed over the topmost tread, his head nodding up and down as
he watched the flight of the ball. Then I had to carry him down and
restart the fun and games. He never tired of it, but after a long day in
the office I did. However, it was rewarding to see how rapidly he
developed the use of his hind legs and the strength of his muscles,
not to mention at least some sort of rudimentary co-ordination between that almost useless front flipper and the rest of him.

These evening games went well until, one day, he attempted to
descend the stairs as the ping-pong ball bounced downwards. He fell
with his chest on the top tread, paused to get his balance, then brought
his back legs down, rather awkwardly and with a crab-wise shuffle of
the body, with a little skip and jump. He then repeated the performance, step after careful step, until he finally arrived at the foot
of the stairs at his very first attempt. He then leapt on the elusive
ping-pong ball, sent it flying and plodded after it.

By Christmas, only three months after his accident, Uncle
Whiskers was able to get about the house at will, upstairs or down,
even if his progress was slow compared with that of a normal cat—
especially so if he was descending. His magnificent coat of fur had
completely recovered its pristine glory, his stripes a rich, glowing
orange and a healthy sheen on every hair. He had very soon learnt to
groom himself perfectly, having plenty of time on his paws, so to
speak, which more than made up for any slowness in his toiletry.
Better still, he had now learnt to make use of his one remaining front
leg to wash his face in the approved feline fashion. He no longer had
recourse to first licking the paw and then rubbing his face against it,
for now he had at least a little use of the shoulder muscles on that
side. So he sat upright on his strong haunches, tail stretched out
rigidly behind him to ensure a firm balance, then licked the paw and
rubbed it over his face. He would repeat the operation a dozen times
or more until he was satisfied that his face passed muster, remaining
rigidly upright all the time. He was now not only able to do what a
normal cat cannot achieve—sit bolt upright on his hams—but he
could maintain this unique position for minutes on end, looking this
way or that as anything might catch his eye, the more than half-useless front flipper draped diagonally across his chest.

A cat normally stretches its limbs after a sleep by digging the
claws of its front paws into the ground, carpet (or even the back of
an upholstered chair until it has been cured of this destructive habit)

and then pulling backwards against them. Having no viable front paws, Uncle Whiskers could no longer do this. Instead he regularly stretched himself upwards, upwards, upwards, whilst sitting on his haunches, until he looked almost incredibly tall and attenuated.

Uncle Whiskers strongly resented using an earth-box to meet the demands of nature. For some weeks after his accident he had no choice but once he recovered some mobility he would plod off to the kitchen door and start mewing softly to be let out. During daylight we used to allow him to go unless the weather was very wet, watching over him whilst he limped off to a border and dug himself some sort of a hole. With his sole, half-paralysed front leg he found this hole-digging business very difficult at first, although he became more proficient as time went by. He would sit half-upright on his haunches and flip away with the front leg with great vigour and at least some success. Then he would rest that leg and one could see the stump of his missing leg working away under the fur, all to no purpose, of course. Uncle Whiskers, as I believe this story will show, was a remarkably intelligent, practical and courageous animal but all through his long life he never seemed to comprehend that all the hard work with this sewn-in stump was simply a waste of effort.

*   *   *   *

Uncle Whiskers spent a good deal of his time in the house during that first winter following his accident—certainly much more than he would have liked. Although he could now plod about the house, jump up on chairs, beds and window-sills and even perform a fair imitation of a sprint when going upstairs, his degree of mobility was still only fractional compared with that of a normal cat. He had, however, made great progress from the virtually immobile state in which he had been returned to us by the vet at the end of September. He was certainly now capable of thoroughly enjoying himself in a restricted sort of way, giving every evidence of being happy enough in spite of manifest handicaps, always breaking into a purr of delight even if he was only spoken to, let alone fondled. At least my first, very real, fears that he might have been condemned to lead a life of misery had by now been proved absolutely groundless. His biggest difficulty lay in getting down from any height. If, for instance, he jumped off a chair his maimed foreleg was useless as a means of taking any weight or buffering the shock. He used to land on his chest with a horrible thud, followed by a quite frightening snoring grunt as the breath was involuntarily expelled from his lungs. However, the performance, horrifying though it was to watch, did not appear to hurt him, for as soon as he had landed he would set off in the direction he had made up his mind to go, "rowing" away with his gammy forepaw. Only in moments of over-enthusiasm did he try to move his very strong hind legs too fast so that, as he had done so frequently only a few months earlier, he turned a somersault. Even this no longer seemed to upset him. It was fortunate that, even over a long period when he was unable to take any exercise, he never put on an ounce of superfluous weight. He remained a lightweight throughout his life.

As the winter gave way to spring and the days grew both longer and warmer it became more and more obvious that Uncle Whiskers was frustrated by his somewhat restricted life and was becoming desperately anxious to get out and about, as he had always been able to do for the first year of his life. Whilst we breakfasted he would sit up on his haunches for minutes on end, peering out through the french windows, watching the birds and anything else which might be moving about in the garden. As I have explained, at this time we had only dared to allow him to wander abroad when either my wife or I could spare the time to keep a constant eye on his exploits. At week-ends I gave a pretty good whack of my time to this somewhat monotonous but rewarding job. In cold weather, nevertheless, merely standing about for much of the time could be unpleasant because, unlike the cat, one did not enjoy the advantage of a first-class fur coat. My wife did her stints when I was away during the working week and I have no doubt that these frequent outdoor forays were not only much enjoyed by Uncle Whiskers but that they helped greatly in strengthening his muscles and in enabling him the better to co-ordinate the movements of his good hind legs and the one apology for a foreleg which still remained to him. What a vital possession of his was that wonky front-limb! It may have been half-paralysed, twisted and, even at its best, more than half-useless, yet almost everything depended upon it so far as Uncle Whiskers' future was concerned. My own philosophy is never to worry about disasters that may never happen but throughout the whole twelve years of his life after the disastrous accident I must admit that I was haunted by fears that that one remnant of a foreleg might get crushed or broken in some way or another or else that it might wither away completely through lack of proper use.

*   *   *   *

It was one of those still, clear summer evenings, cool enough after the heat of the day to feel almost crisp. Moths were not in good supply. I had watched Uncle Whiskers, not best-pleased with the moth famine, leaping up at two or three of them as they passed him by. Then, quite unexpectedly (for both of us, I think) Uncle Whiskers leapt up and snapped at and succeeded in catching a fair-sized moth in his mouth. He fell with it, thudding on to the hard turf with his chest, the force of the fall expelling all the wind from his lungs which, in turn, blew the moth out of his mouth. The moth was injured and fluttered rather purposelessly over the short grass but even before the idea had entered my head to give it the benefit of a mercy-killing, Uncle Whiskers had taken a gigantic leap and, with astonishingly good judgment of the jump, landed so precisely that he was able to seize the insect in his mouth. He must have given it a killing crunch and disliked the taste. He spat it out and the dead moth lay in front of him. After hundreds, if not thousands of vain leapings, that one dead moth meant a great deal to Uncle Whiskers. He wriggled and rolled about in a great ecstasy of triumph and when I called him a "fine boy-o" he rolled about even more and burst into a great purr of happiness. Intelligence overcame instinct, so far as Uncle Whiskers was concerned. As far as I know he never again attempted to catch and kill by trying to use striking paws that he had lost forever when only just over a year old. It was the teeth that could do the trick—and now he knew it. So far as his hunting was concerned, Uncle Whiskers had suddenly changed from a cat to a terrier.

* * * *

Uncle Whiskers now had enormous scope for his activities and this gave him the opportunity to overcome his severe physical handicaps to such a degree that he was soon to become more successful as a hunter than the majority of his kind. Perhaps it may still be difficult for the reader fully to comprehend how a cat without any effective forelegs could possibly overcome such a grievous handicap but Uncle Whiskers certainly did so. We had arrived at our new residence when the late summer days were still long and the cat usually wanted to go out as soon as dawn broke. He would be absent for an hour or so, exploring his new and intriguing domains, returning at breakfast time with the appetite of a tiger. He would spend a good part of the day sleeping, indoors if it were wet and outside, tucked away in one of the many retreats known only to himself, if the sun shone. In the late afternoon, when all was quiet again, he would go off on the prowl, usually returning for his supper about sunset or soon after. By that time he was fairly weary from his long travels and was happy enough to stay indoors and sleep until daybreak; it was only when the days really started to shorten that he became something of a night-bird. . . .

Keen as he was as a hunter and although he had now learnt that the only way in which he could seize and kill his prey was by using his teeth, for some weeks Uncle Whiskers caught nothing more remarkable than a few butterflies and moths and the odd mouse and shrew. Lepidoptera were merely practice targets. He objected to having them in his mouth and only his urge to hunt overcame this distaste. He never ate either a mouse or a shrew but brought them back over long distances to deposit them on the doorstep. He would then sit upright on his haunches and flip the door with his forepaw so violently that he could raise quite a noise. If, by any chance, this brought no response, he would leap up on the ledge of our sitting-room window and bang away at it in fine style. The moment he saw anybody move he would jump down so that, by the time one of us had got to the door and opened it, he would be standing upright over his dead quarry, immensely proud of himself and fairly singing his head off with delight. The moment he was congratulated he would roll about on the ground in sheer ecstasy, raising no objection when you seized the prey by its tail and took it off to the kitchen fire for cremation.

One week-end afternoon in September we were sitting over tea when I heard Uncle Whiskers rapping on the door with his flipper. I went to open it, wondering if I should have the pleasure of congratulating him on catching a mouse or shrew which he would have deposited, as usual, on the doorstep. There was nothing on the step but when I opened the door wide to welcome Uncle Whiskers in to the home, he immediately turned away, moving towards a small courtyard at the western end of the house. I watched him, puzzled by his behaviour. After he had rowed himself rapidly and with obvious intent for a few paces he looked round at me, then sat up on his haunches, gazing first directly at me, then towards the courtyard which was hidden from me by the corner of the house. Then he gazed back at me again. As I still did not move, he stumped two or three paces back towards me, then repeated the sitting-up performance.

I was intrigued by this curious behaviour, so I walked out. The moment I moved in his direction, Uncle Whiskers set off towards the courtyard at his very best pace, which was now equal, over short distances, to a brisk walk. He led me round the angle of the house and diagonally across the yard. Even before he reached it I spotted the body of the dead rat. He went on up to it, then sat up and stood over it, gammy forepaw dangling across his chest, looking from the rat to me and then back again as much as to say: "All my own work, you know!" When I congratulated him in my most dulcet, "good boy" tone of voice, Uncle Whiskers went berserk. He leaped in the air and then proceeded to wriggle and roll over on his back, jerking convulsively from one side to the other, in a rare display of satisfied abandonment, the whole gymnastic exhibition being accompanied by loud, rattling purrs of delight.

"All my own work, you know!" Well, Uncle Whiskers seemed mighty pleased with himself but I didn't believe that he had killed that rat. How could he do it, when he possessed no striking paws or claws? If he had killed that rat, then the rat must have been blind and walked straight into his mouth. I don't like rats but I picked up that corpse and it was still warmish, so that it could not have been dead for more than a very few minutes. There were wounds in the neck, where a little trickle of blood had coagulated, which had surely been made by teeth. I knew that Uncle Whiskers certainly had two useful assets—fine, sharp teeth and tremendous strength in his jaws. By his behaviour (he was still rolling about at my feet like some intoxicated drunkard) he certainly gave me the impression that he had killed the rat and the deep incisions round the beast's neck could be accepted as supporting evidence. But unless the rat had literally committed suicide by running into the jaws of the cat, it was impossible to conceive how the cat could possibly have murdered it. Although Uncle Whiskers' mobility was increasing from month to month, he could not possibly have any chance of outrunning a healthy rat—nor ever would, for that matter. But I gave him the benefit of my serious doubts, tickling his tummy and singing his praises and he nearly blew his top with the excitement of it all.

A few days later there was a repeat performance. This time, however, when there was no offering on the doorstep and Uncle Whiskers stumped off towards the courtyard I had learned the drill and followed at once. He had something he wanted to show me. He led me to what he wanted me to suppose was his second rat, which displayed exactly the same symptoms in death as the first one. I found it more difficult, this time, to believe that the dead rat was not all his own work but I was still completely baffled by the problem of how he could conceivably catch and kill one with his limited armament and mobility. I presumed that he did not bring the rats back to the doorstep, as he always had done with mice and shrews, because they were too heavy for him. I was wrong. Uncle Whiskers loathed rats and once he had caught and killed one he would hurl it aside and never touch it again. He seldom ate mice and shrews but when he had killed one he would often toss the corpse up into the air several times before he set off home to present it to us. But he would scarcely sniff at a rat once he had killed it, let alone carry it back to the house.

Although he still roamed far afield and spent some of his time, especially for an hour or so after daybreak, among his beloved (?) rabbits, Uncle Whiskers began to haunt that courtyard and I was lucky enough to be able to watch the way in which he stalked and killed his third rat. He was sitting, waiting and watching, somewhere near the middle of the courtyard. The irregular configuration of the house blocked the east side of the courtyard and around the southern and western sides there was a high brick wall at the end of which were a pair of wrought-iron gates giving access to the greenhouses and a walled garden.

Whilst I was watching, standing stock-still at the angle of the house, a fat rat slipped under the gate and started to move down close under the base of the west wall. Although he scarcely twitched a muscle, I got the strong impression that Uncle Whiskers was aware of the entry of the rat almost at once. I think he may have moved his head very slightly, in order to get the rat squarely in his sights. Certainly he followed the unsuspecting rodent as it moved slowly and furtively towards the southwest corner of the courtyard, for I could see Uncle Whiskers gently, almost imperceptibly, moving his head to follow the rat's movements. Apart from this movement of the head he might have been carved out of a piece of marble, not even betraying his excitement by even the twitch of his tail-tip.

The rat went on slowly moving down under the west wall until it was three-quarters of the way to the corner where the south wall made a right-angle with it. Until then Uncle Whiskers made no real movement but now he rose up on his haunches and remained looking at his intended victim. I think the rat became aware of the cat almost at once. Certainly the rat paused, turned half-round, and appeared to be looking at Uncle Whiskers, although the two were still fully seven or eight yards apart—perhaps more. Had the rat chosen, at that moment, to bolt back under the wall and through the gate I am sure that Uncle Whiskers would not have had the remotest chance of getting to terms with it. I would make a shrewd guess that this particular feline mind had no intention of letting his instincts get the better of his hard-earned reason and was content to play a waiting game. Had he moved at this juncture, it must have been odds on that the rat would have bolted back to safety. Uncle Whiskers, still sitting up on his haunches, hardly twitched a whisker. What followed was not only both fascinating and thrilling but it proved to my satisfaction I was the owner of a cat with an exceptionally high feline IQ.

Uncle Whiskers, after that long pause sitting up rigid on his haunches, lowered himself very slowly to the ground. Almost imperceptibly and certainly very cautiously, with prolonged and frequent pauses, he entered upon a stalk which lasted several minutes. He moved (perhaps shuffled might be the better word) not diagonally across the courtyard directly towards the rat but towards the west wall, on a track which would lead him to a position between his quarry and the gate under which it had entered the yard. When he was two or three yards from the wall, Uncle Whiskers came to a stop, settled down and remained motionless, facing towards the rat. If the rat chose to bolt back under the wall to the gateway it crossed my mind that Uncle Whiskers might try a prodigious leap but he could not be quick enough to intercept his prey. I was a little worried that, should he try such a leap, he might well bash his brains out against the brick wall. It was a very tense, if slow-moving, drama.

Cat and rat, both scarcely twitching a whisker, stared at one another over a distance of several yards for what seemed a long time. I, myself, scarcely dared to breathe. Then the rat crept very slowly a little farther along under the west wall, away from the gate and also away from the cat. With almost exaggerated caution Uncle Whiskers proceeded to close the distance, then squatted again, now within about six feet of the wall. To cut a longish story a little short, the rat again shifted, followed slowly by the cat, until eventually the former was in the corner of the angle of the west and south walls with Uncle Whiskers facing it, still two yards from the west wall but three or four from the southern one. If the rat chose to bolt under the south wall, it semed impossible that the cat could leap at it, although he might still be able to cut off its retreat.

There was another long pause, with neither party apparently prepared to make a move. Suddenly, unexpectedly, the rat made a bolt for it under the west wall, intent on going back the way he had come and making his escape through the gate. I had been watching the rat rather than the cat but I saw Uncle Whiskers airborne in a flying leap. A split second later I thought there was a squeak and Uncle Whiskers had his teeth into the rat. The rat, however, was still very much alive. It even succeeded in dragging the cat round, for Uncle Whiskers had no forepaws to steady himself. It was a good-sized rat and I had to hope that the cat could hold on with his sharp teeth. He managed to do so. As the rat weakened he shook it, terrier-fashion, and dragged it backwards. Since his accident Uncle Whiskers had learnt to walk backwards, shuffling on his powerful hind legs. I have never known any other cat which could perform in this way.

He had the dying rat very firmly in his vice-like jaws. Victory was at hand. He stood up on his haunches, so that only the rat's tail trailed on the ground, shaking it so violently that he momentarily lost his balance but not, luckily, his grip on his victim. Actually the rat was now as good as dead. The cat sat up on his haunches again, shook the rat several times, then flung it aside. The legs of the prey were still twitching but these were only death-reflexes. Uncle Whiskers seemed to look at it for a few seconds, as if contemplating the sheer size of his prize, then turned round and began moving towards the house with the obvious intention of fetching my wife or me to inspect the evidence of his triumph. But I was already walking towards him and I was so impressed by his almost uncanny skill that I picked him up and gave him a rare good cossetting, holding him on the crook of my arm with his head on my left shoulder. He fairly roared away in my left ear, purring his head off and when I put him down he indulged himself in a whole series of victory rolls.

There was, this time, no room to doubt that "All my own work!" attitude of the cat. Certainly a four-legged cat could not possibly have put up a better performance, either in the patience demanded by the long stalk or in the almost incredible judgment in leaping in for the kill. Once airborne on that final leap, Uncle Whiskers could not, surely, alter his trajectory in any way. I still find it difficult to understand how he did it, but that he did there was no doubt whatsoever. He was, in effect, a two-legged cat with powerful jaws, the heart of a lion and a great deal more "up top" than most of his kind.

Solomon the Great

DOREEN TOVEY

Siamese cats are too much!

Even their owners (when pressed) admit it, while fiercely defending the breed against their humbler cousins. I've never owned one myself, but I do know what I'm missing because I have friends who live with Siamese. I can visit Shiska and Pya or Chang and Soo-ling (whoever heard of a Siamese named Fred?) and admire them for their undoubted beauty and intelligence, and then, when they go on a howling rampage, I can go gratefully home to my modest, quiet alley cat.

But I have to admire people like Doreen Tovey and her husband who have raised litters of the manic creatures and never give up, despite the horrors that Doreen Tovey hilariously recounts in her "Cats in the Belfry," "Cats in Cahoots," and other delightful books. These are so filled with Siamese charm and mischief that it was hard to make selections. You've already met Sugieh of "Cats in the Belfry." Here is her favorite son Solomon, who doesn't really belong in this book at all, for if there ever was an uncool cat, Solomon is it! But he tried, and if he was seldom an achiever like his mother and his sister, Sheba, he is all the more endearing for it and I just couldn't leave him out.

A few days after that the Smiths brought James to tea for the first time since the kittens were born and Solomon assaulted him. We should have anticipated something like that. Ever since the loss of his whiskers, which he seemed to regard as some sort of accolade, Solomon had been quite unbearable. Head of the Family he said he was, and though the head of the family was more often than not seen disappearing ignominiously round a corner on his back to have his ears washed, it was obviously asking for trouble to have a strange cat in the place.

The snag was, we couldn't ask the Smiths without James. They took him everywhere from the post office to the rectory garden party.

If they didn't, they said—and as Siamese owners ourselves we quite understood—he kicked up hell, and the neighbors complained.

I bet he wouldn't have complained if he'd known what was coming to him that afternoon. I can see him now, stalking elegantly up the garden path in his bright red harness and stopping every now and then to smell the wallflowers. Sugieh greeted him at the door. A little suspiciously, perhaps—but then Sugieh always greeted people suspiciously; it made social occasions so much more interesting. The pair of them walking side by side into the living room where, said Sugieh, her family was simply *dying* to meet him. And the awful moment when Solomon, his one-sided whiskers simply bristling with hate, shot out from under the table, drew himself up to his full six inches, and spat.

Before it had even started our polite country tea party was bedlam. Sugieh, screaming that he had Attacked her Son, pitched into James. James, who hadn't done a thing but wasn't stopping to argue, took off through the cucumber sandwiches. And Solomon, completely beside himself with excitement, bit Mrs. Smith in the leg.

Long after James had been driven home shaking like a leaf and we had swept up the remains of the Copeland bowl that used to stand in the window, Solomon was still telling us about Mrs. Smith's leg.

"And after that I bit *James*," he chanted, sitting on the kitchen table where we were wearily cutting up rabbit for their supper. "And then I chased him up the *curtains*. And then I bit him *again* . . ."

Actually he hadn't done anything of the sort. It was Sugieh who bit James. The moment Mrs. Smith screamed Solomon had dived under the bureau like a rocket with the rest of the kittens and all we had seen of him for the next twenty minutes was a pair of eyes as round as marbles gazing dumfounded at the devastation. That, however, was Solomon all over. To add to our other troubles he had turned out to be a feline Walter Mitty.

We usually locked the kittens in the hall when we got their food. Four of them clinging to his legs like Morris bells and Sugieh drooling hungrily in his ear were, as Charles said the day he cut his finger with the chopping knife, more than any man could stand. When the dishes were on the floor, however, and the hall door was opened, it was no ordinary litter of kittens that trooped forth to supper. It was a sheriff's posse with Solomon in the lead. Ears flat, tails raised, they drummed in a solid body through the living room, along the passage, and into the kitchen, with Sugieh hard behind charging as enthusiastically—if a little self-consciously—as any of them.

One day the garden door happened to be open as well and

Solomon, whose two ambitions in life were to Eat and Be Out, had absent-mindedly galloped the posse out into the yard before he realized it. Father Adams, who was passing at the time, was loud in his admiration of the way in which he skidded to a halt in a cloud of dust, turned, and with a mighty roar led the charge hotfoot back to the feeding bowls. If he'd been a hoss, he said, the little black 'un would have made a mighty fine hunter.

Solomon remembered that. The time was to come when he thought he was a horse, and a pretty fine dance he led us. Meanwhile he was busy being head of the family, and a fine job he made of that too.

In the mornings, when the posse tore out of the front door and up the damson tree so fast it hurt your eyes—half their time they spent in the damson tree spying down through the leaves at unsuspecting passers-by and the other half they spent with their noses pressed to the hall window complaining there was somebody interesting going by Right This Moment and now they'd Missed Him—it was always Solomon, who led the way, shouting This Morning he'd be first at the Top. It was always Solomon, too, who after an initial leap big enough to take him clean over the roof, was left clinging desperately to the trunk about two feet up yelling to us to Catch Him Quick, he was feeling Giddy.

The only time he ever did get to the top—we imagined he must have been carried up bodily by the rush of kittens behind him—he was so overcome with excitement when the rector went by that he fell out onto his head. Neither of them was hurt, though the rector—red in the face and the nearest I ever knew him to swearing—said if we had to give him a biblical name it should have been Beelzebub, and after that whenever he came to call he always used to stop at a safe distance and look up into the damson tree before opening the gate. He needn't have worried. Solomon never did it again. Our little black-faced dreamer, though he woke the whole household at five every morning shouting to hurry up and let him out, he knew he could make it This Time, couldn't climb for toffee.

We were always rescuing him from somewhere. If it wasn't from the damson tree it was, more often than not, from the fourth bar of the five-barred gate which led into the lane. Sugieh, who had an eye for effect, was always encouraging her family up there. The idea was obviously to present people walking through the woods with a tableau of Mother and Kittens on a Gate that would absolutely stun them. Very effective it would have been too, if only Solomon had been able to make it. When visitors came past, however, Solomon, wailing with mortification, was always completely and hopelessly stuck on the top bar but one while Sugieh, instead of smirking at them with coy, half-closed eyes from a nest of cuddly kittens as planned, lay flat on her stomach frantically trying to hook him up with her paw.

Failing to climb the damson tree never worried Solomon a scrap, but for some odd psychological reason not being able to get on top of the gate did. In the end he gave up trying. When the other kittens hurled themselves up the gatepost with squeals of delight, to balance-walk across the top with their absurd tails raised like little raft-masts and shrieks of excitement as every now and then somebody slipped and dangled dangerously by one paw, Solomon would stomp off all by himself and sit on top of the cotoneaster.

It was a *cotoneaster horizontalis*, it reached quite three feet up the coalhouse wall, and Solomon solemnly sitting on the top of it trying to look as if he had conquered Everest was absolutely heart-rending. Even the other kittens felt sorry for him. One day when Sugieh issued her clarion call to come and be pretty on the gate they all went up the cotoneaster with Solomon instead. Unfortunately Solomon wasn't expecting them and in the heat of the moment he fell off and sprained his paw. Whatever happened, he just couldn't win.

The one thing in which he did surpass the other kittens—other than having the biggest feet and the largest appetite—was his voice. Being Siamese, of course, they all had enormous voices. Even the she-kitten, who was much quieter than her brothers and given to periods of silent contemplation on top of the curtain rail, occasionally startled visitors by emitting a cracked soprano "Waaaaah" from ceiling level when struck by some particularly profound thought.

Solomon, however, even as a kitten, had a voice only to be compared with a bullfrog. And he never stopped talking. We used to hear him sometimes talking in the middle of the night. When we went in to see what was wrong—we never ignored noises in the night since the time we found Blondin hanging behind a door, trying to suffocate himself in the sleeve-lining of a coat—there, invariably, were the other three kittens snoring away peacefully like little white angels, Sugieh lying on her side with one eye open, obviously wishing him to the devil—and Solomon, bolt upright in the basket, talking to a spider on the wall.

Solomon loved spiders. When he found one too old or infirm to get away he ate it noisily with his mouth open—a habit he had inherited from Sugieh—talking and chewing appreciatively at the same time. It took us quite a time to discover which kitten it was who gave an ecstatic "Woohoohoo" at intervals while eating rabbit, like a small damp train going through the Rockies, but in the end that turned out to be Solomon too.

He had a vocabulary all his own, which for our own good we quickly learned to understand. A black head appearing round the living room door when we had company and uttering a small but urgent "Wooooh" meant he was sorry to intrude but the earth-box was dirty, and he wanted it changed in a hurry. Solomon didn't like dirty earth-boxes. A raucous "Waaow" accompanied by banging noises from the kitchen as he tried valiantly to open the pantry door meant that he was hungry. Loud and prolonged wailing from somewhere up on the hillside behind the cottage meant that Solomon, after setting out with the others all bluff and bustle and Head of the

Family, had once more got left behind and wanted to be rescued. The only time he couldn't talk was when he was feeding from Sugieh and if he opened his mouth he lost his place. Then, instead of talking, he waggled his big bat ears so frantically he looked as if he were about to take off.

*   *   *   *

Solomon was all right. It was just that his weight—his favorite pastime just then was eating and he was, I regret to say, familiarly known as Podgebelly—had brought down not only the curtains but the blocks on which they were screwed to the wall as well. He was in any case not entirely to blame. He was only copying Sheba, who often swung upside down on the curtains to amuse Charles.

He was always copying Sheba. Brash though he was, always noisy, always in trouble—underneath it all Solomon was a small, wistful clown, valiantly striving to be most important and best at everything and pathetically conscious that he was not. Sheba, on the other hand, was a veritable prodigy. Frail and tiny as a flower, she could run like the wind, climb like a monkey, and had the stamina of an ox.

What Solomon envied most was her prowess as a hunter. Solomon was hopeless at hunting. Not because of any physical incapacity but because he just hadn't got a clue in his big, bat-brained head. His idea of catching mice in the garden wall was not, like Sheba, to lie patiently in wait for them. That, he said, was girl's stuff. He blew threateningly down the hole and then, when they wouldn't come out and fight like men, thrust in a long black paw and tried to hook 'em out.

Any time he did sit down with her to watch something—very impressive he looked, too; head narrowed, dark nose pointing eagerly, every inch Rin-Tin-Tin on the trail—five minutes without action and Solomon was either sound asleep from sheer boredom or, with his head swiveled back to front, busy talking to a passing butterfly.

The result was that, while his sister slaughtered mice and shrews by the dozen, Solomon never caught anything firsthand in his life. Unless you count his snake, which was quite six inches long, and he got so excited when he found it that he jumped on its tail instead of its head and it got away.

It was, we knew, his secret sorrow. The look on his face as he watched Sheba prancing and posturing with her trophies before laying them Eastern-fashion at our feet was pathetic. Sometimes, when he could bear it no longer, he would dawdle up on his long, sad, spidery legs, head down so that Sheba shouldn't see what he was carrying, and present us with a soggy leaf. Then he would sit down and look soulfully up into our faces, imploring us with all his small Siamese heart to make believe that he had caught something too. It was a heart-rending scene—marred only by the fact that the moment he managed to grab Sheba's booty away from her Solomon was a different cat altogether.

Then, tossing it high into the air, leaping after it and catching it in his paws, flinging it spectacularly across the room—it was just as well to be out of range when he got to that stage; Charles once fielded a boundary right in his cup and it put him off tea for days— Solomon's ego was back with a bang.

It was His Mouse, he said, panting fiercely over the corpse at Sheba and daring her to pant back. But you couldn't catch Sheba out. She just sat smirking at Charles saying didn't Solomon look silly showing off like that and it was only an old one anyway. It was His Mouse, he said, crouching defensively over it when the rector called—adding, quite untroubled by conscience, that he'd Caught It All Himself. He went on yelling about it being his mouse until either everybody was fed to the teeth and Sheba went and sat on a door or else, taking him completely by surprise—on one occasion indeed frightening him so much he leaped several feet into the air—the mouse got up and ran away.

Calvin

CHARLES DUDLEY WARNER

Admirable though this celebrated essay is, I was at first re-
luctant to include it here because it has appeared in so many
anthologies. But its unusual distinction and its place as a
classic of cat literature won out at last. Perhaps there are
readers who will renew with pleasure their acquaintance
with this exceptional cat: "the least obtrusive of beings,"
whose "individuality always made itself felt." And un-
doubtedly there are some who have never discovered this
eloquent little masterpiece.

Charles Dudley Warner was a prolific writer, an esteemed
editor, and co-author with Mark Twain of "The Gilded
Age." Yet it is one of the ironies of literary fame that this
quiet, moving memoir of Calvin is his most enduring work.

Calvin is dead. His life, long to him, but short for the rest of us, was
not marked by startling adventures, but his character was so uncom-
mon and his qualities were so worthy of imitation, that I have been
asked by those who personally knew him to set down my recollections
of his career.

His origin and ancestry were shrouded in mystery; even his age
was a matter of pure conjecture. Although he was of the Maltese
race, I have reason to suppose that he was American by birth as he
certainly was in sympathy. Calvin was given to me eight years ago by
Mrs. Stowe, but she knew nothing of his age or origin. He walked
into her house one day out of the great unknown and became at once
at home, as if he had been always a friend of the family. He appeared
to have artistic and literary tastes, and it was as if he had inquired at
the door if that was the residence of the author of *Uncle Tom's*
Cabin, and, upon being assured that it was, had decided to dwell
there. This is, of course, fanciful, for his antecedents were wholly
unknown, but in his time he could hardly have been in any household
where he would not have heard *Uncle Tom's Cabin* talked about.
When he came to Mrs. Stowe, he was as large as he ever was, and
apparently as old as he ever became. Yet there was in him no appear-

ance of age; he was in the happy maturity of all his powers, and you would rather have said in that maturity he had found the secret of perpetual youth. And it was as difficult to believe that he would ever be aged as it was to imagine that he had ever been in immature youth. There was in him a mysterious perpetuity.

After some years, when Mrs. Stowe made her winter home in Florida, Calvin came to live with us. From the first moment, he fell into the ways of the house and assumed a recognized position in the family,—I say recognized, because after he became known he was always inquired for by visitors, and in the letters to the other members of the family he always received a message. Although the least obtrusive of beings, his individuality always made itself felt.

His personal appearance had much to do with this, for he was of royal mould, and had an air of high breeding. He was large, but he had nothing of the fat grossness of the celebrated Angora family; though powerful, he was exquisitely proportioned, and as graceful in every movement as a young leopard. When he stood up to open a door—he opened all the doors with old-fashioned latches—he was portentously tall, and when stretched on the rug before the fire he seemed too long for this world—as indeed he was. His coat was the finest and softest I have ever seen, a shade of quiet Maltese; and from his throat downward, underneath, to the tips of his feet, he wore the whitest and most delicate ermine; and no person was ever more fastidiously neat. In his finely formed head you saw something of his aristocratic character; the ears were small and cleanly cut, there was a tinge of pink in the nostrils, his face was handsome, and the expression of his countenance exceedingly intelligent—I should call it even a sweet expression if the term were not inconsistent with his look of alertness and sagacity.

It is difficult to convey a just idea of his gaiety in connection with his dignity and gravity, which his name expressed. As we know nothing of his family, of course it will be understood that Calvin was his Christian name. He had times of relaxation into utter playfulness, delighting in a ball of yarn, catching sportively at stray ribbons when his mistress was at her toilet, and pursuing his own tail, with hilarity, for lack of anything better. He could amuse himself by the hour, and he did not care for children; perhaps something in his past was present to his memory. He had absolutely no bad habits, and his disposition was perfect. I never saw him exactly angry, though I have seen his tail grow to an enormous size when a strange cat appeared upon his lawn. He disliked cats, evidently regarding them as feline and treacherous, and he had no association with them. Occasionally there would be heard a night concert in the shrubbery. Calvin would ask to have the door opened, and you would hear a rush and a "pestzt," and the concert would explode, and Calvin would quietly come in and resume his seat on the hearth. There was no trace of anger in his manner, but he wouldn't have any of that about the house. He had the rare virtue of magnanimity. Although he had fixed notions about his own rights, and extraordinary persistency in getting them, he never showed temper at a repulse; he simply and firmly persisted till he had what he wanted. His diet was one point; his idea was that of the scholars about dictionaries,—to "get the best." He knew as well as anyone what was in the house, and would refuse beef if turkey was to be had; and if there were oysters, he would wait over the turkey to see if the oysters would not be forthcoming. And yet he was not a gross gourmand; he would eat bread if he saw me eating it, and thought he was not being imposed on. His habits of feeding, also, were refined; he never used a knife, and he would put up his hand and draw the fork down to his mouth as gracefully as a grown person. Unless necessity compelled, he would not eat in the kitchen, but insisted upon his meals in the dining room, and would wait patiently, unless a stranger were present; and then he was sure to importune the visitor, hoping that the latter was ignorant of the rule of the house, and would give him something. They used to say that he preferred as his table-cloth on the floor a certain well-known church journal; but this was said by an Episcopalian. So far as I know, he had no religious prejudices, except that he did not like the association with Romanists. He tolerated the servants, because they belonged to the house, and would sometimes linger by the kitchen stove; but the moment visitors came in he rose, opened the door, and marched into the drawing-room. Yet he enjoyed the company of his equals, and never withdrew, no matter how many callers—whom he recognized as of his society—might come into the drawing-room. Calvin was fond of company, but he wanted to choose it; and I have no doubt that his was an aristocratic fastidiousness rather than one of faith. It is so with most people.

The intelligence of Calvin was something phenomenal, in his rank of life. He established a method of communicating his wants, and even some of his sentiments; and he could help himself in many things. There was a furnace register in a retired room, where he used to go when he wished to be alone, that he always opened when he desired more heat; but never shut it, any more than he shut the door after himself. He could do almost everything but speak; and you would declare sometimes that you could see a pathetic longing to do that in his intelligent face. I have no desire to overdraw his qualities, but if there was one thing in him more noticeable than another, it was his fondness for nature. He could content himself for hours at a low window, looking into the ravine and at the great trees, noting the smallest stir there; he delighted, above all things, to accompany me walking about the garden, hearing the birds, getting the smell of the fresh earth, and rejoicing in the sunshine. He followed me and gambolled like a dog, rolling over on the turf and exhibiting his delight in a hundred ways. If I worked, he sat and watched me, or looked off over the bank, and kept his ear open to the twitter in the cherry-trees. When it stormed, he was sure to sit at the window, keenly watching the rain or the snow, glancing up and down at its falling; and a winter tempest always delighted him. I think he was genuinely fond of birds, but, so far as I know, he usually confined himself to one a day; he never killed, as some sportsmen do, for the sake of killing, but only as civilized people do,—from necessity. He was intimate with the flying-squirrels who dwell in the chestnut-trees,—too intimate, for almost every day in the summer he would bring in one, until he nearly discouraged them. He was, indeed, a superb hunter, and would have been a devastating one, if his bump of destructiveness had not been offset by a bump of moderation. There was very little of the brutality of the lower animals about him; I don't think he enjoyed rats for themselves, but he knew his business, and for the first few months of his residence with us he waged an awful campaign against the horde, and after that his simple presence was sufficient to deter them from coming on the premises. Mice amused him, but he usually considered them too small game to be taken seriously; I have seen him play for an hour with a mouse, and then let him go with a royal condescension. In this whole matter of "getting a living," Calvin was a great contrast to the rapacity of the age in which he lived.

I hesitate a little to speak of his capacity for friendship and the affectionateness of his nature, for I know from his own reserve that he would not care to have it much talked about. We understood each other perfectly but we never made any fuss about it; when I spoke his name and snapped my fingers, he came to me; when I returned home at night, he was pretty sure to be waiting for me near the gate, and would rise and saunter along the walk, as if his being there were purely accidental,—so shy was he commonly of showing feeling; and when I opened the door he never rushed in, like a cat, but loitered, and lounged, as if he had had no intention of going in, but would condescend to. And yet, the fact was, he knew dinner was ready, and he was bound to be there. He kept the run of dinner-time. It happened sometimes, during our absence in the summer, that dinner would be early, and Calvin, walking about the grounds, missed it and came in late. But he never made a mistake the second day. There was one thing he never did,—he never rushed through an open doorway. He never forgot his dignity. If he had asked to have the door opened, and was, eager to go out, he always went deliberately; I can see him now, standing on the sill, looking about at the sky as if he was thinking whether it were worth while to take an umbrella, until he was near having his tail shut in.

His friendship was rather constant than demonstrative. When we returned from an absence of nearly two years, Calvin welcomed us with evident pleasure, but showed his satisfaction rather by tranquil happiness than by fuming about. He had the faculty of making us glad to get home. It was his constancy that was so attractive. He liked companionship, but he wouldn't be petted, or fussed over, or sit in anyone's lap a moment; he always extracted himself from such familiarity with dignity and with no show of temper. If there was any petting to be done, however, he chose to do it. Often he would sit looking at me, and then, moved by a delicate affection, come and pull at my coat and sleeve until he could touch my face with his nose, and then go away contented. He had a habit of coming to my study in the morning, sitting quietly by my side or on the table for hours, watching the pen run over the paper, occasionally swinging his tail round for a blotter, and then going to sleep among the papers by the ink-stand. Or, more rarely, he would watch the writing from a perch on my shoulder. Writing always interested him, and, until he understood it, he wanted to hold the pen.

He always held himself in a kind of reserve with his friend, as if he had said, "Let us respect our personality, and not make a 'mess' of friendship." He saw, with Emerson, the risk of degrading it to trivial conveniency. "Why insist on rash personal relations with your friend?" "Leave this touching and clawing." Yet I would not give an unfair notion of his aloofness, his fine sense of the sacredness of the me and the not-me. And, at the risk of not being believed, I will relate an incident, which was often repeated. Calvin had the practice of passing a portion of the night in the contemplation of its beauties, and would come into our chamber over the roof of the conservatory through the open window, summer and winter, and go to sleep on the foot of my bed. He would do this always exactly in this way; he never was content to stay in the chamber if we compelled him to go upstairs and through the door. He had the obstinacy of General

Grant. But this is by the way. In the morning, he performed his toilet and went down to breakfast with the rest of the family. Now, when the mistress was absent from home, and at no other time, Calvin would come in the morning, when the bell rang, to the head of the bed, put up his feet and look into my face, follow me about when I rose, "assist" at the dressing, and in many purring ways show his fondness, as if he had plainly said, "I know that she has gone away, but I am here." Such was Calvin in rare moments.

He had his limitations. Whatever passion he had for nature, he had no conception of art. There was sent to him once a fine and very expressive cat's head in bronze, by Frémiet. I placed it on the floor. He regarded it intently, approached it cautiously and crouchingly, touched it with his nose, perceived the fraud, turned away abruptly, and never would notice it afterward. On the whole, his life was not only a successful one, but a happy one. He never had but one fear, so far as I know: he had a mortal and a reasonable terror of plumbers. He would never stay in the house when they were here. No coaxing could quiet him. Of course he didn't share our fear about their charges, but he must have had some dreadful experience with them in that portion of his life which is unknown to us. A plumber was to him the devil, and I have no doubt that, in his scheme, plumbers were foreordained to do him mischief.

In speaking of his worth, it has never occurred to me to estimate Calvin by the worldly standard. I know that it is customary now, when anyone dies, to ask how much he was worth, and that no obituary in the newspapers is considered complete without such an estimate. The plumbers in our house were one day overheard to say that, "They say that *she* says that *he* says that he wouldn't take a hundred dollars for him." It is unnecessary to say that I never made such a remark, and that, so far as Calvin was concerned, there was no purchase in money.

As I look back upon it, Calvin's life seems to me a fortunate one, for it was natural and unforced. He ate when he was hungry, slept when he was sleepy, and enjoyed existence to the very tips of his toes and the end of his expressive and slow-moving tail. He delighted to roam about the garden, and stroll among the trees, and to lie on the green grass and luxuriate in all the sweet influences of summer. You could never accuse him of idleness, and yet he knew the secret of repose. The poet who wrote so prettily of him that his little life was rounded with a sleep understated his felicity; it was rounded with a good many. His conscience never seemed to interfere with his slumbers. In fact, he had good habits and a contented mind. I can see him now walk in at the study door, sit down by my chair, bring his tail artistically about his feet, and look up at me with unspeakable happiness in his handsome face. I often thought that he felt the dumb limitation which denied him the power of language. But since he was denied speech, he scorned the inarticulate mouthings of the lower animals. The vulgar mewing and yowling of the cat species was beneath him; he sometimes uttered a sort of articulate and well-bred ejaculation, when he wished to call attention to something that he considered remarkable, or to some want of his, but he never went whining about. He would sit for hours at a closed window, when he desired to enter, without a murmur, and when it was opened he never admitted that he had been impatient by "bolting" in. Though speech he had not, and the unpleasant kind of utterance given to his race he would not use, he had a mighty power of purr to express his measureless content with congenial society. There was in him a musical organ with stops of varied power and expression, upon which I have no doubt he could have performed Scarlatti's celebrated cat's-fugue.

Whether Calvin died of old age, or was carried off by one of the diseases incident to youth, it is impossible to say; for his departure was as quiet as his advent was mysterious. I only know that he appeared to us in this world in his perfect stature and beauty, and that after a time, like Lohengrin, he withdrew. In his illness there was nothing more to be regretted than in all his blameless life. I suppose there never was an illness that had more of dignity and sweetness and resignation in it. It came on gradually, in a kind of listlessness and want of appetite. An alarming symptom was his preference for the warmth of a furnace-register to the lively sparkle of the open wood-fire. Whatever pain he suffered, he bore it in silence, and seemed only anxious not to obtrude his malady. We tempted him with the delicacies of the season, but it soon became impossible for him to eat, and for two weeks he ate or drank scarcely anything. Sometimes he made the effort to take something, but it was evident that he made the effort to please us. The neighbors—and I am convinced that the advice of neighbors is never good for anything— suggested catnip. He wouldn't even smell it. We had the attendance of an amateur practitioner of medicine, whose real office was the cure of souls, but nothing touched his case. He took what was offered, but it was with the air of one to whom the time for pellets was passed. He sat or lay day after day almost motionless, never once making a display of those vulgar convulsions or contortions of pain which are so disagreeable to society. His favorite place was on the brightest spot of a Smyrna rug by the conservatory, where the sunlight fell and he could hear the fountain play. If we went to him and exhibited our interest in his condition, he always purred in recognition of our sympathy. And when I spoke his name, he looked up with an expression that said, "I understand it, old fellow, but it's no use." He was to all who came to visit him a model of calmness and patience in affliction.

I was absent from home at the last, but heard by daily postal-card of his failing condition; and never again saw him alive. One sunny morning, he rose from his rug, went into the conservatory (he was very thin then), walked around it deliberately, looking at all the plants he knew, and then went to the bay-window in the dining room, and stood a long time looking out upon the little field, now brown and sere, and toward the garden, where perhaps the happiest hours of his life had been spent. It was a last look. He turned and walked away, laid himself down upon the bright spot in the rug, and quietly died.

It is not too much to say that a little shock went through the neighborhood when it was known that Calvin was dead, so marked was his individuality; and his friends, one after another, came to see him. There was no sentimental nonsense about his obsequies; it was felt that any parade would have been distasteful to him. John, who acted as undertaker, prepared a candle-box for him, and I believe assumed a professional decorum; but there may have been the usual levity underneath, for I heard that he remarked in the kitchen that it was the "dryest wake he ever attended." Everybody, however, felt a fondness for Calvin, and regarded him with a certain respect. Between him and Bertha there existed a great friendship, and she apprehended his nature; she used to say that sometimes she was afraid of him, he looked at her so intelligently; she was never certain that he was what he appeared to be.

When I returned, they had laid Calvin on a table in an upper chamber by an open window. It was February. He reposed in a candle-box, lined about the edge with evergreen, and at his head stood a little wine-glass with flowers. He lay with his head tucked down in his arms—a favorite position of his before the fire,—as if asleep in the comfort of his soft and exquisite fur. It was the involuntary exclamation of those who saw him, "How natural he looks!" As for myself, I said nothing. John buried him under the twin hawthorn-trees,—one white and the other pink,—in a spot where Calvin was fond of lying and listening to the hum of summer insects and the twitter of birds.

Perhaps I have failed to make appear the individuality of character that was so evident to those who knew him. At any rate, I have set down nothing concerning him but the literal truth. He was always a mystery. I do not know whence he came; I do not know whither he has gone. I would not weave one spray of falsehood in the wreath I lay upon his grave.

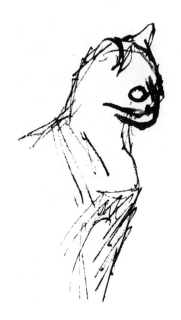

Abner of the Porch

GEOFFREY HOUSEHOLD

*If the word sweetness could be used today in a non-deroga-
tory sense I'd choose it to describe this gentle story by an
author better known for his tales of derring-do. There's
some pleasant one-upmanship between MacGillivray the
terrier and Abner the cat, and the author handles their
skirmishes with skill and humor, and the barest whisper of
suspense.*

When my voice broke, even Abner and MacGillivray understood
my grief. I did not expect sympathy from MacGillivray, for he had
no reason to like me. But he knew what it was to be excluded from
cathedral ceremonies. He was the Bishop's dog.

Abner was masterless. I would not claim that he appreciated the
alto's solo in the Magnificat when the organ was hushed and there
was no other sound in the million and a half cubic feet of the
Cathedral but the slender purity of a boy's voice; yet he would
patronize me after such occasions with air of the master alto which
he might have been. Though not a full Tom, he knew the ancestral
songs which resemble our own. To our ears the scale of cats is distasteful, but one cannot deny them sustained notes of singular love-
liness and clarity.

Abner's career had followed a common human pattern. My father
was the gardener, responsible for the shaven lawns and discreet
flower beds of the cathedral close. Some three years earlier he had
suffered from an invasion of moles—creatures of ecclesiastical subtlety
who avoided all the crude traps set for them by a mere layman. The
cat, appearing from nowhere, took an interest. After a week he had
caught the lot, laying out his game-bag each morning upon the
tarpaulin which covered the mower.

Fed and praised by my father, he began to pay some attention to
public relations and attracted the attention of visitors. Officially
recognized as an ornament of the Cathedral when his photograph
appeared in the local paper, he ventured to advance from the lawns
and tombstones to the porch. There he captivated the Dean, always

politely rising from the stone bench and thrusting his noble flanks against the gaitered leg. He was most gracious to the Bishop and the higher clergy, but he would only stroke the Dean. He knew very well from bearing and tone of voice, gentle though they were, that the Cathedral belonged to him. It was the Dean who christened him Abner.

To such a personage the dog of our new Bishop was a disaster. MacGillivray was of respectable middle age, and had on occasion a sense of dignity; but when dignity was not called for he behaved like any other Aberdeen terrier and would race joyously round the Cathedral or across the close, defying whatever human being was in charge of him to catch the lead which bounced and flew behind.

His first meeting with his rival set the future tone of their relations. He ventured with appalling temerity to make sport of the cathedral cat. Abner stretched himself, yawned, allowed MacGillivray's charge to approach within a yard, leaped to the narrow and rounded top of a tombstone and, draping himself over it, went ostentatiously to sleep. MacGillivray jumped and yapped at the tail tip which graciously waved for him, and then realized that he was being treated as a puppy. After that the two passed each other politely but without remark. In our closed world of the Cathedral such coolness between servants of Dean and servants of Bishop was familiar.

MacGillivray considered that he should be on permanent duty with his master. Since he was black, small and ingenious, it was difficult to prevent him. So devoted a friend could not be cruelly chained—and in summer the French windows of the Bishop's Palace were always open.

He first endeared himself to choir and clergy at the ceremony of the Bishop's installation. Magnificent in mitre and full robes, the Bishop at the head of his procession knocked with his crozier upon the cathedral door to demand admission. MacGillivray, observing that his master was shut out and in need of help, hurtled across the close, bounced at the door and added his excited barks to the formal solemnity of the Bishop's order.

Led away in disapproving silence, he took the enormity of his crime more seriously than we did. On his next appearance he behaved with decent humility, following the unconscious Bishop down the chancel and into the pulpit with bowed head and tail well below the horizontal.

Such anxious piety was even more embarrassing than bounce. It became my duty, laid upon me by the Bishop in person, to ensure on all formal occasions that MacGillivray had not evaded the butler and was safely confined. I was even empowered to tie him up to the railings on the north side of the close in cases of emergency.

I do not think the Bishop ever realized what was troubling his friend and erring brother, MacGillivray—normally a dog of sense who could mind his own business however great his affection for his master. When he accompanied the Bishop around the diocese he never committed the solecism of entering a parish church and never used the vicar's cat as an objective for assault practice.

His indiscipline at home was, we were all sure, due to jealousy of Abner. He resented with Scottish obstinacy the fact that he was ejected in disgrace from the Cathedral whereas Abner was not. He could not be expected to understand that Abner's discreet movements were beyond human control.

The Dean could and did quite honestly declare that he had never seen that cat in the Cathedral. Younger eyes, however, which knew where to look, had often distinguished Abner curled up on the ornate stone canopy over the tomb of a seventeenth-century admiral. In winter he would sometimes sleep upon the left arm of a stone crusader in the cavity between shield and mailed shirt—a dank spot, I thought, until I discovered that it captured a current of warm air from the grating beside the effigy. In both his resting-places he was, if he chose to be, invisible. He was half Persian, tiger-striped with brownish grey on lighter grey, and he matched the stone of the Cathedral.

As the summer went by, the feud between Abner and MacGillivray became more subtle. Both scored points. MacGillivray, if he woke up feeling youthful, used to chase the tame pigeons in the close. One morning, to the surprise of both dog and bird, a pigeon failed to get out of the way in time and broke a wing. MacGillivray was embarrassed. He sniffed the pigeon, wagged his tail to show that there was no ill feeling and sat down to think.

Abner strolled from the porch and held down the pigeon with a firm, gentle paw. He picked it up in his mouth and presented it with liquid and appealing eyes to an elegant American tourist who was musing sentimentally in the close. She swore that the cat had asked her to heal the bird—which, by remaining a whole week in our town in and out of the vet's consulting room, she did. Personally I think that Abner was attracted by the feline grace of her walk and was suggesting that, as the pigeon could be of no more use to the Cathedral, she might as well eat it. But whatever his motives he had again made MacGillivray look a clumsy and impulsive fool.

MacGillivray's revenge was a little primitive. He deposited bones

and offal in dark corners of the porch and pretended that Abner had put them there. That was the second worst crime he knew—to leave on a human floor the inedible portions of his meals.

The verger was deceived and submitted a grave complaint in writing to the Dean. The Dean, however, knew very well that Abner had no interest in mutton bones, old or new. He was familiar with the cat's tastes. Indeed it was rumoured from the Deanery that he secreted a little box in his pocket at meals, into which he would drop such delicacies as the head of a small trout or the liver of a roast duck.

I cannot remember all the incidents of the cold war. And, any way, I could not swear to their truth. My father and the Dean read into the animals' behaviour motives which were highly unlikely and then shamelessly embroidered them, creating a whole miscellany of private legend for the canons and the choir. So I will only repeat the triumph of MacGillivray and its sequel, both of which I saw myself.

That fulfillment of every dog's dream appeared at first final and overwhelming victory. It was September 1st, the feast of St. Giles, our patron saint. Evensong was a full choral and instrumental service, traditional, exquisite, and attracting a congregation whose interest was in music rather than religion. The Bishop was to preach. Perhaps the effort of composition, of appealing to well-read intellectuals without offending the simpler clergy, had created an atmosphere of hard work and anxiety in the Bishop's study. At any rate MacGillivray was nervous and mischievous.

While I was ensuring his comfort before shutting him up, he twitched the lead out of my hand and was off on his quarter-mile course round the Cathedral looking for a private entrance. When at last I caught him, the changes of the bells had stopped. I had only five minutes before the processional entry of the choir. There wasn't even time to race across the close and tie him up to the railings.

I rushed into the north transept with MacGillivray under my arm, pushed him down the stairs into the crypt and shut the door behind him. I knew that he could not get out. Our Norman crypt was closed to visitors during the service, and no one on a summer evening would have reason to go down to the masons' and carpenters' stores, the strong-room or the boilers. All I feared was that MacGillivray's yaps might be heard through the gratings in the cathedral floor.

I dived into my ruffled surplice and took my place in the procession, earning the blackest possible looks from the choirmaster. I just had time to explain to him that it was the fault of MacGillivray. I was not forgiven, but the grin exchanged between choirmaster and Precentor suggested that I probably would be—if I wasn't still panting by the time that the alto had to praise all famous men and our fathers that begat us.

St. Giles, if he still had any taste for earthly music, must have approved his servants that evening. The Bishop, always an effective preacher, surpassed himself. His sinewy arguments were of course beyond me, but I had my eye—vain little beast that I was—on the music critics from the London papers, and I could see that several of them were so interested that they were bursting to take over the pulpit and reply.

Only once did he falter, when the barking of MacGillivray, hardly perceptible to anyone but his master and me, caught the episcopal ear. Even then his momentary hesitation was put down to a search for the right word.

I felt that my desperate disposal of MacGillivray might not be appreciated. He must have been audible to any of the congregation sitting near the gratings of the northern aisle. So I shot down to release him immediately after the recessional. The noise was startling as soon as I opened the door. MacGillivray was holding the stairs against a stranger in the crypt.

The man was good-dogging him and trying to make him shut up. He had a small suit-case by his side. When two sturdy vergers, attracted by the noise, appeared hot on my heels, the intruder tried to bolt—dragging behind him MacGillivray with teeth closed on the turn-ups of his trousers. We detained him and opened the suit-case. It contained twenty pounds weight of the cathedral silver. During the long service our massive but primitive strong room door had been expertly opened.

The congregation was dispersing, but Bishop, Dean, Archdeacon and innumerable canons were still in the Cathedral. They attended the excitement just as any other crowd. Under the circumstances Mac-Gillivray was the centre of the most complimentary fuss. The canons would have genially petted any dog. But this was the Bishop's dog. The wings of gowns and surplices flowed over him like those of exclamatory seagulls descending upon a stranded fish.

Dignity was represented only by our local superintendent of police and the terrier himself. When the thief had been led away Mac-Gillivray reverently followed his master out of the Cathedral; his whole attitude reproached us for ever dreaming that he might take advantage of his popularity.

At the porch, however, he turned round and loosed one short, triumphant bark into the empty nave. The Bishop's chaplain unctuously suggested that it was a little voice of thanksgiving. So it was

—but far from pious. I noticed where MacGillivray's muzzle was pointing. That bark was for a softness of outline, a shadow, a striping of small stone pinnacles upon the canopy of the Admiral's Tomb.

For several days—all of ten I should say—Abner deserted both the Cathedral and its porch. He then returned to his first friend, helping my father to make the last autumn cut of the grass and offering his catch of small game for approval. The Dean suggested that he was in need of sunshine. My father shook his head and said nothing. It was obvious to both of us that for Abner the Cathedral had been momentarily defiled. He reminded me of an old verger who gave in his resignation—it was long overdue any way—after discovering a family party eating lunch from paper bags in the Lady Chapel.

He went back to the porch a little before the Harvest Festival, for he always enjoyed that. During a whole week while the decorations were in place he could find a number of discreet lairs where it was impossible to detect his presence. There may also have been a little hunting in the night. We did not attempt to fill the vastness of the Cathedral with all the garden produce dear to a parish church, but the Dean was fond of fat sheaves of wheat, oats and barley, bound round the middle like sheaves on a heraldic shield.

It was his own festival in his own Cathedral, so that he, not the Bishop, conducted it. He had made the ritual as enjoyable as that of Christmas, reviving ancient customs for which he was always ready to quote authority. I suspect that medieval deans would have denied his interpretation of their scanty records, but they would have recognized a master of stage management.

His most effective revival was a procession of cathedral tenants and benefactors, each bearing some offering in kind which the Dean received on the altar steps. Fruit, honey and cakes were common, always with some touch of magnificence in the quality, quantity or container. On one occasion the landlord of the Pilgrim's Inn presented a roasted peacock set in jelly with tail feathers erect. There was some argument about this on the grounds that it ran close to advertisement. But the Dean would not be dissuaded. He insisted that any craftsman had the right to present a unique specimen of his skill.

That year the gifts were more humble. My father, as always, led the procession with a basket tray upon which was a two-foot bunch of black grapes from the vinery in the Canons' garden. A most original participant was a dear old nursery gardener who presented a plant of his new dwarf camellia which had been the botanical sensation of the year and could not yet be bought for money. There was also a noble milk-pan of Alpine strawberries and cream—which, we hoped, the Cathedral School would share next day with the Alms Houses.

While the file of some twenty persons advanced into the chancel, the choir full-bloodedly sang the 65th Psalm to the joyous score of our own organist. The Dean's sense of theatre was as faultless as ever. Lavish in ritual and his own vestments, he then played his part with the utmost simplicity. He thanked and blessed each giver almost conversationally.

Last in the procession were four boys of the Cathedral School bearing a great silver bowl of nuts gathered in the hedgerows. The gift and their movements were traditional. As they separated, two to the right and two to the left, leaving the Dean alone upon the altar steps, a shadow appeared at his feet and vanished so swiftly that by the time our eyes had registered its true, soft shape it was no longer there.

The Dean bent down and picked up a dead field-mouse. He was not put out of countenance for a moment. He laid it reverently with the other gifts. No one was present to be thanked; but when the Dean left the Cathedral after service and stopped in the porch to talk to Abner he was—to the surprise of the general public—still wearing his full vestments, stiff, gorgeous and suggesting the power of the Church to protect and armour with its blessing the most humble of its servants.

The She-cat

DORIS LESSING

Very different from "The Princess," but also from "Particularly Cats," is this moving recollection of an episode from Miss Lessing's African girlhood. It is a fine example of the resourcefulness of cats and the courage one of them showed in going against her instinct to seek human aid in an emergency.

There was a she-cat, all those years ago. I don't remember why it went wild. Some awful battle must have been fought, beneath the attention of the humans. Perhaps some snub was administered, too much for cat pride to bear. This old cat went away from the house for months. She was not a pretty beast, an old ragbag patched and streaked in black and white and grey and fox-colour. One day she came back and sat at the edge of the clearing where the house was, looking at the house, the people, the door, the other cats, the chickens—the family scene from which she was excluded. Then she crept back into the bush. Next evening, a silent golden evening, there was the old cat. The chickens were being shooed into the runs for the night. We said, perhaps she is after the chickens, and shouted at her. She flattened herself into the grass and disappeared. Next evening, there she was again. My mother went down to the edge of the bush and called to her. But she was wary, would not come close. She was very pregnant: a large gaunt beast, skin over prominent bones, dragging the heavy lump of her belly. She was hungry. It was a dry year. The long dry season had flattened and thinned the grass, cauterized bushes: everything in sight was skeleton, dry sticks of grass; and the tiny leaves fluttering on them, merely shadows. The bushes were twig; trees, their load of leaf thinned and dry, showed the plan of their trunk and branches. The veld was all bones. And the hill our house was on, in the wet season so tall and lush and soft and thick, was stark. Its shape, a low swelling to a high ridge, then an abrupt fall into a valley, showed beneath a stiff fringe of stick and branch. The birds, the rodents, had perhaps moved away to lusher spots. And the cat was not wild enough to move after them, away from the place she still thought of as home.

Perhaps she was too worn by hunger and her load of kittens to travel.

We took down milk, and she drank it, but carefully, her muscles tensed all the time for flight. Others cats from the house came down to stare at the outlaw. When she had drunk the milk, she ran away back to the place she was using to hide in. Every evening she came to the homestead to be fed. One of us kept the other resentful cats away; another brought milk and food. We kept guard till she had eaten. But she was nervous: she snatched every mouthful as if she were stealing it; she kept leaving the plate, the saucer, then coming back. She ran off before the food was finished; and she would not let herself be stroked, would not come close.

One evening we followed her, at a distance. She disappeared halfway down the hill. It was land that had at some point been trenched and mined for gold by a prospector. Some of the trenches had fallen in—heavy rains had washed in soil. The shafts were deserted, perhaps had a couple of feet of rain water in them. Old branches had been dragged across to stop cattle falling in. In one of these holes, the old cat must be hiding. We called her, but she did not come, so we left her.

The rainy season broke in a great dramatic storm, all winds and lightning and thunder and pouring rain. Sometimes the first storm can be all there is for days, even weeks. But that year we had a couple of weeks of continuous storms. The new grass sprang up. The bushes, trees, put on green flesh. Everything was hot and wet and teeming. The old cat came up to the house once or twice; then did not come. We said she was catching mice again. Then, one night of heavy storm, the dogs were barking, and we heard a cat crying just outside the house. We went out, holding up storm lanterns into a scene of whipping boughs, furiously shaking grass, rain driving past in grey curtains. Under the verandah were the dogs, and they were barking at the old cat, who crouched out in the rain, her eyes green in the lantern-light. She had had her kittens. She was just an old skeleton of a cat. We brought out milk for her, and chased away the dogs, but that was not what she wanted. She sat with the rain whipping over her, crying. She wanted help. We put raincoats on over our nightclothes and sloshed after her through a black storm, with the thunder rolling overhead, lightning illuminating sheets of rain. At the edge of the bush we stopped and peered in—in front of us was the area where the old trenches were, the old shafts. It was dangerous to go plunging about in the undergrowth. But the cat was in front of us, crying, commanding. We went carefully with storm lanterns, through waist-high grass and bushes, in the thick pelt of the rain. Then the cat was not to be seen, she was crying from somewhere beneath our feet. Just in front of us was a pile of old branches. That meant we were on the edge of a shaft. Cat was somewhere down it. Well, we were not going to pull a small mountain of slippery dead branches off a crumbling shaft in the middle of the night. We flashed the light through interstices of the branches, and we thought we saw the cat moving, but were not sure. So we went back to the house, leaving the poor beasts, and drank cocoa in a warm lamplit room, and shivered ourselves dry and warm.

But we slept badly, thinking of the poor cat, and got up at five with the first light. The storm had gone over, but everything was dripping. We went out into a cool dawnlight, and red streaks showed in the east where the sun would come up. Down we went into the soaked bush, to the pile of old branches. Not a sign of the cat.

This was a shaft about eighty feet deep, and it had been cross-cut twice, at about ten feet, and then again much deeper. We decided the cat must have put her kittens into the first cut, which ran for about twenty feet, downwards at a slant. It was hard to lift off those heavy wet branches: it took a long time. When the mouth of the shaft was exposed, it was not the clean square shape it had been. The earth had crumbled in, and some light branches and twigs from the covering heap had sunk, making a rough platform about fifteen feet down. On to this had been washed and blown earth and small stones. So it was like a thin floor—but very thin: through it we could see the gleam of rain water from the bottom of the shaft. A short way down, not very far now that the mouth of the shaft had sunk, at about six feet, we could see the opening of the cross-cut, a hole about four feet square, now that it, too, had crumbled. Lying face down on the slippery red mud, holding onto bushes for safety, you could see a good way into the cut—a couple of yards. And there was the cat's head, just visible. It was quite still, sticking out of the red earth. We thought the cut had fallen in with all that rain, and she was half buried, and probably dead. We called her: there was a faint rough sound, then another. So she wasn't dead. Our problem then was, how to get to her. Useless to fix a windlass onto that soaked earth which might landslide in at any moment. And no human could put weight onto that precarious platform of twigs and earth: hard to believe it had been able to take the weight of the cat, who must have been jumping down to it several times a day.

We tied a thick rope to a tree, with big knots in it at three-foot intervals, and let it down over the edge, trying not to get it muddied and slippery. Then one of us went down on the rope with a basket, until it was possible to reach into the cut. There was the cat, crouched against the soaked red soil—she was still with cold and wet. And beside her were half a dozen kittens, about a week old and still blind. Her trouble was that the storms of that fortnight had blown so much rain into the cut that the sides and roof had partly fallen in; and the lair she had found, which had seemed so safe and dry, had become a wet crumbling death trap. She had come up to the house so that we could rescue the kittens. She had been frightened to come near the house because of the hostility of the other cats and the dogs, perhaps because she now feared us, but she had overcome her fear to get help for the kittens. But she had not been given help. She must have lost all hope that night, as the rain lashed down, as earth slid in all around her, as the water crept up behind her in the dark collapsing tunnel. But she had fed the kittens, and they were alive. They hissed and spat as they were lifted into the basket. The cat was too stiff and cold to get out by herself. First the angry kittens were taken up, while she crouched in the wet earth waiting. The basket descended again, and she was lifted into it. The family were taken up to the house, where she was given a corner, food, protection. The kittens grew up and found homes; and she stayed a house cat—and presumably went on having kittens.

Amber

GLADYS TABER

Gladys Taber, known for her many popular books about Stillmeadow Farm, is an impartial animal lover, having raised dogs as well as cats. But I suspect that a special place in her heart has been filled by the exquisite little Abyssinian of whom she writes with such sensible affection in "Amber, A Very Personal Cat."

There may be some stolid cats, but I have never known one. A cat has a naturally lively mind, and my life with Amber has kept me lively too. As for discipline and training—we have learned from each other.

Amber does not care too much for toys that are meant for cats, but sometimes in the night I hear her pouncing in the living room. If I am still up watching a late show, I investigate. I find she has been taking the cigarettes from the small pewter mug and tossing them all over the floor. Every cigarette is full of pin-sized holes.

I learned very soon to keep a cigarette on her counter so she could attack it.

She has also taught me to appreciate pencils. I like soft drawing pencils and so does she. She takes a newly sharpened one and knocks it to the floor, scoops it up, and tosses it and shoves it under the radiator where I cannot reach it. When I retrieve it with the dust mop, the point is gone and the whole pencil mangled.

She does have a few habits which some people might consider need disciplining, but I am learning to accept them.

She enjoys doing over bouquets, especially roses. I keep a half-dozen sweetheart roses in my grandmother's silver teapot and spend some time arranging them just so. Amber watches, with her head cocked, and as soon as possible she takes the best rose and plays games with it. Next to chicken and roast beef and White Lilac perfume, rose is her favorite scent. She prefers it to catnip.

In a short time, petals are all over the floor and she is pouncing on the rose leaves. When I come in the room, she looks up with innocent eyes and with a rose petal under one paw. She indicates she likes roses and I explain that I do not know whether or not they would be a good thing in her small insides. Many house plants, I am told, are poisonous to cats. So I distract her with a small bit of chicken while I hastily sweep up the rose leaves.

The next thing I know she is inside the television set and I am terrified that she may be electrocuted. The television repairman told me terrible tales of this happening. I fish her out, complaining. Then I glue the television cord up on the bookcase with Scotch tape. (I wonder why they call it Scotch?)

As I have said earlier, one of her favorite sports is playing with water. I have learned to be careful about turning on the hot water. Lately she has become a flower-water addict too, so it is hard to keep flower vases filled. It is her theory that water tastes better if roses or daffodils are standing in it. In April she lowered the level in the forsythia pitcher until the pale gold flowers turned paler and paler. She can elongate her neck and somehow make her head slide around stems.

The vacuum cleaner is a delight for her, which is one of the few things we do not have in common. My hostility to the vacuum cleaner is no secret, but I think more kindly of mine since it means so much to Amber. That long snaky hose which trips me and winds around chair legs is a special treat to her. In the beginning, I wondered whether she might be sucked in by that hose, but she never was.

We have disagreed about one other thing. I cannot type when that golden head is in the key well and two deft paws are picking up the keys. It bothers my concentration and makes the keys knot up and stick. Also I have had to discourage her from unrolling the ribbon—I have trouble enough changing it even when that becomes absolutely necessary.

Then there is the matter of kitchen safety. The kitchen at Still-meadow is U-shaped and the refrigerator, which goes almost to the ceiling, bisects one set of counters. I was happy about this when Amber came because it meant I had plenty of counter space inaccessible to her. The range was protected. And the counter under the window was free so that she could eat, play and doze in the sun there while I did kitchen chores.

But one night I got up to have a snack and turned on the kitchen lights. From the top of the refrigerator a small wedge-shaped face peered at me. The next minute she flew through the air and landed in the sink. From there it was easy to leap to the range.

No problem at all, she assured me.

Her feat was comparable to my leaping to the top of the two-hundred-year-old sugar maples. It was equally dangerous. I uttered my most anguished No and she vanished. But the next morning when I went out to plug in the coffee pot, a little golden face hung over the refrigerator top.

By standing on tiptoe, I reached her, and for the first time I spanked her. Now when I go into the kitchen, she flies from the refrigerator top and vanishes. But when I am safely in my room typing, I can hear the thud which means she has pushed the roll of aluminum foil from the top of the refrigerator. And by the time I run out, I find a beautiful Abyssinian tail waving in the sink.

This is probably good for my housekeeping because I cannot leave a single morsel of food on any counter in the kitchen and dishing-up goes at sixty miles an hour. Stacking the soiled plates is not feasible either, so they get washed immediately. I decided this when I found her eating broiled mushrooms that were on a breakfast plate. No cat expert ever said anything about mushrooms on a cat diet. How did I know they wouldn't poison her?

In fact, they agreed with her so well I wondered whether in the wild state cats ever nibble a mushroom on the way to a hunt.

Her games seldom cause me any bother.

When it comes to regular kitten toys, as I have said, Amber finds them dull. She cast a tentative paw over those she got for her first Christmas and settled for munching the ribbon and the tissue paper they came in. A paper grocery bag is better, according to her. She did enjoy taking ornaments from the Christmas tree, and I spent some sleepless hours wondering whether she had really eaten any of those bangles and baubles or just hidden them in cracks in the old floor.

String, erasers, rubber bands, pens, bits of kindling from the wood basket and my best stockings are on the honor list. Crumpled balls of aluminum foil she often drags around, and a ripe olive lifted from the cocktail tray is delightful.

If all else fails, she scoops up a corner of the irreplaceable wool rug and builds a cave in it and chews off nubbins of wool. She also likes bed linen and I often hear Millie, the friend who comes to help me with the weekly household chores, advising her that this time she cannot punch holes in the sheets because these are the *good* ones! Next week, Millie promises, she will use the patched one and it will be all right. A few pillowcases have acquired frayed edges but are still usable, so I do not go into the No-No routine on those.

I have strong opinions on discipline. It should, I think, be sparing. If life is one long negative, nobody is benefited whether it be a child, a pet, or a husband or wife. Most of the problems of living might be solved if we emphasized only the essential.

Cats traditionally do not respond to commands as dogs easily do. I think perhaps the reason Amber obeys me when I say No is that I use it so seldom. If she is pulling the stuffing out of a shabby worn chair I keep quiet. If it is a chair covered with a documentary print, I firmly speak the word "No" as loudly as my rather light voice permits. She gives me an incredulous stare and rakes one last streak down the upholstery and then stops. In three minutes she forgives me and jumps in my lap.

Also, I am sure the reason she always comes when I call her is that I only call her when it is necessary. Ninety per cent of the time when I worry about whether she has gotten stuck in a drawer or under the sink, I silently hunt. But if a strange dog is coming or unknown children (who invariably leave the door open), I call her. She has never failed to materialize from somewhere when I do call. She seems to know that this is not an idle exercise of authority but that it is important.

I admit it has been my theory as a dog raiser for years that much of the trouble owners have is their own doing. As my favorite reader once said, enough is too much of everything. Incessant repetition of commands, which is really nagging, works no better with animals than with humans.

My list of essential negatives for Amber has resulted in her paying attention to them. She knows she cannot slip into the refrigerator just because the door is open and I am getting out the lamb chops. She knows she cannot leap on the stove (although I always put a pan of water over a recently used burner, just in case). She knows she cannot rush out of the door when the groceryman comes in with a carton of groceries. And she knows she should not claw the newly upholstered sofa; when she hears this particular negative command, she flies over to her scratching post and claws at that, watching me with limpid innocent eyes.

One special characteristic of Amber's would melt the stones at Stonehenge. When I combine the No-No-No with a cuff (as when she chews the television wire), she might be expected to run away and hide. Instead she flies to me. Then we comfort each other! This certainly does not add to ease in discipline. I think a psychologist might say she feels I am her protector in time of trouble, and that I still am even when I myself cause the trouble.

This morning we had a new adventure. Over the fireplace on the Cape, two carved pale-gold-and-brown whales are silhouetted against a sea-gray background. They were copied by a gifted artist from a very old engraving. They each have two holes in the backs which fit supports about as big as broom handles in diameter and about two or three inches long.

It is a big fireplace and the whales are placed well above where a mantel would be if there were one. They are probably the most valuable pieces of art in the entire house, and seem to symbolize the whole mystery of the ocean as they swim forever on the imitation deep.

Early this morning for some reason Amber woke up and discovered the whales. They were not just decorations, they were creatures. Now the only fish she has ever seen is her own flounder fillet, which is headless, tailless, just a flat bit of pinky sweetness. But some deep instinct invaded her—the Abyssinian is said to have been the fishing cat of the Egyptians 4,000 years ago and who can know. . . .

I heard the sound and jumped out of bed, reaching the living room just as Amber landed on the right-hand whale, knocking it loose from one peg. Fortunately I just caught it before it crashed and cracked. Amber's leap was halfway to the ceiling from a flat take-off with no window sill or shelf as a help. The back of the whale she landed on is about ¼ inch thick and would not quite accommodate all of her.

She was preparing for another launch when I used a seldom-word very sharply. No-No-No. Then I started out to fix coffee and looked back to see her tensed on the chair top nearest the fireplace, gazing up with passion at the two somnolent whales. In the end, I added a small slap to the No-No-No.

I am grateful I do not have to say "No" often. It is upsetting to discipline a kitten and have her rush to you to be comforted immediately afterward.

Mr. Cat's Immolation

GEORGE FREEDLEY

One of the most important attributes of the knowing cat is
that he/she is a survivor. I have read that if life becomes
unendurable some cats will go off in a corner and quietly
die, but most of them put up a stiff fight to stay alive.

From George Freedley's "Mr. Cat," I have selected the
chapter about the cat's entrapment, one of the best stories
about survivor cats.

At this moment it seems forever ago, but it was only a little over five
years ago that Mr. Cat disappeared for a second time. It was on a
June morning that I awoke early and there were no signs of him
beside my bed. I was more annoyed than apprehensive, however, as
I dressed and left for the day.

"He's probably fallen asleep on the roof," I grumbled. "Or else he's
gone and gotten himself trapped in somebody's apartment again."
He had done that once and had to wait two days until they returned
from their week-end.

For the past few nights he had been in and out of the apartment
so often via the fire escape, that I felt sure I would hear his
trumpeting call even before I left the building. And of course, he
now wore a harness with his identification so he couldn't get lost.

At lunchtime, I telephoned the Superintendent. He looked into the
apartment and reported it empty. At dinner time when he had not
returned and his food was still untouched, my alarm grew but I
realized that there was little to do but sit and hope. I went to bed
shortly after dinner, but every sound in the old house awakened me
with vain hope that the Prodigal had returned.

At last, I had to face the inevitable and telephoned the ASPCA
and once again placed advertisements in the newspapers. No Persian
had been turned in, and no reply came from the advertisements
except from friends and neighbors who called to inquire.

One lady telephoned and said she was positive that she had seen a
Persian hiding under an automobile in Beekman Place nearly a mile
from his home. She had tried to coax him out, recognizing that he

was "somebody's" but he had gotten away. I thanked her though I doubted that it was Mr. Cat.

With the help of a friend, I placed a mimeographed description of the lost one complete with departure time and date, telephone number and my home and office telephone numbers. We left them in all the mailboxes of the neighborhood, and the Beekman Place area as well. We even left them in Fifth Avenue and Madison Avenue shops and office buildings, remembering Mr. Cat's last experience.

The local police were alerted until they must have been sick of my voice. Our building superintendent spread the word to all his confreres at their local "club," a bar on Lexington Avenue. (Unfortunately, as it turned out, one superintendent did not belong to their club.) They neglected no rumor, whether it was of Persian or Maltese, gray, white or what have you.

And now days grew into weeks until it got to the point that a kindly inquiry became a source of pain. When I answered the telephone now, it was sure to be some friend asking if there were any news. My replies got less and less polite, though perhaps more resigned. Where was Mr. Cat?

When it came to the fifth week, I could no longer believe that I would ever see Himself again. I could not believe that he would ever consent to accept a new home, no matter what inducements were offered. The best I could hope was that he had been kidnapped again, and some day would get free and find his way back to me.

As the fifth week drew to a close, the telephone rang at lunch time. A strange voice asked, "Are you Mr. Freedley? Have you lost a cat?"

My voice shook as I answered that I was, and I had. "Have—have you found him?"

"I found his harness" the voice replied, "with his name, and yours, so I called you up. I'm the superintendent over at 16 East 56th, the Fiberglass place. We're putting in air-conditioning and the hole in the floor in the secretary's room was covered with a board. We are re-flooring tomorrow, so I lifted up the board and looked down the hole, and found this harness."

"Do you think . . ." I ventured.

"Don't get your hopes up," said the superintendent. "I called through the hole and there was no answer. You say it was almost six weeks ago, and it's been hot as blazes. Maybe he was there and got away. Maybe he is there, but . . ."

I could not understand why he had not gotten the mimeographed paper we had left at every building including his, but there was no time for that now. The office closed at five, and I was to come over then.

It was the longest afternoon I ever spent. I tried to be rational. Six weeks! And the hottest July we had for years. It was only common sense that he couldn't be alive after being shut up there for six weeks without food or water. If he were there, would his inquiring eyes still be bright and ready to greet me?

I dressed in my oldest clothes in anticipation of climbing between floors, and I hauled out his old carrier as well as some of his dangle toys. The sight of them made my eyes grow wet. Cold reason made me bring along an old silence cloth as well. Cats had been known to go mad . . .

A lone secretary was at her desk when I arrived there with the superintendent. First, we called up the ASPCA: "Was it true," I asked, "that you rescue cats from between buildings or from under floors?"

They assured me that they would come and tear up the whole floor if there were the slightest hope.

I lifted up the board and called his name.

"Mr. Cat," I called. "Mr. Cat."

There was silence. Then from afar, a faint mew answered me!

Six weeks!

I was shaking with excitement as I continued to call down into the hole and spoke to him. The face of the superintendent was a study as he lent me his flashlight. The secretary's jaw dropped open.

I knelt down and put my hand into the hole. A small paw patted my hand.

I was afraid to do more lest in his fear he would withdraw altogether. I dangled his favorite cellophane ball and I saw him slowly appear. Slowly, I drew the ball towards me, and slowly he followed it. What were the memories that went through his mind as he saw and heard that homely wad of cellophane which had once been such a source of innocent pleasure to a lovely kitten? He trembled and the whole of his body came into view. I dropped the cord and gently but firmly grabbed at him and pulled him up.

Then, in my amazement, I almost dropped him! He had weighed almost fifteen pounds when I lost him; he had wasted away until he was little more than one pound. His long fur had concealed his emaciation until I held him in my arms. Only his eyes seemed larger and brighter, but that of course was in comparison with the rest of his frame.

Then he talked to me quite plainly: "Well, it's time you got here," he seemed to say. "Where on earth have you been?"

"Six weeks," marveled the superintendent.

We called the ASPCA and cancelled our request for help but the wagon was already on the way so a friend of mine was asked to come by and inform them what had happened. I gently laid Mr. Cat into the carrier, using the silence cloth as a cushion. Thank Heavens, I had not needed it!

What passers-by on Madison Avenue in that early August dusk thought when they saw a man hurry by with an animal carrier, a handful of toys, and tears streaming down his face, I shall never know. Nor shall I care. Mr. Cat was safe.

When I got him home, I lifted him out of the carrier and set him on his feet. He tried to follow me into the kitchen but he sagged over from weakness. I held him in my arms as I warmed a little milk and put him down beside the saucer. He smelled it, but made no effort to touch it. He had forgotten how to eat.

Finally, I dipped my finger in the milk and held it to his lips. He licked it like a newly weaned kitten. I repeated this until he gradually got accustomed to lap the milk himself. In this way, I fed him every ten minutes for two hours until we both dropped off to sleep.

The friend who had waited for the ASPCA wagon came by the next morning. He told me that the attendant had listened with impassive face to the piteous tale and had jotted down on his report sheet the laconic notation:

"Got cat out himself."

Lillian

DAMON RUNYON

Had it not been for Wilbur Willard's picking up a scrawny black kitten out of a snow drift when he was "all mulled up to a million," she might have ended up a randy old hoyden like Don Marquis's mehitabel. As it turned out, Lillian became quite a lady, and a heroine at that, and she can take her prideful place among the unforgettable cast of characters who inhabit the never-never land that is Damon Runyon's Broadway.

What I always say is that Wilbur Willard is nothing but a very lucky guy, because what is it but luck that has him teetering along Forty-ninth Street one cold snowy morning when Lillian is mer-owing around the sidewalk looking for her mamma?

And what is it but luck that has Wilbur Willard all mulled up to a million, what with him having been sitting out a few seidels of Scotch with a friend by the name of Haggerty in an apartment over in Fifty-ninth Street? Because if Wilbur Willard is not mulled up he will see Lillian is nothing but a little black cat, and give her plenty of room, for everybody knows that black cats are terribly bad luck, even when they are only kittens.

But being mulled up like I tell you, things look very different to Wilbur Willard, and he does not see Lillian as a little black kitten scrabbling around in the snow. He sees a beautiful leopard; because a copper by the name of O'Hara, who is walking past about then, and who knows Wilbur Willard, hears him say:

"Oh, you beautiful leopard!"

The copper takes a quick peek himself, because he does not wish any leopards running around his beat, it being against the law, but all he sees, as he tells me afterwards, is this rumpot ham, Wilbur Willard, picking up a scrawny little black kitten and shoving it in his overcoat pocket, and he also hears Wilbur say:

"Your name is Lillian."

Then Wilbur teeters on up to his room on the top floor of an old fleabag in Eighth Avenue that is called the Hotel de Brussels, where he lives quite a while, because the management does not mind actors, the management of the Hotel de Brussels being very broad-minded, indeed.

There is some complaint this same morning from one of Wilbur's neighbors, an old burlesque doll by the name of Minnie Madigan, who is not working since Abraham Lincoln is assassinated, because she hears Wilbur going on in his room about a beautiful leopard, and calls up the clerk to say that a hotel which allows wild animals is not respectable. But the clerk looks in on Wilbur and finds him playing with nothing but a harmless-looking little black kitten, and nothing comes of the old doll's beef, especially as nobody ever claims the Hotel de Brussels is respectable anyway, or at least not much.

Of course when Wilbur comes out from under the ether next afternoon he can see Lillian is not a leopard, and in fact Wilbur is quite astonished to find himself in bed with a little black kitten, because it seems Lillian is sleeping on Wilbur's chest to keep warm. At first Wilbur does not believe what he sees, and puts it down to Haggerty's Scotch, but finally he is convinced, and so he puts Lillian in his pocket, and takes her over to the Hot Box night club and gives her some milk, of which it seems Lillian is very fond.

Now where Lillian comes from in the first place of course nobody knows. The chances are somebody chucks her out of a window into the snow, because people are always chucking kittens, and one thing and another, out of windows in New York. In fact, if there is one thing this town has plenty of, it is kittens, which finally grow up to be cats, and go snooping around ash cans, and mer-owing on roofs, and keeping people from sleeping good.

Personally, I have no use for cats, including kittens, because I never see one that has any too much sense, although I know a guy by the name of Pussy McGuire who makes a first-rate living doing nothing but stealing cats, and sometimes dogs, and selling them to old dolls who like such things for company. But Pussy only steals Persian and Angora cats, which are very fine cats, and of course Lillian is no such cat as this. Lillian is nothing but a black cat, and nobody will give you a dime a dozen for black cats in this town, as they are generally regarded as very bad jinxes.

Furthermore, it comes out in a few weeks that Wilbur Willard can just as well name her Herman, or Sidney, or not, but Wilbur sticks to Lillian, because this is the name of his partner when he is in vaudeville years ago. He often tells me about Lillian Withington when he is mulled up, which is more often than somewhat, for Wilbur is a great hand for drinking Scotch, or rye, or bourbon, or gin, or whatever else there is around for drinking, except water. In fact, Wilbur Willard is a high-class drinking man, and it does no good to tell him it is against the law to drink in this country, because it only makes him mad, and he says to the dickens with the law, only Wilbur Willard uses a much rougher word than dickens.

"She is like a beautiful leopard," Wilbur says to me about Lillian Withington. "Black-haired, and black-eyed, and all ripply, like a leopard I see in an animal act on the same bill at the Palace with us once. We are headliners then," he says, "Willard and Withington, the best singing and dancing act in the country.

"I pick her up in San Antonio, which is a spot in Texas," Wilbur says. "She is not long out of a convent, and I just lose my old partner, Mary McGee, who ups and dies on me of pneumonia down there. Lillian wishes to go on the stage, and joins out with me. A natural-born actress with a great voice. But like a leopard," Wilbur says. "Like a leopard. There is cat in her, no doubt of this, and cats and women are both ungrateful. I love Lillian Withington. I wish to marry her. But she is cold to me. She says she is not going to follow the stage all her life. She says she wishes money, and luxury, and a fine home, and of course a guy like me cannot give a doll such things.

"I wait on her hand and foot," Wilbur says. "I am her slave. There is nothing I will not do for her. Then one day she walks in on me in Boston very cool and says she is quitting me. She says she is marrying a rich guy there. Well, naturally it busts up the act and I never have the heart to look for another partner, and then I get to belting that old black bottle around, and now what am I but a cabaret performer?"

Then sometimes he will bust out crying, and sometimes I will cry with him, although the way I look at it, Wilbur gets a pretty fair break, at that, in getting rid of a doll who wishes things he cannot give her. Many a guy in this town is tangled up with a doll who wishes things he cannot give her, but who keeps him tangled up just the same and busting himself trying to keep her quiet.

Wilbur makes pretty fair money as an entertainer in the Hot Box, though he spends most of it for Scotch, and he is not a bad entertainer, either. I often go to the Hot Box when I am feeling blue to hear him sing Melancholy Baby, and Moonshine Valley, and other sad songs which break my heart. Personally, I do not see why any doll cannot love Wilbur, especially if they listen to him sing such songs as Melancholy Baby when he is mulled up good, because he is a tall, nice-looking guy with long eyelashes, and sleepy brown eyes, and his voice has a low moaning sound that usually goes very big with the dolls. In fact, many a doll does do some pitching to Wilbur when he is singing in the Hot Box, but somehow Wilbur never gives them a tumble, which I suppose is because he is thinking only of Lillian Withington.

Well, after he gets Lillian, the black kitten, Wilbur seems to find a new interest in life, and Lillian turns out to be right cute, and not bad-looking after Wilbur gets her fed up good. She is blacker than a yard up a chimney, with not a white spot on her, and she grows so fast that by and by Wilbur cannot carry her in his pocket any more, so he puts a collar on her and leads her around. So Lillian becomes very well known on Broadway, what with Wilbur taking her many places, and finally she does not even have to be led around by Willard, but follows him like a pooch. And in all the Roaring Forties there is no pooch that cares to have any truck with Lillian, for she will leap aboard them quicker than you can say scat, and scratch and bite them until they are very glad indeed to get away from her.

But of course the pooches in the Forties are mainly nothing but Chows, and Pekes, and Poms, or little woolly white poodles, which are led around by blonde dolls, and are not fit to take their own part against a smart cat. In fact, Wilbur Willard is finally not on speaking terms with any doll that owns a pooch beween Times Square and Columbus Circle, and they are all hoping that both Wilbur and Lillian will go lay down and die somewhere. Furthermore, Wilbur has a couple of battles with guys who also belong to the dolls, but Wilbur is no sucker in a battle if he is not mulled up too much and leg-weary.

After he is through entertaining people in the Hot Box, Wilbur generally goes around to any speakeasies which may still be open, and does a little offhand drinking on top of what he already drinks down in the Hot Box, which is plenty, and although it is considered very risky in this town to mix Hot Box liquor with any other, it never seems to bother Wilbur. Along toward daylight he takes a couple of bottles of Scotch over to his room in the Hotel de Brussels and uses them for a nightcap, so by the time Wilbur Willard is ready to slide off to sleep he has plenty of liquor of one kind and another inside him, and he sleeps pretty good.

Of course nobody on Broadway blames Wilbur so very much for being such a rumpot, because they know about him loving Lillian Withington, and losing her, and it is considered a reasonable excuse in this town for a guy to do some drinking when he loses a doll, which is why there is so much drinking here, but it is a mystery to one and all how Wilbur stands off all this liquor without croaking. The cemeteries are full of guys who do a lot less drinking than Wilbur, but he never even seems to feel extra tough, or if he does he keeps it to himself and does not go around saying it is the kind of liquor you get nowadays.

He costs some of the boys around Mindy's plenty of dough one winter, because he starts in doing most of his drinking after hours in Good Time Charley's speakeasy, and the boys lay a price of four to one against him lasting until spring, never figuring a guy can drink very much of Good Time Charley's liquor and keep on living. But Wilbur Willard does it just the same, so everybody says the guy is just naturally superhuman, and lets it go at that.

Sometimes Wilbur drops into Mindy's with Lillian following him on the lookout for pooches, or riding on his shoulder if the weather is bad, and the two of them will sit with us for hours chewing the rag about one thing and another. At such times Wilbur generally has a bottle on his hip and takes a shot now and then, but of course this does not come under the head of serious drinking with him. When Lillian is with Wilbur she always lays as close to him as she can get and anybody can see that she seems to be very fond of Wilbur, and that he is very fond of her, although he sometimes forgets himself and speaks of her as a beautiful leopard. But of course this is only a slip of the tongue, and anyway if Wilbur gets any pleasure out of thinking Lillian is a leopard, it is nobody's business but his own.

"I suppose she will run away from me some day," Wilbur says, running his hand over Lillian's back until her fur crackles. "Yes, although I give her plenty of liver and catnip, and one thing and another, and all my affection, she will probably give me the shake. Cats are like women, and women are like cats. They are both very ungrateful."

"They are both generally bad luck," Big Nig, the crap shooter, says. "Especially cats, and most especially black cats."

Many other guys tell Wilbur about black cats being bad luck, and advise him to slip Lillian into the North River some night with a sinker on her, but Wilbur claims he already has all the bad luck in the world when he loses Lillian Withington, and that Lillian, the cat, cannot make it any worse, so he goes on taking extra good care of her, and Lillian goes on getting bigger and bigger until I commence thinking maybe there is some St. Bernard in her.

Finally I commence to notice something funny about Lillian. Sometimes she will be acting very loving towards Wilbur, and then again she will be very unfriendly to him, and will spit at him, and snatch at him with her claws, very hostile. It seems to me that she is all right when Willard is mulled up, but is as sad and fretful as he is himself when he is only a little bit mulled. And when Lillian is sad and fretful she makes it very tough indeed on the pooches in the neighborhood of the Brussels.

In fact, Lillian takes to pooch-hunting, sneaking off when Wilbur is getting his rest, and running pooches bowlegged, especially when she finds one that is not on a leash. A loose pooch is just naturally cherry pie for Lillian.

Well, of course this causes great indignation among the dolls who own the pooches, particularly when Lillian comes home one day carrying a Peke as big as she is herself by the scruff of the neck, and with a very excited blonde doll folowing her and yelling bloody murder outside Wilbur Willard's door when Lillian pops into Wilbur's room through a hole he cuts in the door for her, still lugging the Peke. But it seems that instead of being mad at Lillian and giving her a pasting for such goings on, Wilbur is somewhat pleased, because he happens to be still in a fog when Lillian arrives with the Peke, and is thinking of Lillian as a beautiful leopard.

"Why," Wilbur says, "this is devotion, indeed. My beautiful leopard goes off into the jungle and fetches me an antelope for dinner."

Now of course these is no sense whatever to this, because a Peke is certainly not anything like an antelope, but the blonde doll outside Wilbur's door hears Wilbur mumble, and gets the idea that he is going to eat her Peke for dinner and the squawk she puts up is very terrible. There is plenty of trouble around the Brussels in chilling the blonde doll's beef over Lillian snagging her Peke, and what is more the blonde doll's ever-loving guy, who turns out to be a tough Ginney bootlegger by the name of Gregorio, shows up at the Hot Box the next night and wishes to put the slug on Wilbur Willard.

But Wilbur rounds him up with a few drinks and by singing Melancholy Baby to him, and before he leaves the Ginney gets very sentimental towards Wilbur, and Lillian, too, and wishes to give Wilbur five bucks to let Lillian grab the Peke again, if Lillian will promise not to bring it back. It seems Gregorio does not really care for the Peke, and is only acting quarrelsome to please the blonde doll and make her think he loves her dearly.

But I can see Lillian is having different moods, and finally I ask Wilbur if he notices it.

"Yes," he says, very sad, "I do not seem to be holding her love. She is getting very fickle. A guy moves onto my floor at the Brussels the other day with a little boy, and Lillian becomes very fond of this kid at once. In fact, they are great friends. Ah, well," Wilbur says, "cats are like women. Their affection does not last."

I happen to go over to the Brussels a few days later to explain to a guy by the name of Crutchy, who lives on the same floor as Wilbur Willard, that some of our citizens do not like his face and that it may be a good idea for him to leave town, especially if he insists on bringing ale into their territory, and I see Lillian out in the hall with a youngster which I judge is the kid Wilbur is talking about. This kid is maybe three years old, and very cute, what with black hair, and black eyes, and he is wooling Lillian around the hall in a way that is most surprising for Lillian is not such a cat as will stand for much wooling around, not even from Wilbur Willard.

I am wondering how anybody comes to take such a kid to a joint like the Brussels, but I figure it is some actor's kid, and that maybe there is no mamma for it. Later I am talking to Wilbur about this, and he says:

"Well, if the kid's old man is an actor, he is not working at it. He sticks close to his room all the time, and he does not allow the kid to go anywhere but in the hall, and I feel sorry for the little guy, which is why I allow Lillian to play with him."

Now it comes on a very cold spell, and a bunch of us are sitting in Mindy's along toward five o'clock in the morning when we hear fire engines going past. By and by in comes a guy by the name of Kansas, who is named Kansas because he comes from Kansas, and who is a crap shooter by trade.

"The old Brussels is on fire," this guy Kansas says.

"She is always on fire," Big Nig says, meaning there is always plenty of hot stuff going on around the Brussels.

About this time who walks in but Wilbur Willard, and anybody can see he is just naturally floating. The chances are he comes from Good Time Charley's, and is certainly carrying plenty of pressure. I never see Wilbur Willard mulled up more. He does not have Lillian with him, but then he never takes Lillian to Good Time Charley's because Charley hates cats.

"Hey, Wilbur," Big Nig says, "your joint, the Brussels, is on fire."

"Well," Wilbur says, "I am a little firefly, and I need a light. Let us go where there is fire."

The Brussels is only a few blocks from Mindy's, and there is nothing else to do just then, so some of us walk over to Eighth Avenue with Wilbur teetering along ahead of us. The old shack is certainly roaring good when we get in sight of it, and the firemen are tossing water into it, and the coppers have the fire lines out to keep the crowd back, although there is not much of a crowd at such an hour in the morning.

"Is it not beautiful?" Wilbur Willard says, looking up at the flames. "Is it not like a fairy palace all lighted up this way?"

You see, Wilbur does not realize the joint is on fire, although guys and dolls are running out of it every which way, most of them half dressed, or not dressed at all, and the firemen are getting out the life nets in case anybody wishes to hop out of the windows.

"It is certainly beautiful," Wilbur says. "I must get Lillian so she can see this."

And before anybody has time to think, there is Wilbur Willard walking into the front door of the Brussels as if nothing happens. The firemen and the coppers are so astonished all they can do is holler at Wilbur, but he pays no attention whatever. Well, naturally everybody figures Wilbur is a gone gosling, but in about ten minutes he comes walking out of this same door through the fire and smoke as cool as you please, and he has Lillian in his arms.

"You know," Wilbur says, coming over to where we are standing with our eyes popping out, "I have to walk all the way up to my floor because the elevators seem to be out of commission. The service is getting terrible in this hotel. I will certainly make a strong beef to the management about it as soon as I pay something on my account."

Then what happens but Lillian lets out a big mer-ow, and hops out of Wilbur's arms and skips past the coppers and the firemen with her back all humped up, and the next thing anybody knows she is tearing through the front door of the old hotel and making plenty of speed.

"Well, well," Wilbur says, looking much surprised, "there goes Lillian."

And what does this daffy Wilbur Willard do but turn and go marching back into the Brussels again, and by this time the smoke is pouring out of the front doors so thick he is out of sight in a second. Naturally he takes the coppers and firemen by surprise, because they are not used to guys walking in and out of fires on them.

This time anybody standing around will lay you plenty of odds—two and a half and maybe three to one that Wilbur never shows up again, because the old Brussels is now just popping with fire and smoke from the lower windows, although there does not seem to be quite so much fire in the upper story. Everybody seems to be out of the joint, and even the firemen are fighting the blaze from the outside because the Brussels is so old and ramshackly there is no sense in them risking the floors.

I mean everybody is out of the joint except Wilbur Willard and Lillian, and we figure they are getting a good frying somewhere inside, although Feet Samuels is around offering to take thirteen to five for a few small bets that Lillian comes out okay, because Feet claims that a cat has nine lives and that is a fair bet at the price.

Well, up comes a swell-looking doll all heated up about something and pushing and clawing her way through the crowd up to the ropes and screaming until you can hardly hear yourself think, and about this same minute everybody hears a voice going ai-lee-hi-hee-hoo, like a Swiss yodeler, which comes from the roof of the Brussels, and looking up what do we see but Wilbur Willard standing up there on the edge of the roof, high above the fire and smoke, and yodeling very loud.

Under one arm he has a big bundle of some kind, and under the other he has the little kid I see playing in the hall with Lillian. As he stands up there going ai-lee-hi-hee-hoo, the swell-dressed doll near us begins yipping louder than Wilbur is yodeling, and the firemen rush over under him with a life net.

Wilbur lets go another ai-lee-hi-hee-hoo, and down he comes all spraddled out, with the bundle and the kid, but he hits the net sitting down and bounces up and back again for a couple of minutes before he finally settles. In fact, Wilbur is enjoying the bouncing, and the chances are he will be bouncing yet if the firemen do not drop their hold on the net and let him fall to the ground.

Then Wilbur steps out of the net, and I can see the bundle is a rolled-up blanket with Lillian's eyes peeking out of one end. He still has the kid under the other arm with his head stuck out in front, and his legs stuck out behind, and it does not seem to me that Wilbur is handling the kid as careful as he is handling Lillian. He stands there looking at the firemen with a very sneering look, and finally he says:

"Do not think you can catch me in your net unless I wish to be caught. I am a butterfly, and very hard to overtake."

Then all of a sudden the swell-dressed doll who is doing so much hollering, piles on top of Wilbur and grabs the kid from him and begins hugging and kissing it.

"Wilbur," she says, "God bless you, Wilbur, for saving my baby! Oh, thank you, Wilbur, thank you! My wretched husband kidnaps and runs away with him, and it is only a few hours ago that my detectives find out where he is."

Wilbur gives the doll a funny look for about half a minute and starts to walk away, but Lillian comes wiggling out of the blanket, looking and smelling pretty much singed up, and the kid sees Lillian and begins hollering for her, so Wilbur finally hands Lillian over to the kid. And not wishing to leave Lillian, Wilbur stands around somewhat confused, and the doll gets talking to him, and finally they go away together, and as they go Wilbur is carrying the kid, and the kid is carrying Lillian, and Lillian is not feeling so good from her burns.

Furthermore, Wilbur is probably more sober than he ever is before in years at this hour in the morning, but before they go I get a chance to talk some to Wilbur when he is still rambling somewhat, and I make out from what he says that the first time he goes to get Lillian he finds her in his room and does not see hide or hair of the little kid and does not even think of him, because he does not know what room the kid is in, anyway, having never noticed such a thing.

But the second time he goes up, Lillian is sniffing at the crack under the door of a room down the hall from Wilbur's and Wilbur says he seems to remember seeing a trickle of something like water coming out of the crack.

"And," Wilbur says, "as I am looking for a blanket for Lillian, and it will be a bother to go back to my room, I figure I will get one out of this room. I try the knob but the door is locked, so I kick it in, and walk in to find the room is full of smoke, and fire is shooting through the windows very lovely, and when I grab a blanket off the bed for Lillian, what is under the blanket but the kid?"

"Well," Wilbur says, "the kid is squawking, and Lillian is mer-ow-ing, and there is so much confusion generally that it makes me nervous, so I figure we better go up on the roof and let the stink blow off us, and look at the fire from there. It seems there is a guy stretched out on the floor of the room alongside an upset table between the door and the bed. He has a bottle in one hand, and he is dead. Well, naturally there is no percentage in lugging a dead guy along, so I take Lillian and the kid and go up on the roof, and we just naturally fly off like humming birds. Now I must get a drink," Wilbur says. "I wonder if anybody has anything on their hip?"

Well, the papers are certainly full of Wilbur and Lillian the next day, especially Lillian, and they are both great heroes.

But Wilbur cannot stand the publicity very long, because he never has no time to himself for his drinking, what with the scribes and the photographers hopping on him every few minutes wishing to hear his story, and to take more pictures of him and Lillian, so one night he disappears, and Lillian disappears with him.

About a year later it comes out that he marries his old doll, Lillian Withington-Harmon, and falls into a lot of dough, and what is more he cuts out the liquor and becomes quite a useful citizen one way and another. So everybody has to admit that black cats are not always bad luck, although I say Wilbur's case is a little exceptional because he does not start out knowing Lillian is a black cat, but thinking she is a leopard.

I happen to run into Wilbur one day all dressed up in good clothes and jewelry and chucking quite a swell.

"Wilbur," I say to him, "I often think how remarkable it is the way Lillian suddenly gets such an attachment for the little kid and remembers about him being in the hotel and leads you back there a second time to the right room. If I do not see this come off with my own eyes, I will never believe a cat has brains enough to do such a thing, because I consider cats are extra dumb."

"Brains nothing," Wilbur says. "Lillian does not have brains enough to grease a gimlet. And what is more she has no more attachment for the kid than a jack rabbit. The time has come," Wilbur says, "to expose Lillian. She gets a lot of credit which is never coming to her. I will now tell you about Lillian, and nobody knows this but me.

"You see," Wilbur says, "when Lillian is a little kitten I always put a little Scotch in her milk, partly to help make her good and strong, and partly because I am never no hand to drink alone, unless there is nobody with me. Well, at first Lillian does not care so much for this Scotch in her milk, but finally she takes a liking to it, and I keep making her toddy stronger until in the end she will lap up a good big snort without any milk for a chaser, and yell for more. In fact, I suddenly realize that Lillian becomes a rumpot, just like I am in those days, and simply must have her grog, and it is when she is good and rummed up that Lillian goes off snatching Pekes, and acting tough generally.

"Now," Wilbur says, "the time of the fire is about the time I get home every morning and give Lillian her schnapps. But when I go into the hotel and get her the first time I forget to Scotch her up, and the reason she runs back into the hotel is because she is looking for her shot. And the reason she is sniffing at the kid's door is not because the kid is in there but because the trickle that is coming through the crack under the door is nothing but Scotch running out of the bottle in the dead guy's hand. I never mention this before because I figure it may be a knock to a dead guy's memory," Wilbur says. "Drinking is certainly a disgusting thing, especially secret drinking."

"But how is Lillian getting along these days?" I ask Wilbur Willard.

"I am greatly disappointed in Lillian," he says. "She refuses to reform when I do and the last I hear of her she takes up with Gregorio, the Ginney bootlegger, who keeps her well Scotched up all the time so she will lead his blonde doll's Peke a dog's life."

The Cat's Behavior in Two Worlds

FRANCES AND RICHARD LOCKRIDGE

Like many professional writers, the Lockridges were wise in the ways of cats, which often played a significant role in their enjoyable mystery novels.
In this chapter from their thoughtful and amusing book "Cats and People," their astute conclusions about cat behavior were drawn from observation of their own admirable pets, Martini, Gin, Pammy, Jerry, and the others.

It may be that the cat lives emotionally in two worlds, the human and his own, and that this is more true of him than of the other animals who associate with man, although it is to some degree true of all of them. Even chickens, creatures of exceptional stupidity and little emotional warmth, seem dimly to adjust to man's habits. Dogs, although always knocking hopefully at the door of man's world, have also a world of their own and it is conceivable that cows, gathering at the pasture gate toward the hour of going home, think mistily bovine thoughts while waiting for the herdsman. But it may be that no other animal makes the distinction so sharply as it is made in the logical mind of the cat.

As he moves between the two worlds, the cat speaks languages suitable to the comprehension of the other denizens—speaks in one fashion to men and women and in quite another to his fellow cats, and to the mice and birds and, lamentably, dogs who share or intrude upon the feline world. To show affection for another cat, a cat licks it and the greatest affection is shown by licking the other cat's face. When a cat wishes to join another, or several others, in a preempted place—a box, a warm ledge, a cushion—the newcomer must first lick, if only in token, the cat or cats who got there first. Failure to do this is bad manners and may lead to ejection by the resident. Now and then, the cat who has been moved in on may comment audibly, giving permission or expressing disapproval, but this is unusual, even among quite talkative cats. Except in anger or other passion, and as between mother cats and kittens, audible conversation is the exception between cat and cat. Beyond hissing, which is done by curling the tongue up at the sides, making it into a kind of trough, cats have little to say to dogs, and a minor growl will do for a rat or mouse.

But with humans who, as the cat has noticed, communicate with one another by making sounds, almost all cats talk audibly and some talk a good deal. (Siamese are traditionally, and in our experience actually, the most frequent talkers.) They speak abruptly when they want out or want dinner; some of them talk uninterruptedly while their meals are being prepared; they purr when stroked (as, although more rarely, they purr when licked by one another); many of them respond, usually in a monosyllable or two, when spoken to in greeting; Martini has a special quick ejaculation used only when she wishes to jump to human shoulders—it is at once request and warning, although more the latter than the former. If offended by a human, a cat will growl briefly in admonition—as it will with another cat; if sufficiently alarmed by human, as by dog or other cat, a cat will hiss.

The cat has discovered, however, that humans are slow of understanding and so adds pantomime to words, as humans do when seeking to explain something to other humans of imperfect understanding—as, for example, foreigners. Thus a cat wanting dinner may add to his vocal announcement the pantomimic explanation of going to the place in which food is prepared; Gin, when the ordeal of waiting for food to be warmed becomes unbearable, when her most audible instructions to hurry up—can't you see I'm starving?—do not produce the speed she wishes, goes to a pile of paper plates and paws at the topmost, knowing that it is the one on which food will eventually—but how long, oh God?—be served.

All cats go to the door and speak there when they want to go out, many reach toward the knob or latch, not a few learn to manipulate the lock and go out by themselves if the door opens away from them. Gin used to climb into a chair which stood near an outer door and do her talking from there because then, since the door opened inward, she was out of the path of its swing and could go out faster. All cats know that people speak cat imperfectly and that the simplest things have to be acted out, as in a charade. Some of these performances become so familiar, and so stylized, that cats probably hardly know they are engaged in them and people take them for granted. Thus even Dr. Shaler no doubt took for granted that when a cat said he was hungry, and then acted as if he was hungry, he was hungry. Almost without knowing what he did, he took the cat's word for it—the cat's words and actions.

But often, in any cat's life in the human world, situations arise which require greater thought on the part of both feline and human if communication is to be established. If the thing to be expressed has to do with an objective matter, this need not long baffle an intelligent or a reasonably attentive human. Thus Martini once communicated to one of us an emergency which had arisen in connection with her toilet pan, and did it with an explicitness which no one could fail to understand.

Martini was, when living in town, "broken" to torn-up newspaper. The quotation marks are used because, as is usually true of cats, we did not "break" her to this sanitary arrangement. We provided pan and torn-up papers and, although the result is by no means a cat's idea of toilet facilities, it was better than anything else available. Being a reasonable person, no holder-out for unobtainable perfection, Martini promptly used pan and paper and, when it became necessary, pointed out the pan to her kittens. Thereafter, all three used the same pan.

The flaw in this, from the cats' point of view and ours, was that we and our maid had always to be thinking of whether the pan was clean and dry and that our minds too often wandered from this, to the cats, essential, preoccupation. On the day when Martini explained things to one of us, we had apparently been thinking for some hours of lesser matters. Martini probably spoke about it several times and got no answer, which gave her a low view of our intelligence and also annoyed her considerably, since she is uncommonly fastidious and insists on a dry pan.

So she came to the room where one of us was working and gave that one a final chance. She got onto a couch and spoke so loudly, so insistently, that no concentration could withstand her voice. The human turned and said, "What's the matter, Teeney?"

Martini spoke again, more briefly. Then she assumed a characteristic and unmistakable position on the couch.

"Teeney!" the human said, very loudly, in surprise and shock. "Teeney!" The human also got up. "You bad—" the human began.

But then Teeney left the couch. She left hurriedly, and resumed her vocal instructions. She also went toward the kitchen, in which the pan was kept. She went hurriedly. The one of us summoned went after her and found her standing in front of the pan, looking at it, her upper lip slightly curled back, as cats curl back their lip when they encounter something unpleasant. She let the human see this attitude of hers. Then she looked up. Then she said, "Yah!"

The human changed the pan. Martini used it.

Now this, while requiring some ingenuity on Martini's part, was not too complicated for a bright cat and it does not, one would think, admit of more than one explanation. Martini wanted something done and saw it was done. Presumably a person who knows little of cat's habits might argue that she had really intended to use the couch, so that her actions were not pantomimic but real. There are several things against this. Healthy cats, except females in season, almost never break habit; Martini, locked up in the Brewster cabin for hours together—the cats reasonably enough decline to use the pan in the country and Martini, for reasons of her own, for a time abandoned the fireplace—waits until she is let out, no matter how long the waiting is. (Cats have unhuman control in such matters.) And, if she had been going to break habit on the couch, she would certainly not have announced it to one of us, nor have used a cushioned surface in an occupied room.

But often cats must talk with humans on subjects more abstract— must communicate such emotions as jealousy, hurt feelings and, most frequently of all, affection. Some of them seem to feel these emotions more keenly than do others; some are more adept at communicating them. But neither of us ever knew a cat who could not, in one way or another, express himself on these matters and who did not do so when the need arose. It seems to us, as it does to most people who have spent any appreciable time around cats, that a cat's expression of, for example, love for a human is often quite as clear as a cat's expression of a desire to go out doors.

There was, for example, the case of the cat called Pammy who, like Martini later, was a very special cat—a cat about whom one would like to write a book, as Michael Joseph did about Charles; or such an essay as Charles Dudley Warner wrote about the incomparable Calvin, who used to turn on a furnace register "in a retired room, where he used to go when he wished to be alone" and when he required more heat. (Any writer would like to have done either of these perceptive pieces, as a craftsman even if not as a cat lover.)

Pammy, who as we have said is dead now, was a longish gray cat, with a white collar; her mother was Siamese and her father anybody, and she came to us years ago with her brother Jerry. Of these two, and of other cats of ours, we may tell more on later pages; what is significant here is that, from the time she was a small kitten, Pammy formed a special attachment for one of us—the one, as it happened, the more aggressive Jerry did not prefer. He would slap her down if she approached Frances. All the affection of a very gentle cat was thus channeled toward one human, and it was shown in soft sounds, in purring, in a desire always to be close—in all the little ways which are convincing to those less adamant than the Dr. Shalers.

But then the war came and for a couple of months it became necessary for the one to whom Pammy was devoted to be away. The room in which he worked, and in which Pammy tried, with soft paws, with endearments, to keep him from working, was temporarily otherwise occupied. And Pammy was brokenhearted—one does not like to use terms so extreme, but other terms are inadequate. The bottom dropped out of Pammy's life.

She would go to the door of the small room in which the man should have been, had always been. She did not need to enter to know that he was not there; there was another smell there, even when the room was empty. She would look into the room and raise her head and give a small, hopeless cry. Then she would turn away and wander the apartment restlessly, and return to the room and again find it empty—find it worse than empty, because someone else was occupying it. She would turn away again and then, perhaps, she would hear the front door opening a flight below. Then, instantly, she was all a listening animal, but only for an instant. The sound of footsteps was as wrong as the scent had been and again she would cry, and begin to wander.

For the first few weeks she would have nothing to do with the one who remained. She displayed the detached courtesy she always showed; she was never a rude cat. But the affection freely offered by one who was lonely too, in a human fashion, was accepted only absent-mindedly, did not touch the cat. Pammy continued to eat; there was no change there, except that she seemed to eat with no great pleasure. (The one who was gone had almost never fed her.) But she did not play with her brother; she merely drifted through the apartment, searching; merely listened at the door, hoping.

Finally, she appeared more or less to give up, but that was after weeks. She began to look up into the human face which remained and, although she still expressed her loneliness with a little cry, it was clear that she also sought friendship and reassurance. Finally, after about six weeks, she appeared to accept her loss and to make the new adjustment. When the wanderer returned she was clearly very glad to see him and sat as much as possible on his lap. But she was never again a one-man cat; she had learned, as humans most often have to, that there is danger in channeling love too narrowly; she had widened her emotional field.

But if, during those weeks, she did not feel deeply the loss of someone she loved, then the actions of cats and men make no sense at all, and the words we use have no meaning. We may guess that emotions were inchoate in her mind; that she did not form an "idea" of her loss, although in this we may well be wrong. But she did all a sentient being could to reveal that underlying disappointment, that feeling of depression, which, for some time after an affectional trauma, also underlies the human consciousness, is never quite absent even when the surface mind is busiest.

Martini, in all respects a more violent person and not a cat to take anything sitting down, showed a similar response when it was necessary for both of us to leave her at a crucial time in her life. We had to go away for ten days or so when the kittens were very small and she was their only source of sustenance. Martini merely quit eating and, since she continued to provide food, she faded alarmingly. The person who was, very generously, acting as cat sitter became alarmed and summoned the veterinarian. Martini retired to an inaccessible position, prepared in advance, and growled and hissed. She would not allow herself to be touched; she met coaxing with angry warnings. And, since she had never been a cat to fool with, she was allowed her way, which was to continue to refuse food. When we returned, she swore at us for a couple of days, and would not let us touch her or the kittens, but she ate.

Obviously, if one of the things so many people "know" about cats had been true of Martini, none of this would have happened. She was in a familiar place, and places, many people tell one another, are all cats care about. She was not even with a strange person; her sitter was one she had known and liked since she was a kitten. She had been deserted by people she loved and, being the kind of person she is, this made her furious; Martini is of a temperament to kill the things she loves; she is very proud and one rejects her at his peril. Her love is violent.

It is more violent than that of most cats we have known even when nothing in particular has happened to upset her, even in its day-to-day expression. When she chooses to express affection— usually toward Frances, whom she owns—there is nothing half way about it. Lap sitting, quiet purring, is not enough. She lies up a chest, with her whiskers tickling a cheek; she puts paw to face, and arms about neck. When she is in this position she expects to be talked to, touched gently, to hear her name often spoken in a soft voice. During this period, the occupied person must sit quietly, must not try to read, must not answer the telephone if it rings. A movement, any wavering in concentration on cat, and Martini is down with an oath, is on the floor, sitting with back to the offender, not answering if spoken to. She is not to be lightly wooed, our major cat; she has no patience with casual affection.

She and her daughters always greet us when we return after an absence; they are always sitting at the door before we reach it. Martini usually moves a little away from the others and rolls over on her back. She expects to be greeted first; it is wise not to notice the others until her emotional needs are gratified. Then one may speak to Gin and Sherry, who are rubbing against legs, purring furiously. (Martini herself has a very small purr; often it is almost soundless, and merely a matter of vibrating cat.)

If we have been gone for some hours, the cats—after being greeted —usually run excitedly through the house, wrestling with one another, leaping onto things and off of them, emitting sharp cries of excitement. Martini at such times, and often at other times, forgets the dignity of a matron and romps furiously, leaping half across a room, her tail bushy, to land almost upon another cat, to lock with it and roll it on the floor, pretending to tear it apart with tooth and claw. Both of them are larger cats than she, and stronger; both have been under her paw since they were kittens.

Not all of our cats have been so demonstrative in the world they share with humans. Pammy was, in her fashion. She, also, met us at doors. Jerry did sometimes, when he happened to think of it, but perhaps only because Pammy did, and he wondered—in his rather vague fashion—what she was up to. Jerry liked attention well enough, but he did not seem to be a deeply affectionate cat. Pete was wont merely to look up when we entered, smile faintly, and go back to sleep again. Sometimes he would roll over to be rubbed, but not always. But he was a great cat to follow us around, as Martini also is. Pete kept an eye on us and did not let us wander far afield. One night, when we stayed too long with friends at a near-by cabin, Pete came across the fields after us, looked in the window, opened the screen door, and entered to tug at our clothing and to tell us it was high time we came home with him.

Pete lived longer than the others a semi-migratory existence between town and country, since during the earlier of the ten years or so he lived with us we stayed most of our time in New York and got to the country only for weekends and for vacations. Pete traveled, usually by car but now and then by train, always in a carrying case which he hated thoroughly. But he never showed any signs of a place fixation; if he was in the apartment, that was all right; if he was in the country, that was fine. After his first visit to the country it never seemed to surprise him, although for some time, of course, it required investigation. There was never any thought in our minds, or apparently in his, that he might try to walk back to New York. Home was where we were; he might have been contented in the traveling box if it had been convenient for one of us to ride in it with him.

The more recent cats have all shared his indifference to places and addiction to people; we have, indeed, never known a cat who felt otherwise, nor have we ever heard of one at firsthand. (If cat stories have any value—which many dispute—they have it only at firsthand; what somebody has heard about somebody else's cat is seldom instructive and never evidence.) But the cats we have known, and know most about, were cats who, in their homes, were treated as persons, not as furniture. Presumably a cat treated like a piece of furniture would begin to act like one, at least to human eyes. He would not feel like one, but he might come to feel like part of the house.

The Cat

MARY E. WILKINS FREEMAN

I think the reason Mrs. Freeman's "The Cat" has so often been reprinted—certainly the reason it is a favorite of mine —is its absolute believability. Although it describes a situation—a cat's struggle for survival against nature at its harshest—that could only be imagined by the author, every word rings true. Even the cat's relationship with the two men, which in less talented hands could be very sticky, comes across as true and memorable.

The snow was falling, and the Cat's fur was stiffly pointed with it, but he was imperturbable. He sat crouched, ready for the death-spring, as he had sat for hours. It was night—but that made no difference—all times were as one to the Cat when he was in wait for prey. Then too, he was under no constraint of human will, for he was living alone that winter. Nowhere in the world was any voice calling him; on no hearth was there a waiting dish. He was quite free except for his own desires, which tyrannized over him when unsatisfied as now. The Cat was very hungry—almost famished, in fact. For days the weather had been very bitter, and all the feebler wild things which were his prey by inheritance, the born serfs to his family, had kept, for the most part, in their burrows and nests, and the Cat's long hunt had availed him nothing. But he waited with the inconceivable patience and persistency of his race; besides, he was certain. The Cat was a creature of absolute convictions, and his faith in his deductions never wavered. The rabbit had gone in there between those low-hung pine boughs. Now her little doorway had before it a shaggy curtain of snow, but in there she was. The Cat had seen her enter, so like a swift grey shadow that even his sharp and practised eyes had glanced back for the substance following, and then she was gone. So he sat down and waited, and he waited still in the white night, listening angrily to the north wind starting in the upper heights of the mountains with distant screams, then swelling into an awful crescendo of rage, and swooping down with furious white wings of snow like a flock of fierce eagles into the valleys and ravines. The Cat was on the

175

side of a mountain, on a wooded terrace. Above him a few feet away towered the rock ascent as steep as the wall of a cathedral. The Cat had never climbed it—trees were the ladders to his heights of life. He had often looked with wonder at the rock, and miauled bitterly and resentfully as man does in the face of a forbidding Providence. At his left was the sheer precipice. Behind him, with a short stretch of woody growth between, was the frozen perpendicular wall of a mountain stream. Before him was the way to his home. When the rabbit came out she was trapped; her little cloven feet could not scale such unbroken steeps. So the Cat waited. The place in which he was looked like a maelstrom of the wood. The tangle of trees and bushes clinging to the mountain-side with a stern clutch of roots, the prostrate trunks and branches, the vines embracing everything with strong knots and coils of growth, had a curious effect, as of things which had whirled for ages in a current of raging water, only it was not water, but wind, which had disposed everything in circling lines of yielding to its fiercest points of onset. And now over all this whirl of wood and rock and dead trunks and branches and vines descended the snow. It blew down like smoke over the rock-crest above; it stood in a gyrating column like some death-wraith of nature, on the level, then it broke over the edge of the precipice, and the Cat cowered before the fierce backward set of it. It was as if ice needles pricked his skin through his beautiful thick fur, but he never faltered and never once cried. He had nothing to gain from crying, and everything to lose; the rabbit would hear him cry and know he was waiting.

It grew darker and darker, with a strange white smother, instead of the natural blackness of night. It was a night of storm and death superadded to the night of nature. The mountains were all hidden, wrapped about, overawed, and tumultuously overborne by it, but in the midst of it waited, quite unconquered, this little, unswerving, living patience and power under a little coat of grey fur.

A fiercer blast swept over the rock, spun on one mighty foot of whirlwind athwart the level, then was over the precipice.

Then the Cat saw two eyes luminous with terror, frantic with the impulse of flight, he saw a little, quivering, dilating nose, he saw two pointing ears, and he kept still, with every one of his fine nerves and muscles strained like wires. Then the rabbit was out—there was one long line of incarnate flight and terror—and the Cat had her.

Then the Cat went home, trailing his prey through the snow.

The Cat lived in the house which his master had built, as rudely as a child's block-house, but stanchly enough. The snow was heavy on the low slant of its roof, but it would not settle under it. The two windows and the door were made fast, but the Cat knew a way in. Up a pine-tree behind the house he scuttled, though it was hard work with his heavy rabbit, and was in his little window under the eaves, then down through the trap to the room below, and on his master's bed with a spring and a great cry of triumph, rabbit and all. But his master was not there; he had been gone since early fall and it was now February. He would not return until spring, for he was an old man, and the cruel cold of the mountains clutched at his vitals like a panther, and he had gone to the village to winter. The Cat had known for a long time that his master was gone, but his reasoning was always sequential and circuitous; always for him what had been would be, and the more easily for his marvellous waiting powers so he always came home expecting to find his master.

When he saw that he was still gone, he dragged the rabbit off the rude couch which was the bed to the floor, put one little paw on the carcass to keep it steady, and began gnawing with head to one side to bring his strongest teeth to bear.

It was darker in the house than it had been in the wood, and the cold was as deadly, though not so fierce. If the Cat had not received his fur coat unquestioningly of Providence, he would have been thankful that he had it. It was a mottled grey, white on the face and breast, and thick as fur could grow.

The wind drove the snow on the windows with such force that it rattled like sleet, and the house trembled a little. Then all at once the Cat heard a noise, and stopped gnawing his rabbit and listened, his shining green eyes fixed upon a window. Then he heard a hoarse shout, a halloo of despair and entreaty; but he knew it was not his master come home, and he waited, one paw still on the rabbit. Then the halloo came again, and then the Cat answered. He said all that was essential quite plainly to his own comprehension. There was in his cry of response inquiry, information, warning, terror, and finally, the offer of comradeship; but the man outside did not hear him, because of the howling of the storm.

Then there was a great battering pound at the door, then another, and another. The Cat dragged his rabbit under the bed. The blows came thicker and faster. It was a weak arm which gave them, but it was nerved by desperation. Finally the lock yielded, and the stranger came in. Then the Cat, peering from under the bed, blinked with a sudden light, and his green eyes narrowed. The stranger struck a match and looked about. The Cat saw a face wild and blue with hunger and cold, and a man who looked poorer and older than his poor old master, who was an outcast among men for his poverty and lowly mystery of antecedents; and he heard a muttered, unintelligible voicing of distress from the harsh piteous mouth. There was in it both profanity and prayer, but the Cat knew nothing of that.

The stranger braced the door which he had forced, got some wood from the stock in the corner, and kindled a fire in the old stove as quickly as his half-frozen hands would allow. He shook so pitiably as he worked that the Cat under the bed felt the tremor of it. Then the man, who was small and feeble and marked with the scars of suffering which he had pulled down upon his own head, sat down in one of the old chairs and crouched over the fire as if it were the one love and desire of his soul, holding out his yellow hands like yellow claws, and he groaned. The Cat came out from under the bed and leaped up on his lap with the rabbit. The man gave a great shout and start of terror, and sprang, and the Cat slid clawing to the floor, and the rabbit fell inertly, and the man leaned, gasping with fright, and ghastly, against the wall. The Cat grabbed the rabbit by the slack of its neck and dragged it to the man's feet. Then he raised his shrill, insisent cry, he arched his back high, his tail was a splendid waving plume. He rubbed against the man's feet, which were bursting out of their torn shoes.

The man pushed the Cat away, gently enough, and began searching about the little cabin. He even climbed painfully the ladder to the loft, lit a match, and peered up in the darkness with straining eyes. He feared lest there might be a man, since there was a cat. His experience with men had not been pleasant, and neither had the experience of men been pleasant with him. He was an old wandering Ishmael among his kind; he had stumbled upon the house of a brother, and the brother was not at home, and he was glad.

He returned to the Cat, and stooped stiffly and stroked his back, which the animal arched like the spring of a bow.

Then he took up the rabbit and looked at it eagerly by the firelight. His jaws worked. He could almost have devoured it raw. He fumbled—the Cat close at his heels—around some rude shelves and a table, and found, with a grunt of self-gratulation, a lamp with oil in it. That he lighted; then he found a frying-pan and a knife, and skinned the rabbit, and prepared it for cooking, the Cat always at his feet.

When the odour of the cooking flesh filled the cabin, both the man and the Cat looked wolfish. The man turned the rabbit with one hand and stooped to pat the Cat with the other. The Cat thought him a fine man. He loved him with all his heart, though he had known him such a short time, and though the man had a face both pitiful and sharply set at variance with the best of things.

It was a face with the grimy grizzle of age upon it, with fever hollows in the cheeks, and the memories of wrong in the dim eyes, but the Cat accepted the man unquestioningly and loved him. When the rabbit was half cooked, neither the man nor the Cat would wait any longer. The man took it from the fire, divided it exactly in halves, gave the Cat one, and took the other himself. Then they ate.

Then the man blew out the light, called the Cat to him, got on the bed, drew up the ragged coverings, and fell asleep with the Cat in his bosom.

The man was the Cat's guest all the rest of the winter, and winter is long in the mountains. The rightful owner of the little hut did not return until May. All that time the Cat toiled hard, and he grew rather thin himself, for he shared everything except mice with his guest; and sometimes game was wary, and the fruit of patience of days was very little for two. The man was ill and weak, however, and unable to eat much, which was fortunate, since he could not hunt for himself. All day long he lay on the bed, or else sat crouched over the fire. It was a good thing that fire-wood was ready at hand for the picking up, not a stone's-throw from the door, for that he had to attend to himself.

The Cat foraged tirelessly. Sometimes he was gone for days together, and at first the man used to be terrified, thinking he would never return; then he would hear the familiar cry at the door, and stumble to his feet and let him in. Then the two would dine together, sharing equally; then the Cat would rest and purr, and finally sleep in the man's arms.

Towards spring the game grew plentiful; more wild little quarry were tempted out of their homes, in search of love as well as food. One day the Cat had luck—a rabbit, a partridge, and a mouse. He could not carry them all at once, but finally he had them together at the house door. Then he cried, but no one answered. All the mountain streams were loosened, and the air was full of the gurgle of many waters, occasionally pierced by a bird-whistle. The trees rustled with a new sound to the spring wind; there was a flush of rose and gold-green on the breasting surface of a distant mountain seen through an opening in the wood. The tips of the bushes were swollen and glistening red, and now and then there was a flower; but the Cat had nothing to do with flowers. He stood beside his booty at the house door, and cried and cried with his insistent triumph and complaint and

pleading, but no one came to let him in. Then the cat left his little treasures at the door, and went around to the back of the house to the pine-tree, and was up the trunk with a wild scramble, and in through his little window, and down through the trap to the room, and the man was gone.

The Cat cried again—that cry of the animal for human companionship which is one of the sad notes of the world; he looked in all the corners; he sprang to the chair at the window and looked out; but no one came. The man was gone and he never came again.

The Cat ate his mouse out on the turf beside the house; the rabbit and the partridge he carried painfully into the house, but the man did not come to share them. Finally, in the course of a day or two, he ate them up himself; then he slept a long time on the bed, and when he waked the man was not there.

Then the Cat went forth to his hunting-grounds again, and came home at night with a plump bird, reasoning with his tireless persistency in expectancy that the man would be there; and there was a light in the window, and when he cried his old master opened the door and let him in.

His master had strong comradeship with the Cat, but not affection. He never patted him like that gentler outcast, but he had a pride in him and an anxiety for his welfare, though he had left him alone all winter without scruple. He feared lest some misfortune might have come to the Cat, though he was so large of his kind, and a mighty hunter. Therefore, when he saw him at the door in all the glory of his glossy winter coat, his white breast and face shining like snow in the sun, his own face lit up with welcome, and the Cat embraced his feet with his sinuous body vibrant with rejoicing purrs.

The Cat had his bird to himself, for his master had his own supper already cooking on the stove. After supper the Cat's master took his pipe, and sought a small store of tobacco which he had left in his hut over winter. He had thought often of it; that and the Cat seemed something to come home to in the spring. But the tobacco was gone; not a dust left. The man swore a little in a grim monotone, which made the profanity lose its customary effect. He had been, and was, a hard drinker; he had knocked about the world until the marks of its sharp corners were on his very soul, which was thereby calloused, until his very sensibility to loss was dulled. He was a very old man.

He searched for the tobacco with a sort of dull combativeness of persistency; then he stared with stupid wonder around the room. Suddenly many features struck him as being changed. Another stove-lid was broken; an old piece of carpet was tacked up over a window to keep out the cold; his fire-wood was gone. He looked and there was no oil left in his can. He looked at the covering on his bed; he took them up, and again he made that strange remonstrant noise in his throat. Then he looked again for his tobacco.

Finally he gave it up. He sat down beside the fire, for May in the mountains is cold; he held his empty pipe in his mouth, his rough forehead knitted, and he and the Cat looked at each other across that impassable barrier of silence which has been set between man and beast from the creation of the world.

Cat with a Telephone Number

FRED SPARKS

Endowed with a gregarious nature and the ability to defend himself when the circumstances required, Stoop was also supplied by his owner with a distinct advantage over his fellow street cats—a tag with his telephone number.

While pet cats shouldn't roam the streets, New York was a friendlier place in the days of Stoop's freedom, and that little tag led him—and his master—into some very pleasant adventures.

It's a humiliating confession for a bachelor to make, but whenever my phone rings the call most likely concerns not me but my cat, name of Stoop. We live, Stoop and I, in a New York apartment one flight up. The branch of an oak tree brushes the railing of our back terrace, providing a feline staircase that enables Stoop to live a double life, civilized and sedentary within the apartment, completely uninhibited when he climbs down the tree and prowls the outside world.

I first met Stoop three years ago. I was walking home on a bitterly cold night when I saw a tangerine red kitten sitting on a snowy brownstone stoop. As I approached, the creature tried to stand, wobbled, then fell down a step, half-frozen.

I wrapped the few ounces of shivering fur in my scarf and got an immediate purr of confidence. At home, Stoop (an obvious christening) responded immediately to an eyedropper-feeding of warm milk lightly laced with brandy. Within a week he was frisking around my place, and by spring, thanks to the spreading oak tree, he had discovered the exotic world of New York's sidewalks.

When his excursions lasted longer and longer, I bought a light collar and had a tag inscribed:

> THIS IS NOT A STRAY.
> IN EMERGENCY PHONE
> FRED SPARKS, BU 8- — — — —

Unlike full-time alley cats, who flee anything on two legs, Stoop is trusting. As he wanders through the neighborhood, strangers stop to pet him. Attracted by the tag, dozens of them have phoned me. They seem under the impression that Stoop has run away or was lost. They sound disappointed when I assure them that he can find his own way home.

A gentleman I hadn't seen in years called up and said, "Well, well, it *is* a small world. I stop to pet a cat and find you're back in town. Remember that $20 you owe me?"

That wasn't the only time Stoop was expensive. One caller identified himself as the owner of a seafood restaurant down the block. He complained that cats had been raiding his kitchen through a basement window, filching crabs and lobsters. "The only one I could catch had this telephone number," he said. "Please give me your address. I'm going to send you a bill for his share."

I obliged, convinced it was a joke. As I walked away from the phone something crunched under my shoe. A lobster claw.

By the time Stoop had been on the streets for six months, he was a combat veteran of the cement jungle. His nose was crisscrossed with scratches, and his ears were nicked with notches like a Western bad man's belt. But in spite of the horrendous things that supposedly happen to small animals loose in the big city, he shows no evidence of ever having been mistreated. In fact, many of the phone calls come from friendly souls who want to be sure of doing the right thing. "I've got your nice cat with me in a phone booth," a man said recently. "Is he allowed to eat a fig?" Another wanted to know if Stoop could safely handle lamb chop bones.

The wife of a U.N. delegate phoned one Sunday to report that Stoop was a guest at a garden party in her nearby town house. "He just strolled in and is now having an anchovy," she said. "Won't you join us?" I did, and it was a lovely party.

Stoop certainly gets around. One morning he climbed into a cab parked down the street. I heard about it when an excited voice on the phone asked, "You-the-guy-widda-cat?" When I said I was, he rattled on, "Holy smoke! I'm a taxi driver and I thought I'd seen everything. But when I got in line at Grand Central Station, I find this cat sitting in the back seat. With a telephone number, yet!"

"Where is he now?" I asked, apprehensively.

"In a coin locker. Pick up the key at the starter's office and leave me the quarter. And say, Mister! How about a tip or something? Nobody—not even a cat—is supposed to ride free."

Stoop gets around locally, too. A call came late at night, a few months ago, from an indignant female.

"Your *cat* is under my bed!" she snapped. "I got a look at his tag before he ran away from me and hid."

Trying to calm her down, I said, "How do you know that its' a he?"

"Because he's been corrupting *my* cat, a *her*."

Curtly she gave me her name, Helen ———, and her address, a ground-floor apartment across the yard. When I went over to collect my housebreaking cat, I tried to apologize for his bad manners, but she slammed the door on both of us.

Two nights later it happened again. This time I brought along a box of chocolates for Helen and a catnip mouse for her tortoise-shell pet. She found this amusing and I found her really an attractive girl. We agreed to have dinner together.

Stoop doesn't see Helen's cat any more. But I still see Helen. Now when the phone rings, I know that at least sometimes it's for me.

Piazza Vittorio

ELEANOR CLARK

To attempt to introduce Eleanor Clark is presumptuous; I will be brief. Others have written about the cats of Rome, but they were tourists. Miss Clark sees the sights, yes, but she is of that better breed, the traveler. One thinks of Rose Macaulay and Freya Stark, admirable travelers too, with their own precincts. Think of them by all means, but read Eleanor Clark. Read "The Oysters of Locmariaquer," mysterious, evocative. And of course read "Rome and a Villa," of which this essay is a portion.

Some find Miss Clark's writing dense. If so, it is the density of scores of angels dancing on the head of a pin. I would no sooner attempt to count them than I would count the myriad cats that superbly embellish that ancient ruin in the Piazza Vittorio. I can only admire—and marvel.

Thousands of cats; a city of cats, as of fountains and churches, and as naturally. Most of them are not even roaming but in definite asylums, which were never planned any more than the piazzas were, or seem to have been, for human use. They just come about. The cats are drawn for some reason to one place or another, which may remain the haunt of their descendants for centuries, and people come there to feed them. It is not that Romans really consider them a sacred or even superior animal, or think about them much at all, yet some ancient habit of respect seems to apply to them, giving them a unique position among the public cats of the world. There are not many private ones—a Siamese in the house is apt to be a sign of neurosis or international marriage; normal Roman life has no more need or use for pets than for similar attachments within its own species. The cats, like people, are mostly strays, and after their great number the striking fact about them is that very few are thin.

In the old days their most famous spot was Trajan's Forum, this of course before Mussolini and the Via dell' Impero, when the forum was not the propped-up showpiece it is now but a weedy ruin-strewn pit sunk among tenements, with the triumphal column bolt upright in its old-style grandeur at the end; the cats looked natural there. Sometimes the government saw to feeding them, other times just the neighborhood; at night there were the usual back-yard screechings multiplied by a hundred or so but when the fascist authorities, before the final overhauling of the area, tried to remove the nuisance there was such protest from the people it had to back down. But then the tenements went, the excavations began; the jig was up; Empire Street could not be desecrated by cats; anyway the garbage supply had been cut off. Another place, until recently, used to be around the pyramid of Caius Cestius, beside the Protestant cemetery, but that district finally became too unresidential too.

One of the smaller ancestral centers that remains is in back of the Pantheon where there is a colony of twenty or thirty, most likely of Renaissance origin. Another is an alley running from the Via Giulia to the rear of the Palazzo Spada, which some people consider rather sinister, probably because the alley is narrow and barred and usually in shadow and the Council of the State meets in the palace. The cats have a barricaded look; the council sits beside the sinister statue of Pompey that Caesar clutched when he fell. But by far the greatest cat congregation of present-day Rome and possibly of Western civilization is in the huge market square on the other side of town from these two—Piazza Vittorio so-called, really Vittorio Emanuele, for the unifier of Italy.

The name happens to suit the architecture. It is of the early House of Savoy period, airy, sensible and bourgeois; the colonnades around the square are not of any Roman style that survives though in the ancient city there were miles of them; the quarter around has a solid and quite pleasant middle-class look of eighty years ago. It is all most un-Roman, except as Rome like an insectivorous plant can take in anything, even Turin, and make it Rome. Pines and palms grow in the large parklike center of the square, inside the roaring double ring of the market, and from the middle there is a long lyrical view, from Santa Maria Maggiore to Santa Croce in Gerusalemme and way beyond that, clear as angels and snowy sometimes in winter, the peak of Monte Cavo. There is a high jumble of ruins back of the fish stalls; a set of cabalistic carvings on a door nearby from nobody knows what or when, said to contain a formula for making gold; a baroque fountain of stone corroded to an even wilder appeal than usual; and about a hundred and fifty cats.

They are of course at the fish end, and the ruins, of 3rd Century brick, are their backdrop. They never go far from there, or not for long; it is not necessary; an invisible line around that corner of the square marks their precinct, they have made their own atmosphere there, and prefer it.

The ruins have a connection with water, which the cats in their own way keep vivid. The building, big enough to have been a three-story villa or public library, was a monumental fountain or show-off point for the water of one of the big aqueducts coming in through the quarter, and a gaudy show it must have been, from that height. Now it is a craggy rambling mass with a suggestion of enchantment though of the wrong color for a fairy tale, and the cats, who cannot get inside where the keeper of the garden lives, in their idle hours wander and drape themselves over all its levels and sketchy escarpments and juttings, all the way to the top—unhurried, unchased, wonderfully at home and regal in all their motions, not having to play up to anybody. The choreography is excellent.

In a little window at the very top, opening on to nothing, a cat framed in vines lies like a princess drying her hair; another is oddly reclined below on top of a cluster of sharp posts which are end up; somehow in the mercurial way of cats she has made herself comfortable. Others are stretched or curled in the flower beds and on the chunks of fallen marble cornice and Corinthian capitals lying around, or in favorite dents like couches under the bushes. This will be early in the afternoon when they are not hungry any more, although the market has not yet folded up. They are more or less sated; not groggy, and not really sleeping, because there is still a sense of opportunity in the air at this time of day but they have only half an eye open for it. A calico tom with a black neckline like a court decoration decides to investigate a bloody scrap of paper in which there are still a few scraps from one of the meat stalls, pulls his paw across it languidly a couple of times and saunters back to rest among the zinnias. On the first shelf of the ruin two kittens, one white as a sacred calf, box a moment, not having learned to gage their desires, then in disillusion move apart. Here and there older cats take a swipe or two at washing themselves or each other, and are not too drowsy to have their feelings hurt; obscure episodes of pride and disgrace are taking place all through the happy scene, but that is not the fault of Rome.

Nobody is even watching especially. The cats are taken for granted, as many holier things are; besides in the pace and gusto of its own life, in extent too, this is the Saint Peter's among markets. The fascination is general.

You can buy almost anything there—live fowl and any other foodstuff, leather goods, clothes, toys, stolen bicycle parts, and everybody is head over heels in the business not so much for the sake of the business as the life. An aged woman with two teeth, selling carrots, detects you smiling a little at her bellow of publicity, the same tremendous voice as the others but sharper from age, thinks for a second you wanted to buy, then perceiving that you were only laughing at her goes off in a fit of gaiety herself: "Ah, old age! . . . CARROTS!" People go out of their way to touch a midget for good luck, and down a side street a man keeping up a brilliant monologue tells fortunes with dolls that rise in a jar of water that he carries on a peg and white mice running up a string outside. Several of the young girls selling vegetables are of typical Roman beauty and aware of it. There is much too much going on for the cats to be a center of attraction.

Nevertheless they do have a special part in the show, more than if anyone were paying attention to them, and not only through the spectacle they provide. There is something else, something in the apparently offhand human treatment of them that takes you way outside of commerce and common sense, not to religion, not to charity. It puts a bargain in another perspective.

Perhaps in the Roman feeling about the species there is some dim recollection from the days of popular Egyptiana in the city, around the time the present ruin was going up in all its water-glory; or it may be only that cats are a mysterious animal as everyone admits, and Romans are alert to mysteries outside their own nature and fall easily into ways of propitiating them. Or perhaps they came into honor as a check to rats carrying plague in the Middle Ages and after—a kind of honor that only the Roman mind would perpetuate, because if they were of any use in that way it would have been the same anywhere in Europe, and no other city has such sanctuaries or would take them as such a matter of course: there would be societies for preservation, committees for extermination, propaganda for equal treatment of dogs or birds, Malthusian editorials etc., or somebody would decide they ought to be somewhere else.

Not in Rome. The regard they are held in is general and careless; the problem, if there is one, solves itself. No doubt there is some element of primitive religious sense, or call it superstition, at the root of the matter, there usually is in tigerology, but it would be hard to trace. There is no particular emphasis on the animal anywhere in Roman culture ancient or Christian, either as good or as evil; they were never deified, nor the familiars of witches, although at one time there were plenty of witches; they are not even liked for their company; you never read of Roman old maids being found dead in a house with seventeen cats, and nobody goes pussy-pussy, meesha-meesha in Italian, indiscriminately.

But there they are, not worshiped or pampered or feared or in any way consciously honored, but honored just the same, rather as the fountains are; with which after all they do have one function in common. They are a link with the past, that is with all time, having kept a clearer set of original instincts together with more various personality than any other tamed animal. There is nothing transitory about a cat, aside from the individual knack of survival; it is the most ancient of our animals. A dead cat never has the look of finality that a dead dog does; neither does a dead Roman, which is why you never see many people bothering to follow funerals there. The eye of a cat is an eye in the forest and in all time and so even the stupidest cat seems to *know* more than any dog or horse; it knows history; you do not have to believe in the transmigration of souls to feel that a living knowledge of Agrippa continues in back of the Pantheon just as it does in the fountain in front of it.

In any case, what with the view and their numbers and the strange beauty of their dwelling, the cats of Piazzo Vittorio have all the look of a sacred colony even if not officially sanctioned like cows or monkeys in other parts of the world. It is not as if they were scavenging all over the market, or in captivity like the wolf on the Capitoline or creatures in a zoo. There is an air of pleasant natural concord all around, a credit to man and beast and not very characteristic of either party in the case. Romans are not notably kind to other animals nor of any Franciscan spirit in general, and cats are not a usual symbol of the earthly paradise. They simply happen to hit it off; they understand one another; consequently the cats are the most civilized in the world.

They are also of the most extraordinary colors. It is a botanical garden of exotic furs, in every combination: marmalades shading to bronze, orange in trout specklings on grey or black, a single contrasting or striped forearm on a monotone coat, every kind of bib and dashing including the common chest triangle, often only one perky ear of solid color like an insistent strain of nobility through the conglomerate birth; but they are all aristocrats though of dead-end breed, even the ones with backsides and front sides of two utterly incompatible schemes, blue-grey and white in front and black with orange behind, like a blue-faced mandrill or a polychrome bust from the late empire; or say a pansy bed took to sprouting mammals, some plain white with only the golden circles of the eyes or all black as pansies can be, which now stalk or rest among the other furless flowers that they would never permit themselves to break any more than if they were of rare porcelain on a mantelpiece.

They have neither the hyper-dependence of house cats nor the fears of alley ones. They are free of the two greatest sufferings of the species, hunger and loneliness, also from the ravages of human temperament pro or con, not to mention surgical abominations. It is much as humans have imagined heaven, only the cats run no danger of spinelessness; in fact the spine, their most distinctive piece of anatomy, and muscular development in general are spectacular in these cats. Among domestic felines only purebred Siamese leap to such marvelous heights and distances, and they have become a race of neurasthenics. In Piazza Vittorio you are seeing cat life at its healthiest, at least the healthiest possible in such a millennium as ours, but for that matter there can never have been such a sight in the wilderness either. The cats have reverted to true tiger prowess and beauty of form in action, but without ferocity. The ancient jungle-gym they have taken over is ideal for all the play that cats must have, watching, stalking, springing etc., and at any hour there will be a few engaged in it, acting as usual on primeval urgencies but with a look more of Greek athletes, especially in the prowl and the slow gallop, two of their most becoming sports. They have lost the jitters of wild life.

They seem to have lost some of their vices too, though not at any cost to individuality; if you hang around awhile you will see them of every character, from pussy willow to the sphinx. But there is not much stealing or fighting. They would not risk approaching the tubs of squid and other heavenly slobber that lie around them on two sides, but they are unusually well-mannered among themselves as

well; you see hardly any chewed ears and bloody noses. When a passer-by or one of the fish vendors comes over with a package a dozen or two will bound for it, like planes bouncing in to a landing, from their various marble roosts or solitary promenades, but if they are too late they leave quietly; there will be more later, and not only refuse. The big scene is when the government feeder comes, a woman usually, and familiar with cats; otherwise she could be terrified.

They come streaking from the lower branches of the trees and all the heights of the ruin and everywhere around, leaping over the flower beds and fallen fluted columns, and champ and mew and race scratching up to other branches to leap down on her shoulders; in a few seconds there will be seventy or eighty with their crazy coats all in a roil so you would think they would come out of it with somebody else's markings, and their whiskers aquiver like telegraph wires, but there is no real frenzy; they all get something in the end. A high-strung bronze-and-black, leaner than most, stays on her shoulder trying to snatch at the basket from above; she lets him stay, and in fact though fierce of eye he is all humility in his claws—one of the grieving type, who are more anxious to be grabbed from than to grab and will stay thin all their lives; a more politic black one waits alert with neck stretched from a tree trunk; off on the other side a small white baffled Persian that has somehow joined the flock or perhaps was left there and is not yet used to its ways, tries different approaches, then stands at the rim anxiously lifting one forepaw after the other, his eyes following the whole course of every morsel from basket to the final dash for privacy; he was fed alone by a butler until recently.

When it is over they nearly all follow the woman as far as the gravel path which nothing prevents them from crossing but they stop there, and little by little disperse, only to be shot into action ten minutes later by another event: rain.

A cloudburst; there is a human rush for the colonnades; with a subtle shuddering motion the market folds in on itself like a bird into its feathers; tarpaulins appear from nowhere over the destructibles, certain tender points are whisked in altogether, the vendors pull back under their awnings meant for protection from the sun.

This time the motion of the cats is not centripetal. The lines they trace are as fast and straight as before but all in a criss-cross as of night projectiles over a battlefield. It is each not to the nearest cover but the predetermined one, which may be halfway round the ruin or all the way across the lawn, one way to some nook in the structure, another to the sheltering brown pantalettes of a pygmy palm, so for a few seconds the whole ground is a contradiction of flying cat-furs, which resolves itself in a moment without collision or argument or even a swerve of line unless a particular place were taken, when the late-comer shoots off by the same mystic geometry to the nearest alternative. Then there is no further move. Only nursing mothers have stayed where they were, having already chosen some fairly safe location, from which they view the sky's performance with gentle sorrow as others will when all of it comes down.

The rest are watching too, in a different way. There is really no inside room for them at all; they would rather drown in a place fit for guarding than follow the humans into the exposure of the colonnades. They are crouched under every little brick-eave and in clusters under the low-branching pines, all in the same waiting posture and perfectly still, hind paws invisible, the front ones in a plumb line with their noses and shoulder blades, not to spring, only to guard. They will not begin to lick themselves dry until it is over, which is in a couple of minutes.

The sun bursts out; the market is bustling again though not for long—it is nearly packing-up time. Greenery and every kind of impedimenta around the northwest corner begin slowly discharging cats, which revert to their individual natures and ways of doing things and soon are all over the place again with their sinewy purposeful activities and delicate affections: a hundred and fifty personalities, although sooner or later all must dry themselves, at once and thoroughly like fussy housewives or in wayward licks and spinal doublings after racing back to some lone preeminence. Meanwhile they take stock of the damage. Many of their beds are puddles, certain surfaces untrustworthy; even the flowers have become inimical; there are many little new arrangements to be made.

They have another job in common, more than to look after themselves. They are about to be in charge of the empty square, as one cat may be of a grocery store but here it is not so much a question of mice. There is nothing left to attract a mouse. It is astonishing how fast and utterly the enormous market takes itself away; the fantasia of human commodities, wearable, edible, combustible, aesthetic, hygienic and vehicular, the gamut of man's utensils, and all the push and pleasure of life that went into their changing hands, are suddenly gone; booths turn into carts and men into cart horses and everything vanishes. Pizza Vittorio at first glance is a big undistinguished place of northern design, with a park in the middle, where you would imagine little scenes of provincial longing and escape to the movie house. But there is something more.

One cat may be dying. Some will be conceived tonight around the fountain-ruin with horrible shriekings as from the victims of emperors or emperors meeting their own ends, which the people who live above the colonnades will scarcely hear; if they do hear they will turn over and sleep again like children. A more fearful continuity has sprung up where theirs left off; a hundred and fifty charms are working for that neighborhood alone. The cats are not idle at all now, and not playing. Among the vines in the highest window of the jungle palace an eye burns that no human ever saw; between screams a furry figure was caught a second in the streetlight's gleam, in mid-spring, with claws bared to the root sharper than any doctor's tool, plunging to silence and the dark. No troop of Swiss could guard these mysteries.

The market will be back in the morning; for another day Rome is safe; if all were quiet, then you would stay awake.

"The resounding Albunea, the headlong Anio, the grove of Tibur . . ."—HORACE.

Dick Baker's Cat

MARK TWAIN

Although often anthologized, "Dick Baker's Cat" deserves its popularity. Not only is it a superb example of the American tall tale, it is also—unlike many of the species—genuinely funny.

One of my comrades there—another of those victims of eighteen years of unrequited toil and blighted hopes—was one of the gentlest spirits that ever bore its patient cross in a weary exile: grave and simple Dick Baker, pocket-miner of Dead-Horse Gulch. He was forty-six, grey as a rat, earnest, thoughtful, slenderly educated, slouchily dressed and clay-soiled, but his heart was finer metal than any gold his shovel ever brought to light—than any, indeed, that ever was mined or minted.

Whenever he was out of luck and a little downhearted, he would fall to mourning over the loss of a wonderful cat he used to own (for where women and children are not, men of kindly impulses take up with pets, for they must love something). And he always spoke of the strange sagacity of that cat with the air of a man who believed in his secret heart that there was something human about it—maybe even supernatural.

I heard him talking about this animal once. He said: "Gentlemen, I used to have a cat here, by the name of Tom Quartz, which you'd 'a' took an interest in, I reckon—most anybody would. I had him here eight year—and he was the remarkablest cat I ever see. He was a large grey one of the Tom specie, an' he had more hard, natchral sense than any man in this camp—'n' a power of dignity—he wouldn't let the Govner of Californy be familiar with him. He never ketched a rat in his life—'peared to be above it. He never cared for nothing but mining. He knowed more about mining, that cat did, than any man I ever, ever see. You couldn't tell *him* noth'n' 'bout placer-diggin's—'n' as for pocket-mining, why he was just born for it. He would dig out after me an' Jim when we went over the hills prospect'n', and he would trot along behind us for as much as five

197

mile, if we went so fur. An' he had the best judgement about mining-ground—why you never see anything like it. When we went to work, he'd scatter a glance around, 'n' if he didn't think much of the indications, he would give a look as much as to say, 'Well, I'll have to get you to excuse me,' 'n' without another word he'd hyste his nose into the air 'n' shove for home. But if the ground suited him, he would lay low 'n' keep dark till the first pan was washed, 'n' then he would sidle up 'n' take a look, an' if there was about six or seven grains of gold he was satisfied—he didn't want no better prospect 'n' that—'n' then he would lay down on our coats and snore like a steamboat till we'd struck the pocket, an' then get up 'n' superintend. He was nearly lightnin' on superintending.

"Well, by an' by, up comes this yer quartz excitement. Everybody was into it—everybody was pick'n' 'n' blast'n' instead of shovelin' dirt on the hillside—everybody was putt'n' down a shaft instead of scrapin' the surface. Noth'n' would do Jim, but we must tackle the ledges, too, 'n' so we did. We commenced putt'n' down a shaft, 'n' Tom Quartz he begin to wonder what in the Dickens it was all about. He hadn't ever seen any mining like that before, 'n' he was all upset, as you may say—he couldn't come to a right understanding of it no way—it was too many for him. He was down on it too, you bet you—he was down on it powerful—'n' always appeared to consider it the cussedest foolishness out. But that cat, you know, was always agin new-fangled arrangements—somehow he never could abide 'em. You know how it is with old habits. But by an' by Tom Quartz begin to git sort of reconciled a little, though he never could altogether understand that eternal sinkin' of a shaft an' never pannin' out anything. At last he got to comin' down in the shaft hisself, to try to cipher it out. An' when he'd git the blues, 'n' feel kind o' scruffy, 'n' aggravated 'n' disgusted—knowin' as he did, that the bills was runnin' up all the time an' we warn't makin' a cent—he would curl up on a gunny-sack in the corner an' go to sleep. Well, one day when the shaft was down about eight foot, the rock got so hard that we had to put in a blast—the first blast'n' we'd ever done since Tom Quartz was born. An' then we lit the fuse 'n' clumb out 'n' got off 'bout fifty yards—'n' forgot 'n' left Tom Quartz sound asleep on the gunny-sack. In 'bout a minute we seen a puff of smoke bust up out of the hole, 'n' then everything let go with an awful crash, 'n' about four million ton of rocks 'n' dirt 'n' smoke 'n' splinters shot up 'bout a mile an' a half into the air, an' by George, right in the dead centre of it was old Tom Quartz a-goin' end over end, an' a-snortin' an' a-sneez'n', an' a-clawin' an' a-reach'n' for things like all possessed. But it warn't no use, you know,

it warn't no use. An' that was the last we see of *him* for about two minutes 'n' a half, an' then all of a sudden it begin to rain rocks and rubbage an' directly he come down ker-whoop about ten foot off f'm where we stood. Well, I reckon he was p'raps the orneriest-lookin' beast you ever see. One ear was sot back on his neck, 'n' his tail was stove up, 'n' his eye-winkers was singed off, 'n' he was all blacked up with powder an' smoke, an' all sloppy with mud 'n' slush f'm one end to the other. Well, sir, it warn't no use to try to apologize—we couldn't say a word. He took a sort of a disgusted look at hisself, 'n' then he looked at us—an' it was just exactly the same as if he had said—'Gents, maybe you think it's smart to take advantage of a cat that ain't had no experience of quartz-minin', but *I* think *different*' —an' then he turned on his heel 'n' marched off home without ever saying another word.

"That was jest his style. An' maybe you won't believe it, but after that you never see a cat so prejudiced agin quartz-mining as what he was. An' by an' by when he *did* get to goin' down in the shaft ag'in, you'd 'a' been astonished at his sagacity. The minute we'd tetch off a blast 'n' the fuse'd begin to sizzle, he'd give a look as much as to say, 'Well, I'll have to git you to excuse me,' an' it was su'pris'n' the way he'd shin out of that hole 'n' go f'r a tree. Sagacity? It ain't no name for it. 'Twas *inspiration!*"

I said, "Well, Mr. Baker, his prejudice against quartz-mining was remarkable, considering how he came by it. Couldn't you ever cure him of it?"

"*Cure him!* No! When Tom Quartz was sot once, he was *always* sot—and you might 'a' blowed him up as much three million times 'n' you'd never 'a' broken him of his cussed prejudice agin quartz-mining."

The Leopard Cat

LUDWIG KOCH-ISENBURG

Maij is such an irresistible charmer that I had to include her in this book despite her not being, strictly speaking, a domestic cat.

In "The Realm of the Green Buddha," his absorbing book about collecting wild animals in the Far East, the author tells of his patient efforts to domesticate the beautiful little leopard cat.

I have mentioned that Suthat was a police official. He was high enough in the official hierarchy to take vacations when he pleased. Since he was also a passionate amateur naturalist, it was easy to persuade him to undertake an expedition into the southern bamboo forests. And so one day we landed in a village of rice farmers close to the Cambodian border. I listened uncomprehendingly to the lengthy negotiations with a band of handsome, brown-skinned boys and men, for I had learned little of their musical language except a few names of animals. Suthat and I always spoke English together.

Day after day we tramped through the endless groves of bamboo. Splendid green and pearly gray tree lizards, multicolored tree snakes, and tortoises were our principal booty. Above us in the treetops mockingbirds sang and monkeys performed acrobatics. Evenings, when we returned to our quarters from capturing geckos, we had long palavers with our native trappers, whose bird snares and ape traps remained spitefully empty.

One evening, however, an elderly Thai pressed through the crowd of callers around us. He was carrying a covered bamboo basket, and he kneeled down on the ground with it. I was frightfully curious, but I had learned to be patient in dealing with Asiatics. After endless talk between Suthat and the newcomer, I caught a word that rather dashed my hopes: "baby leopard." I asked a question, and the reply was, "Spotted." What in the world would I want with a spotted leopard cub? If it had been a black leopard now—but neither I nor my friends at home had any interest in an ordinary spotted leopard, since this breed multiplies in European zoos with the regularity of house cats. Still, we wanted to see the baby; we would have to take it and pay for it anyhow, or we would severely undermine the morale of our hunters. After all, we could give the cub to the zoo director in Bangkok, since we could not very well return it to its mother.

The lid was opened, and out climbed a delicate, spotted thing, at the sight of which I uttered a cry of joyful surprise. Was this supposed to be a spotted leopard? Not at all—it was the leopard's Lilliputian edition, the leopard cat. Suthat turned to me, smiling and shaking his head. How could an old Thai be so ignorant as to confuse a half-grown leopard cat with its big cousin's baby? In his defense it must be said that the kitten was a faithful image of the leopard in all respects—a perfect spotted leopard the size of a domestic cat. The tawny hide was soft as silk, like close-cropped plush; the big yellow eyes those of a typical leopard. The cat moved with noiseless, inconspicuous gait; the lithe body was flexible as a bamboo pole. Even the characteristic white spots that tigers and leopards have on the back of their ears were there. I myself have never been excessively fond of cats: I am a dog man. Animal lovers the world over may be divided into two great groups, which probably have their deeper roots in character and temperament. As a rule dog lovers are not fond of cats, and cat enthusiasts do not love dogs. Of course I admired cats; they are nature's masterpiece among mammals; but I had never really seriously wanted to have cats about me. In my house dogs were dominant. But this leopard cat took my breath away. It was, aside from my beloved white-hand gibbon, the most endearing creature I had ever set eyes on. The way this cat set down its velvety paws as it padded softly toward us; the way it lifted its finely chiseled little head and gazed at each of us in turn with knowing, intelligent eyes; the way it rubbed, purring, against our hands, glad to be free of its confinement in the basket—all that was the very essence of poetic, ethereal, feline grace.

"But the cat is completely tame. It can't have been captured wild," I said with some excitement. "Where did the man get it?"

It turned out that he had been walking through a jungle village and had seen the cat sitting in front of a peasant hut. The owners had found it as a kitten in the woods and had bottle-raised it. There was no doubt that this leopard cat had lost all fear of men, but it could not transcend its feral nature. Now that it was almost grown, it was beginning to take more of an interest in its owners' hens and ducks than they liked. And so they had given the lovely animal to the old man with a sigh of relief.

How many generations are needed to adapt an animal to the domestic arrangements of human beings? The dog has been attached to human families for some ten thousand years, but even today a thoroughbred English pointer bitch will set upon her master's chickens and carry them to her pups when her litter begins to require solid food. The ancient instincts of the wolf have not yet been completely extinguished, and the dog does what it must do, by the unalterable laws of its predatory nature and the keenness of its maternal instincts. Except when she is looking after her pups, it does not occur to her to attack domestic animals; she knows they are men's property and she respects them. In the cat, whose career as a domestic animal is more recent by thousands of years, the instincts are more deeply and firmly rooted; moreover, the nature of this solitary predator is less flexible and adaptable than that of the submissive dog.

My friend produced several bank notes—he always handled these transactions with the natives and we two settled up afterward—and the lovely cat was mine. Or rather, I thought it was mine. It turned out that my friend was also smitten with the leopard cat and wanted it for himself. In vain I pointed out that he was very much a bird fancier and that a cat was not the ideal animal to have around his aviaries. He shook his head and smiled at all my blandishments. I promised him the finest thoroughbred pigeons from Europe, English pouters, Indian and wig doves, birds that had taken prizes at exhibitions on the Continent, and guaranteed breeders. He, for his part, began suggesting consolations. He would find a little panda for me, and he even went so far as to offer me the Farther Indian tapir, an animal of priceless value, if I would give up the leopard cat. We were well-matched bargainers; he knew as well as I did that it was easier to obtain a hundred wild cats than one tame one.

The drive back to Bangkok took nearly twenty-four hours. During all that time, I returned again and again to the fray. When I could think of no further arguments and no further proposals I tried to resign myself to the idea of giving up the little puss. Never, Suthat later confided, had I so impressed him as such a dyed-in-the-wool European. Buddha teaches, he reminded me, that foolish desires are the source of all human discontent. Desires that are unfulfillable are proved by that very fact alone to be foolish. The Oriental can renounce a desire smilingly; the European clings to it and makes himself unhappy. I professed to be an admirer of the Oriental spirit; well, then, here was my opportunity to put its philosophy into practice. And so I gave up hammering at him, but the disappointment hammered away inside me.

We named the cat Maij—the Thai word for "jungle," and our little beauty was a jungle animal. From the start she showed a special attachment to me. She spent most of her time in my room and slept on my bed at night. If I tried to shut her out she mewed so pathetically that it would have softened a heart of stone. Back in the village, she must have spent the nights on her master's rice-straw mat.

Suddenly, one morning, Suthat informed me that he had thought the matter over and that I could have the cat—in fact he would give her to me as a gift. I was speechless, and even more astonished by the typically Oriental reasoning. "I have often found, when I have brought myself to renounce something, that afterward I have had spiritual or material profit from doing so," he said with an inscrutable smile.

At that very moment the maid announced a visitor. A young man carrying a cardboard box appeared and stood modestly at the door. Asked to enter, he slipped off his sandals and approached us barefoot. The conversation was conducted in Thai, and my interest was aroused only when the lid of the box was opened and a white crow appeared. An albino sport—a white-plumaged bird with red eyes and pale beak and legs—occasionally crops up among almost all varieties of birds. There are white pheasants, blackbirds, sparrows, jays, and even swallows. They are great rarities. In Europe they are regarded as highly interesting but are not especially esteemed: in the land of the white elephant they enjoy an almost religious veneration. Never had I seen Suthat so carried away. He did not haggle about the price for a moment but reached for his wallet and gave the boy eight brand-new hundred-bath notes—equivalent to about forty-five dollars. After the boy left, my friend laughed with sheer delight and gripped both my hands. "What did I tell you? Isn't this an absolutely incredible coincidence? A white crow! Imagine, a pure white crow! I wouldn't exchange it for ten leopard cats."

*   *   *   *

On my visit to northern Thailand, I spent some time in one of those delightful pavilion hotels which provide first-class quarters and gracious Oriental service at fantastically high prices. My own cottage stood on posts to be safe from snakes and ground moisture. It included two large sleeping rooms, connected by a veranda; a shower (baths are little used in Thailand), and a small kitchen in case a guest wished to prepare his own meals. Electric fans on the ceiling hummed incessantly. There was a bell to summon the houseboy, who would run to the main building and bring anything the guest desired, from iced coffee to the hundred tidbits of a Thai rice table.

I was in the habit of rising very early, for anyone who sleeps away those most precious hours of the day in the tropics does not deserve to be a guest in paradise. One day I stood on the veranda in the silvery-gray predawn light, drying myself after my shower. I noticed that an elegant convertible was parked between me and the adjacent pavilion; it had not been there the night before. A screen door squeaked softly, and I instinctively drew back somewhat into the shadows, for some white woman might very easily have arrived at the hotel. Instead out came a tall man in an impeccable white tropical suit. He remained standing at the railing of his veranda for a few minutes, and eyes seemed to be drinking in the unearthly peacefulness of the landscape. The tall spikes of rose mallow that surrounded the cabins were fresh and glowing in the dew, and the noble, lacy heads of the coconut palms made dark silhouettes against the slowly flushing sky. Over all there sounded the flutelike voices of the Himalayan mockingbirds, which inhabited this Garden of Eden by the hundreds.

Just as the man was descending the steps from the veranda to go to his car, a sound like the grating of a badly oiled door hinge broke the silence. I smiled. That was Maij, my tame leopard cat; I had locked her in the shower room because she had been bothering me with her excessive affection. She did not like this at all and publicized her feelings with a succession of cries, each hoarser and "rustier" than the one before. The stranger's head jerked up. That sudden movement had something of the quality of an alarmed stag about it. It was like the response of the sambur deer to the click of a camera. With an almost stealthy movement the stranger approached. I could not very well go on skulking at the back of my veranda, so I greeted him politely.

"Did you hear that?" he asked in English. "That was the cry of a leopard cat."

"Of course," I replied lightly. "It's mine."

"Oh!" he exclaimed. "You have it in your cottage?"

This brief exchange had already told me a great deal. Whereas I had at first taken the man for an army officer, I was now inclined to class him as an experienced forest ranger. It was also evident that he knew a great deal about animals. Not only had he recognized the leopard cat by its voice, but he also seemed properly astonished at finding a tame, domestic cat of this variety. I went and fetched my beautifully spotted pet, and the "wild" animal, which had never known anything but kindness from men, went up to the stranger with grace and dignity and calmly accepted his caresses. "You might raise three hundred leopard cats from kittenhood," the man remarked, looking up at me, "and only one of them would become as friendly and trusting as this one."

*   *   *   *

I had a charming and amusing companion and cabin mate on that stormy homeward voyage—Maij, the spotted leopard cat. On ship-board she behaved exactly as she had in Bangkok. Caged and put away with the other animals, she howled piteously. The upshot was that I took her into my cabin, and there she was forever surprising me by fresh demonstrations of her intelligence. The very first evening she claimed her sleeping place at the foot of my bunk. If she wanted water she jumped into the washbowl, looked over at me, and cried. There had been no plumbing in her first home, and in Bangkok she had never had the opportunity to see pipes and faucets. But the sound of the running water must have taught her the source of it.

There was no sand available on board the ship, so I was somewhat perplexed about what to do for her hygienic needs. I placed several layers of newspaper in a corner and trusted to her cleverness. She promptly used the paper, and I had only to crumple it up and throw it into the sea. She thoroughly enjoyed the endless pitching and roll-ing of our two-week sail to Aden. The apes and even the green spike-bearing peacocks were badly seasick. But Maij did not mind at all. Her appetite was astonishingly good, although I had nothing to offer her but tough beef, which in India—since the Hindus will not slaughter cattle—costs ten times what it is worth. The flying fish that were tossed on deck by the raging monsoon would have been a good source of vitamins for her, but she would not touch them. All she wanted was raw meat or raw egg. During the day she behaved very civilly, but every evening after five o'clock the devil took hold of her. Then she would push manuscripts and newspapers from my desk, jump against the screening over the portholes, and rip towels to shreds. She settled down only after complete darkness fell.

*   *   *   *

Back at home, I collected my animals from the various friends who had been kind enough to care for them. . . .

Maij, the elegant spotted cat, won everybody's heart. She refused to be kept in a pen and moved into our house like a genuine pet. I am convinced this completely tame leopard cat could become the ancestor of a new breed of housecats. We would only have to practice a certain amount of selection, choosing the tamest kittens for breeding for a few generations and keeping the wilder ones not bred. Koko the gibbon and Lambag the monkey could not frighten Maij. She knew both these primates from her native land and had no fear of them. On the contrary, she liked to play with them, and everyone who watched was ravished. Sometimes the two rascals took hold of her, one behind and one in front, and literally stretched her; she would give a few squeals of annoyance but hardly ever lashed out at them. When the gibbon took her into his arms and tenderly hugged her, she would actually purr. However, she was extremely shy of all strangers, like a real wild animal. If she heard a visitor's voice in the hall, through the closed door, we could be certain of not finding her when we entered the room. She had explored the big room thoroughly and knew all its hiding places: we would have to search for a long time before discovering her in the heating shaft of the tile stove, in a fold of the couch cover, behind the draperies, or under a cupboard. She would avoid all strange dogs with firmness, though not with any display of hostility. Her reserve disappeared only when I was alone in the room with her and the door closed. Then she would come purring up to me and with comical capers invite me to play.

When she first caught sight of our two dachshunds, she retreated, spitting and arching her back, but she did not attack them. My dogs knew that every living creature in Master's house and garden was taboo, and although they were great mischief-makers, they respected every chick and every young pigeon that fell from its nest. Once they had become accustomed to the smell and sight of the new member of the household, they did not meddle with her but made a point of keeping their distance. Before long it was the leopard cat who sought a rapprochement. She crept cautiously up to the dogs and made a thorough study of the creatures, sniffing all over them.

Things had reached this promising pass when an event occurred which severely upset the nervous, sensitive feline. A friend asked us to board four dachshund pups. So now there were six lively, short-legged little fellows, and the commotion they made obviously got on the cat's nerves. If a door was opened just a crack, a gang of wild barkers burst into the house and set upon every furred creature in sight. On such occasions Maij would sit enthroned, wearing an expression of disdain, on a bookshelf or the arm of a chair. It was only too obvious that she hated the din and flurry. By the third day she had decided she had had enough of these intolerable conditions, and with one great leap over the backs of the dogs she vanished into the garden. That in itself would have been no tragedy, for the intelligent cat knew us and the house as a safe refuge. She had run off into the garden a number of times before and always had appeared in the hall during the night, for we would leave the door open for her.

But this time the situation was different. Disorder had invaded her beloved quiet house, and it was all too much for a lover of solitude like Maij. For the next few hours I saw her creeping through the shrubbery, which we had let grow for wildlife cover, but she dodged me when I tried to catch her. The property was fenced, of course, but it was no problem for a cat to climb over a fence. We decided to keep the dogs in the house, in order not to drive the cat out of the garden; but unfortunately on that particular day we had several men planting trees in the garden, so Maij found no peace there either. That first night, Maij did not come back, although the door was left open. We continued to leave all doors open for a full month, but there was no trace of our beautiful leopard cat. That summer we had an unending succession of hot days and lovely nights. She must have greatly enjoyed her glorious freedom. Perhaps she might have acted differently if it had been cool and wet, for this delicate child of the tropics detested rain.

Our whole household and all our friends mourned the loss of our lovely and extraordinary cat. They had all given up hope. There was a highway not far from us, and cars tore by at race-track speeds. That did not bode well for an animal crossing the road at night. On the other hand, there were plenty of mice, rabbits, and birds in our vicinity, and all sorts of garden sheds, piles of brush, and impenetrable blackberry thickets. A wild cat would find food and shelter anywhere, and Maij would not let any stranger pick her up—I was certain of that. If she escaped the cars, she would be in no particular danger until winter. I decided that I would try to track her after the first snow fell, and would then set a cat trap on her trail. Somehow I could not believe that I would never see my beautiful leopard cat again. Of course I could not very well imagine that she would have remained tame, for even an ordinary house cat goes wild within a few weeks. Naturally I went on peering into all hedges and possible hiding places. But the camouflage of a spotted coat is so perfect that there is little hope of detecting a leopard small or large in a tangle of shrubbery.

During the following weeks I sometimes noticed very strange behavior on the part of my spike-bearing peacocks. Sometimes, when I sat writing on the veranda, the birds would come flying with piercing cries of terror from the depths of the garden and would drop into the orchard, their long necks turned and peering back. No matter how often I went and looked, I found no reason for their fright. A fox would not venture inside the fence by day, and a wild house cat could scarcely frighten such large fowl as peacocks enough to make them take to their wings. Finally I decided that there must be a polecat or weasel in the garden and rested content with that conclusion. Today I know the reason: the birds had encountered the leopard cat, and since they knew it from their native Thailand as a dangerous predator they were terrified. Once, too, my old dachshund bitch Topsy startled me. She had run down to the edge of the pond, and suddenly I heard her barking with that joyous surprise which she reserved for greeting people she knew. When I went to investigate she ran on into the bushes, barking joyfully and wagging her tail. If the dog had only been able to speak she probably could have told me that she had met a former housemate. As it was, her alert, intelligent eyes followed my motions mutely as I searched the vicinity and then returned, shaking my head in bafflement.

Five weeks passed before we received our first worthwhile information about the cat. One evening a man came to the door to report that just at twilight he had seen a small "leopard" at the edge of an overgrown wilderness of shrubs about six hundred feet from my house. If a strange animal is sighted anywhere in our vicinity, the neighbors know that it probably has escaped from my collection. Once again the search proved fruitless. But at least I knew that the cat was alive and had not left the neighborhood.

Next day, shortly before dusk, just as I was once again setting out to look for the cat, a man came running up to me. "Come quick! A strange spotted cat has just crossed the path." I snatched my net from its hook and rushed off. Only fifty paces from my land, Maij had slipped into a small garden. Haste was essential, and the owner was not in sight, so without hesitation I climbed the fence onto someone else's property. For a while I hunted around among cabbages and currant bushes. Then I suddenly noticed my Maij, as if she had sprung out of the ground, sitting on the garden path in the last rays of sunlight. I stood stock-still and coaxed her, "Here, Maij, here, Maij." At the sound of my voice she lifted her head abruptly and her golden-brown eyes rested on my face. Calmly, without haste, she moved away from me. Her spree in the wilds had gone on too long. She had recognized me, but she would never let me get near her. I would have to capture her. And so I tried, as she trotted along about four yards ahead of me, to drive her against a fence, intending, while she was seeking a way of escape, to drop the net over her head. But try hunting a wild cat! With one graceful leap into a tangle of gooseberry bushes, Maij vanished as though the earth had swallowed her.

But at any rate I now knew that the runaway cat tended to move toward the familiar surroundings of the house when evening fell.

We set up a box trap at a narrow passage between two garden fences, baiting it with two white mice in a small wire cage. I gave the mice hard zwieback to nibble, for I wanted the cat's keen ear to hear the sound of their gnawing, which would travel far in the stillness of the night. But the fence around an acre and a half of land is long, and who can say where a small cat will choose to slip through it? The next morning came a report that Maij had been seen at the eastern end of the garden. This part of our grounds is a wild shrubby meadow. Though four of us made a careful search of the whole terrain, we found no trace of the fugitive. I did notice a hole under the fence which showed signs of having been used frequently; but that might equally well have been an escape route dug secretly by one of the dogs. Still, it seemed clear that the leopard cat was creeping about the place at night and going in and out at will. I might have tried setting twenty traps night after night, but twenty traps are somewhat hard to come by.

Toward ten o'clock that same night—I was reading in bed beside my open window—I heard a truly bone-chilling yelp that brought me to my feet instantly. What was that? A house guest in the adjoining room had also heard it and thought it could only be a cat. Then the sound came again, and this time I identified it as the cry of a rabbit. I realized instantly that the leopard cat was hunting. Half dressed, I rushed out. My house stands close to the fence of my neighbor's property. On the other side is a rather deep trench meant for drainage, which dries out in midsummer. I sent the beam of my flashlight through the fence. At the foot of the trench the blackberry canes stirred, and in the cone of light I saw a spotted coat. I could also discern the gray pelt of a rabbit, which Maij was now hurriedly dragging up the side of the trench. I ran for a ladder, climbed over the fence, got caught in the barbed wire, and stepped into a mudhole in my slippers. But who cared! This time I had to capture my cat. I was counting on a predatory animal's determined hold upon its prey. Perhaps that instinct would be strong enough so that I could approach her. After all, this was not a wild animal, but Maij, who only a short while ago had been my pet. If she was hungry enough I might succeed. Undoubtedly I could expect to be clawed and bitten when I seized her; but I have had plenty of scratches and bites in a lifetime of dealing with animals. If I caught so much as the tip of her tail, nothing would make me let go. But I found nothing.

When I emerged from the muddy trench onto firm ground, I heard nothing whatsoever. I stood absolutely motionless. Where could I search in these overgrown gardens with their fences full of gaps? After some time I heard a faint sound of dragging. Cautiously I crept toward it. But I might just as well have been walking in thudding boots; the cat's sensitive ears could hear my breathing. Wherever I flashed my light I caught no trace of leopard skin. Yet I knew that only a few steps away Maij was probably crouching, ready to flee, staring at me with her big eyes. For her it was bright as day, after all, while I had to search in darkness.

When nothing turned up I walked in a wide arc and began systematically flashing my light into one hiding place after another. Suddenly, in a corner between a pile of wood and a garden shed, there was a reddish gleam, the phosphorescent glow of a cat's eyes. She lay hunched up, ready to dash away. I knew that curious flickering in her eyes. When, during her days as a domestic cat, she had lurked behind a fold in the curtains, waiting for her playmates; or when I held her in my arms against her will; or when she became conscious of the gnawing of a mouse which I had inside a box for her, then this same wild glare would come into her eyes, which ordinarily surveyed her surroundings with such tranquil hauteur. But whenever my little cat was swept by passion—the excitement of play, the hunting urge, or the instinct of self-defense—her wild, amber-yellow eyes seemed to shoot flames.

In my many years of dealings with tamed wild beasts—which interest me more than domestic animals—I have made a point of paying close attention to the light in their eyes. There is no better index to

the alternation of their moods. Often there are only tiny nuances, barely visible vacillations in the barometer of their feelings; but recognizing these can sometimes be a matter of life and death for men, and can at least save him from bad bites and mean scratches. All the cats, both wild and domestic, are creatures of passion. Hence the mysteriously strong attachment that especially warmhearted and temperamental human beings feel for these masterpieces of creation. My Maij hated being touched by strangers, and when I would sometimes put her into the arms of visitors, such flames would dart from her eyes that they would be frightened of her. As soon as I took her back into my own the fire in her eyes would instantly fade. There are "one-man dogs," like the Chinese chow. Maij was and remained a "one-man cat." To her credit, however, it must be said that she never once relapsed into savagery. She growled like a leopard, spat and hissed, but she never bit or scratched. I could pull her out from under a wardrobe by the tail; her needle-sharp teeth could close around my finger, but they never even nicked my skin. I am certain that she would never have bitten strangers either, but no one dared come close to her when she growled. She was a mistress at the art of playing "the beast" and knew quite well that her play-acting did not impress me but was very effective with others.

Now, however, she had lived for weeks out of contact with people. A once wild cat, especially when she is excited by having just caught her prey, will, if cornered, recklessly attack a man. Now my former pet crouched in her corner, eyes glaring dangerously. I stooped down and directed the beam of the flashlight straight at those yellow eyes. It is an old piece of animal lore that predatory animals will never leap into a bright light. Darkness is their friend. In a low, gentle voice I talked to my little fugitive. This was my one chance of laying hands on her again. I would have to make one swift grab at her; otherwise she was lost. For it seemed clear that after this episode so intelligent a jungle animal would forever shun the spot where she had been given such a fright.

Under the steady soothing of the voice that had once been familiar to her, she tucked her forepaws under her body. Her tension slackened; she was calmer now. Carefully avoiding the beam of light, my hand approached inch by inch. A sudden forward thrust, and I had Maij by the collar. But what was this? No savage rearing up, no slashing claws, no desperate bites. The spotted cat snuggled against my hand as she always had. The human contact seemed to have wiped out all defensive reactions as if by magic. Never in my long and varied experience with animals had I encountered anything so surprising.

With the cat in my arm, I cautiously scaled the fence and carried her back to her familiar room. (Our dachshund boarders had long since departed.) And here I had an even greater surprise. I put Maij down on the carpet. She looked around for just a moment, and then all the wildness dropped away from her as if it had been a bad dream. She went to her various favorite spots, sniffed under the tile stove, peered under the wardrobe, let herself be picked up and hugged. We stood in a circle, mute, and a little ashamed of our emotion. The leopard cat raised her head and in her deep, hoarse voice demanded food, as though no time had gone by between the past and present. With intense hunger she fell upon the raw meat we offered her and consumed an incredible quantity in an amazingly short time. She struck us as having grown a little, was long and lean, and her skin was smooth and glossy; but she was so thin that her pelvic bones showed through her skin.

A little while later I was alone in the room with Maij. I lay in bed reading, as she had seen me do so many nights in the past. She had finished her meal and came over to my bed. With a leap she jumped up on it and went to her accustomed place at the foot. Surreptitiously, I observed her. Her rather slanting, slitted Thai eyes rested upon me for long minutes. Then she walked deliberately up the length of the bed and settled down on my chest. With the greatest care she propped her delicate little paws against my cheek and, purring affectionately, began licking my skin. Never before had she expressed her affection in this way. Then she took my hand between her paws and rolled up comfortably, purring like a kettle for sheer happiness. She ran her spread claws very gently over the back of my hand and playfully nibbled my fingers. It was quite plain that she was rapturous at being home again.

Such behavior, of course, is not at all strange in a tame, affectionate pet. But it remains extremely astonishing that after five weeks of freedom, thirty-five nights of hunting warm-blooded prey in keeping with her instincts, all her native savagery should drop away and completely vanish at the first human contact. Hundreds of times I have seen how wild animals bottle-raised by human beings will revert to their inherited patterns and abandon their acquired tameness in a matter of a few days. I know only too well how strong the instincts are, and how superficial the tameness can be. Instincts are the sum of impulses that have become fixed over thousands of years because they are necessary to the continuance of the species. Tameness is an altogether personal acquisition by a single individual. One particular animal among many of the same species can dispense with its instinctive flight and defense reactions because of its peculiar situation as a ward of man. But the species as a whole must remain alert and on its guard.

We consider cats less intelligent than the canine species. Are we mistaken, and are we doing an injustice to the personality of the cat because we understand that personality less? Or is my high-strung sensitive Maij an isolated exception? Has this creature with her fine nervous system, with her radar equipment for sensing the moods of those around her, been capable of so sudden a reversal because she has felt the current of kindness that flows along with the warmth of our hands into her body? In spite of all my knowledge of animals, I must confess that I do not know. An elderly, very wise, and experienced foreign colleague of mine once summed up our whole predicament vis à vis brute creation. "Believe me," he said to me once when we were discussing the problem, "at bottom we know nothing about animals."

As far as I know, no one has made a specific study of the personality of the leopard cat. Consequently there is no way to determine whether all these cats are endowed with such strange sensitivity and receptivity. I should like to make a stab at solving the riddle. I have written to all my friends in Thailand and Burma: "Send me leopard cats by plane, half tamed or entirely wild, no matter which." I would be delighted to lay my hands on a regular spitfire of this species someday.

"Cat Bill" Veto

ADLAI STEVENSON

*The definitive statement on cat versus bird will probably
never be made, but Adlai Stevenson came close in his veto
of the "Cat Bill."*

I herewith return, without my approval, Senate Bill No. 93 entitled,
"An Act to Provide Protection to Insectivorous Birds by Restraining
Cats." This is the so-called "Cat Bill." I veto and withhold my approval from this bill for the following reasons: It would impose fines
on owners or keepers who permitted their cats to run at large off
their premises. It would permit any person to capture, or call upon
the police to pick up and imprison, cats at large. It would permit the
use of traps. The bill would have statewide application—on farms, in
villages, and in metropolitan centers. This legislation has been introduced in the past several sessions of the legislature, and it has, over
the years, been the source of much comment—not all of which has
been in a serious vein. It may be that the General Assembly has now
seen fit to refer it to one who can view it with a fresh outlook. Whatever the reasons for passage at this session, I cannot believe there is
a widespread public demand for this law or that it could, as a practical matter be enforced. Furthermore, I cannot agree that it should be
the declared public policy of Illinois that a cat visiting a neighbor's
yard or crossing the highway is a public nuisance. It is in the nature
of cats to do a certain amount of unescorted roaming. Many live
with their owners in apartments or other restricted premises, and I
doubt if we want to make their every brief foray an opportunity for
a small game hunt by zealous citizens—with traps or otherwise. I
am afraid this bill could only create discord, recrimination and
enmity. Also consider the owner's dilemma: To escort a cat abroad
on a leash is against the nature of the cat, and to permit it to venture
forth for exercise unattended into a night of new dangers is against
the nature of the owner. Moreover, cats perform useful service, particularly in rural areas, in combating rodents—work they necessarily
perform alone and without regard for property lines. We are all in-

terested in protecting certain varieties of birds. That cats destroy some birds, I well know, but I believe this legislation would further but little the worthy cause to which its proponents give such unselfish effort. The problem of cat versus bird is as old as time. If we attempt to resolve it by legislation, who knows but what we may be called upon to take sides as well in the age-old problem of dog versus cat, bird versus bird, even bird versus worm. In my opinion, the State of Illinois and its local governing bodies already have enough to do without trying to control feline delinquency. For these reasons, and not because I love birds the less or cats the more, I veto and withhold my approval from Senate Bill No. 93.

Apotheosis

CARL VAN VECHTEN

Since Carl Van Vechten said so many sensible words about cats, it seems just to give him the last word in this anthology. His monumental work, "The Tiger in the House," of which this is the final chapter, is a deserved classic in literature about the cat in all its many manifestations. It has never been surpassed, nor is it likely to be.

I like to think that if Van Vechten were alive today, he would approve of the selections in this book.

> *Les bêtes sont au bon Dieu;*
> *Mais la bêtise est à l'homme.*
> VICTOR HUGO

I have written, how skilfully, I cannot tell, on the manners and customs of the cat, his graces and calineries, the history of his subjugation of humankind. Through all the ages, even during the dark epoch of witchcraft and persecution, puss has maintained his supremacy, continued to breed and multiply, defying, when convenient, the laws of God and man, now our friend, now our enemy, now wild, now tame, the pet of the hearth or the tiger of the heath, but always free, always independent, always an anarchist who insists upon his rights, whatever the cost. The cat never forms soviets; he works alone.

We have much to learn from the cat, we men who prefer to follow the slavish habits of the dog or the ox or the horse. If men and women would become more feline, indeed, I think it would prove the salvation of the human race. Certainly it would end war, for cats will not fight for an ideal in the mass, having no faith in mass ideals, although a single cat will fight to the death for his own ideals, his freedom of speech and expression. The dog and the horse, on the other hand, perpetuate war, by group thinking, group acting, and serve further to encourage popular belief in that monstrous panacea, universal brotherhood.

For the next war man will build ships which can make sixty or seventy knots an hour; submarines will skim through five thousand leagues of the sea with the speed of sharks; and airships will fly over cities, dropping bundles of TNT. Saïgon, Berlin, Cairo, Paris, Madrid, and even Indianapolis are doomed to disappear. Man himself will become extinct; crude, silly man, always struggling against Nature, rather than with Nature behind him, helping him forward and across, beyond the abysses and torrents and landslides of existence. And presently everything we know will be over, another cycle of years will begin, and a new "civilization" will arise.

For man has persistently, and perhaps a little intentionally, misunderstood the Prometheus legend. Prometheus was the enemy, not the friend, of man. The fire which he brought to earth was a devastating flame and Zeus, the Nature God, chained him to a rock to protect humanity. This misuse of holy things, this turning of good to the account of evil, this misapplication of natural principles to unnatural practices are the commonplaces of history, the foundations of our present state, and the causes of all misery.

But the cat will survive. He is no such fool as man. He knows that he must have Nature behind him. He also knows that it is easier for one

cat alone to fit into the curves of Nature than two cats. So he walks by himself. For Nature here and Nature there are two different Natures and what one cat on one side of the fence has to do is not what another cat on the other side of the fence has to do. But the great principles are obeyed by all cats to such an extent that twenty, a hundred, a thousand cats will willingly give their lives, which they might easily save, to preserve an instinct, a racial memory, which will serve to perpetuate the feline race. The result will be that, after the cataclysm, out of the mounds of heaped-up earth, the piles and wrecks of half-buried cities, the desolated fields of grain, and the tortured orchards, the cat will stalk, confident, self-reliant, capable, imperturbable, and philosophical. He will bridge the gap until man appears again and then he will sit on new hearths and again will teach his mighty lesson to ears and eyes that again are dumb and blind. Shylock's doom was foretold by Shakespeare from the moment the poet asked the poor creature to say, "the harmless necessary cat." For it is possible, nay probable, that the cat, unlike man who forgets his previous forms, remembers, really remembers, many generations back; that what we call instinct may be more profound than knowledge. And so Providence wisely has not allowed the cat to speak any language save his own.

We may dominate dogs, but cats can never be dominated except by force. They can be annihilated, at least a few of them can, but never made servile or banal. The cat is never vulgar. He will not even permit God to interfere with his liberty and if he suffers so much as a toothache he will refuse all food. He would rather die than endure pain. Thus, like the Spartan, he preserves the strength of his stock. He may at any moment change his motto from *Libertas Sine Labore* or *Amica Non Serva* to *Quand Même*.

There is, indeed, no single quality of the cat that man could not emulate to his advantage. He is clean, the cleanest, indeed, of all animals, absolutely without odor or soil when it is within his power to be so. He is silent, walking on padded paws with claws withdrawn, making no sound unless he wishes to say something definite and then he can express himself freely. He believes in free-speech, and not only believes in it, but indulges in it. Nothing will make a cat stop talking when he wants to, except the hand of death.

He is entirely self-reliant. He lives in homes because he chooses to do so, and as long as the surroundings and the people suit him, but he lives there on his own terms, and never sacrifices his own comfort or his own well-being for the sake of the stupid folk with whom he comes in contact. Thus he is the most satisfactory of friends. Among men (or women) it is customary to say, "We're dining with the Ogilvies tonight. We don't want to go but they'll never forgive us if we don't." Meanwhile the Ogilvies are muttering, "Good God! This is the night those horrible Mitchells are coming to dinner. I wish they would telephone that they cannot come. Perhaps their motor will break down on the way!" The cat neither gives nor accepts invitations that do not come from the heart. If he tires of his friends sometimes, so do I. If he wishes to move he does so. Perhaps to another house, perhaps to the wilds. If he is suddenly thrown on his own resources in the country he can support himself on the highway; he can even support himself in town under conditions that would terrify that half-hearted, group-seeking socialist, the dog. The cat is virile, and virility is a quality which man has almost lost. St. George Mivart insisted that the cat rather than man was at the summit of the animal kingdom and that he was the best-fitted of the mammalians to make his way in the world. I agree perfectly with St. George Mivart. I do not see how it is possible for anyone to disagree with him. But the cat makes no boast of his pre-eminent position; he is satisfied to occupy it. He does not call man a "lower animal" although doubtless he regards him in this light. I have dwelt at some length on his occult sense. It can scarcely be overestimated. He has not lost the power of gesture language. With his tail, with his paws, his cocking ears, his eyes, his head, the turn of his body, or the waving of his fur, he expresses in symbols the most cabalistic secrets. He is beautiful and he is graceful. He makes his appearance and his life as exquisite as circumstances will permit. He is modest, he is urbane, he is dignified. Indeed, a well-bred cat never argues. He goes about doing what he likes in a well-bred superior manner. If he is interruptd he will look at you in mild surprise or silent reproach but he will return to his desire. If he is prevented, he will wait for a more favourable occasion. But like all well-bred individualists, and unlike human anarchists, the cat seldom interferes with other people's rights. His intelligence keeps him from doing many of the fool things that complicate life. Cats never write operas and they never attend them. They never sign papers, or pay taxes, or vote for president. An injunction will have no power whatever over a cat. A cat, of course, would not only refuse to obey any amendment whatever to any constitution, he would refuse to obey the constitution iself.

Feathers is very tired of this book. She has told me so more than once lately. Sometimes with her eyes, gazing at me with impatience while I write. Sometimes with her paws, scratching scornfully at the sheets of paper as I toss them to the floor. Sometimes on my writing table she insinuates herself between me and my work. When I began this book she was a kitten, a chrysanthemum-like ball of tawny, orange, white, and black fuzzy fur, and now she is about to become a mother. Yes, while I have been writing a book, Feathers has experienced teething, love, and now soon will come maternity. It makes me feel very small, very unimportant. What I have done in fourteen months seems very little when it is compared with what she has done.

The mystery of life deepens for her. Her eyes are slightly drawn. She is less active and she wishes more repose. She needs the warmth of my knees, where she desires to sleep uninterrupted by the sound of clicking keys. She is pleading with me to come to an end. And I cannot resist her prayer. See, Feathers, I am nearly done. I am writing the last page. You can come to me now and spend the hours of preparation in my lap, and I offer, rather than this poor book, to test myself as a literary man, after Samuel Butler's method, by naming your yet unborn kittens. I shall call them, if Nature gives you five, and the sexes permit, Aurélie, Golden Feathers, Coq d'Or, Prince Igor, and Jurgen.

March 4, 1920
New York

To a Cat

ALGERNON CHARLES SWINBURNE

Stately, kindly, lordly friend,
  Condescend
Here to sit by me, and turn
Glorious eyes that smile and burn,
Golden eyes, love's lustrous meed,
On the golden page I read.

All your wondrous wealth of hair,
  Dark and fair,
Silken-shaggy, soft and bright
As the clouds and beams of night,
Pays my reverent hand's caress
Back with friendlier gentleness.

Dogs may fawn on all and some
  As they come;
You, a friend of loftier mind,
Answer friends alone in kind.
Just your foot upon my hand
Softly bids it understand.